Social Theories of Urban Violence in the Global South

While cities often act as the engines of economic growth for developing countries, they are also frequently the site of growing violence, poverty, and inequality. Yet, social theory, largely developed and tested in the Global North, is often inadequate in tackling the realities of life in the dangerous parts of cities in the Global South. Drawing on the findings of an ambitious five-year, 15-project research programme, *Social Theories of Urban Violence in the Global South* offers a uniquely Southern perspective on the violence–poverty–inequalities dynamics in cities of the Global South.

Through their research, urban violence experts based in low- and middle-income countries demonstrate how "urban violence" means different things to different people in different places. While some researchers adopt or adapt existing theoretical and conceptual frameworks, others develop and test new theories, each interpreting and operationalizing the concept of urban violence in the particular context in which they work. In particular, the book highlights the links between urban violence, poverty, and inequalities based on income, class, gender, and other social cleavages.

Providing important new perspectives from the Global South, this book will be of interest to policymakers, academics, and students with an interest in violence and exclusion in the cities of developing countries.

Jennifer Erin Salahub managed the Safe and Inclusive Cities initiative, a global research programme jointly funded by Canada's International Development Research Centre and the United Kingdom's Department for International Development.

Markus Gottsbacher is senior programme specialist with the Governance and Justice programme at the International Development Research Centre.

John de Boer is managing director of the SecDev Group.

Routledge Studies in Cities and Development

The series features innovative and original research on cities in the Global South, aiming to explore urban settings through the lens of international development. The series particularly promotes comparative and interdisciplinary research targeted at a global readership.

In terms of theory and method, rather than basing itself on any one orthodoxy, the series draws on a broad toolkit taken from across social sciences and built environment studies, emphasizing comparison, the analysis of the structure and processes, and the application of qualitative and quantitative methods.

The series welcomes submissions from established and junior authors on cutting-edge and high-level research on key topics that feature in global news and public debate.

The Politics of Slums in the Global South
Urban Informality in Brazil, India, South Africa and Peru
Edited by Véronique Dupont, David Jordhus-Lier, Catherine Sutherland and Einar Braathen

Social Theories of Urban Violence in the Global South
Towards Safe and Inclusive Cities
Edited by Jennifer Erin Salahub, Markus Gottsbacher and John de Boer

Social Theories of Urban Violence in the Global South

Towards Safe and Inclusive Cities

Edited by Jennifer Erin Salahub, Markus Gottsbacher, and John de Boer

Routledge
Taylor & Francis Group
LONDON AND NEW YORK

International Development Research Centre
Ottawa • Cairo • Montevideo • Nairobi • New Delhi

First published 2018
by Routledge
2 Park Square, Milton Park, Abingdon, Oxon OX14 4RN

and by Routledge
711 Third Avenue, New York, NY 10017

Routledge is an imprint of the Taylor & Francis Group, an informa business

Co-published with the
International Development Research Centre
PO Box 8500, Ottawa, ON K1G 3H9 Canada
info@idrc.ca / www.idrc.ca

The research presented in this publication was carried out with the financial assistance of Canada's International Development Research Centre and the United Kingdom's Department for International Development (DFID). The views expressed herein do not necessarily represent those of IDRC or its Board of Governors, or those of DFID.

British Library Cataloguing-in-Publication Data
A catalogue record for this book is available from the British Library

Library of Congress Cataloging-in-Publication Data
Names: Salahub, Jennifer Erin, editor. | Gottsbacher, Markus, editor. | de Boer, John, editor.
Title: Social theories of urban violence in the global south : towards safe and inclusive cities / edited by Jennifer Erin Salahub, Markus Gottsbacher and John de Boer.
Description: Abingdon, Oxon ; New York, NY : Routledge, 2018. |
Series: Routledge studies in cities and development | Includes bibliographical references and index.
Identifiers: LCCN 2017052862 (print) | LCCN 2017054821 (ebook) | ISBN 9781351254724 (eBook) | ISBN 9780815368397 (hardback)
Subjects: LCSH: Urban violence—Developing countries. | Violence—Developing countries. | Urbanization—Developing countries. | Urban policy—Developing countries. | Sociology, Urban—Developing countries.
Classification: LCC HN981.V5 (ebook) | LCC HN981.V5 S63 2018 (print) | DDC 303.609173/2—dc23
LC record available at https://lccn.loc.gov/2017052862

ISBN: 978-0-815-36839-7 (hbk)
ISBN: 978-1-351-25472-4 (ebk)
ISBN: 978-1-552-50597-7 (IDRC ebk)

Typeset in Sabon
by Out of House Publishing

Contents

Figures and tables

Figures

Tables

Notes on contributors

Foreword

Caroline Moser is an urban social anthropologist and social policy specialist, with more than 40 years of experience relating to urban and social development issues—ranging from academic to policy-focused research, teaching, and training. She has undertaken field-based research on many topics: urban poverty, urban violence, household asset vulnerability and accumulation strategies, gender and development, and the informal sector. Her work has taken her to Ecuador, Guatemala, Jamaica, and other countries. Caroline's empirical research has also included social policy, community participation, the social dimensions of economic reform, human rights, and social protection. Most recently, she has studied urban adaptations to climate change in Mombasa, Kenya, and the role of women's organisations in peace processes in Colombia. Caroline has taught at a number of institutions, both in the UK (the University of Manchester, the London School of Economics, and University College London) and abroad: the New School, New York. She has held senior positions at the World Bank, the Overseas Development Institute, and the Brookings Institution. Caroline has served as an advisor to many donor agencies and has been a member of the United Nations Centre for Human Settlements' (Habitat) Huairou Commission, a visiting professor at the University of Bristol, a research fellow at the World Policy Institute in New York, and a member of the panel on Urban Population Dynamics (US National Academy of Sciences).

Lead editor (Introduction and Conclusion)

Jennifer Erin Salahub managed the Safe and Inclusive Cities initiative, a global research programme jointly funded by Canada's International Development Research Centre and the United Kingdom's Department for International Development. Before joining IDRC, Jennifer was senior researcher and team leader of the Fragile and Conflict-Affected States programme at the North-South Institute (NSI), where she researched topics such as peace-building, fragile states, and legislative effectiveness. Her specific focus was security and development: at NSI, she contributed to the fields of security sector reform, gender equality in fragile states, and gender-sensitive policing. Her interests also include urban violence, poverty, and inequalities. Jennifer holds an MA in Political Science (International Relations) from McGill University in Montreal.

Contributing editors (Introduction and Conclusion)

John de Boer is managing director of The SecDev Group, an international risk consultancy firm; he is also an expert on development, humanitarian, and security challenges in situations of conflict and violence. He was previously senior policy advisor with the United Nations University's Centre for Policy Research, where he researched vulnerability in urban contexts; specific challenges included urban violence and disaster, and organised crime. John was formerly programme leader for Governance, Security, and Justice at Canada's International Development Research Centre. He has worked at the Canadian International Development Agency, where he served on the Afghanistan and Pakistan Task Force. John holds a PhD in Area Studies from the University of Tokyo.

Markus Gottsbacher is senior programme specialist with the Governance and Justice programme at the International Development Research Centre (IDRC). A political scientist and ethnologist by training, he develops and manages research projects in Latin America and the Caribbean to support efforts for peace-building, citizen security, and access to justice. Previously, Markus worked on an IDRC project in Honduras that focused on dealing with conflict over natural resources. He has almost a decade of experience with various UN agencies (mostly in Latin America), and has worked on issues ranging from drugs and crime to HIV/AIDS and the rights of indigenous peoples and women. As a professor at several universities in Mexico, he focused on human security, international development and cooperation, and conflict prevention. Markus has worked for a number of NGOs, and, while at the Austrian Study Centre for Peace and Conflict Resolution, he developed a training programme for peace-builders in conflict areas. Markus holds a PhD in Political Science and an MA in Political Science and Social Anthropology from the University of Vienna.

Chapter authors

Chapter 1

Nausheen H. Anwar is an associate professor at the Institute of Business Administration in Karachi. She teaches City and Regional Planning in the Department of Social Sciences and Liberal Arts. Nausheen received her PhD from Columbia University, New York. Her work focuses on the role policymaking and planning processes play in sustaining urban and regional inequality in the production of space/place.

Sarwat Viqar is a professor of humanities at John Abbott College in Montreal, QC. She has an interdisciplinary PhD in Anthropology, History, and Political Science. Her research focuses on urban politics and forms of informal urban governance. She has also worked as a consultant for the IDRC-supported project Gender and Violence in Urban Pakistan as part of the SAIC programme. She has published articles on Karachi's urban history, on the dynamics of its low-income neighbourhoods, and on fieldwork methodology. Sarwat also has an MA in Architecture, and has worked in Pakistan, Thailand, and Mexico as a consultant and researcher in the fields of low-income housing and informal settlements.

Daanish Mustafa is a reader in politics and environment at the Department of Geography, King's College, London. He received his PhD in Geography from the University of Colorado in 2000. Much of his published work deals with the intersection of water resources, environmental hazards, and development geography. He also maintains an active interest in the critical geographies of violence and terror.

Chapter 2

Esmeralda Mariano holds a PhD in Social and Cultural Anthropology from the Institute for Anthropological Research in Africa, at the University of Leuven, Belgium. She is a professor and researcher with the Faculty of Arts and Social Sciences in the Department of Archaeology and Anthropology at Eduardo Mondlane University (UEM) in Mozambique. She also has a joint appointment in UEM's Faculty of Medicine (Master Program on Public Health). Much of Esmeralda's work deals with the intersection of body, gender, sexuality, and reproductive health issues. She is also engaged in studies of different forms of violence, while maintaining an active interest in human ecology.

Henny Slegh is a PhD candidate in Medical Anthropology at the University of Amsterdam. She is senior researcher and technical advisor for non-profit organisations working on masculinities, culture, and mental health in conflict and post-conflict areas. For 15 years, she worked as a psycho-trauma therapist in the Netherlands, with survivors of sexual and gender-based violence (SGBV), and her 10 years of research in Africa has taken her to Mozambique, Rwanda, DRC, Burundi, and Mali (where she has also coordinated studies for the International Men and Gender Equality

Survey). Henny has conducted several African studies on SGBV, mental health, and masculinity in conflict and post-conflict settings.

Sílvia Roque holds a PhD in International Relations (International Politics and Conflict Resolution) from the University of Coimbra, Portugal, and an MA in African Studies from the University Institute of Lisbon (ISCTE). She has worked as a researcher at the Centre for Social Studies of the University of Coimbra since 2005. Sílvia has conducted field research on the dynamics of gender and youth violence, and on peace-building, in Guinea-Bissau, El Salvador, and Mozambique.

Chapter 3

Julie Stewart is a professor of law at the University of Zimbabwe, where she directs the Southern and Eastern African Regional Centre for Women's Law. The Centre's Masters programmes in Women's Law and in Women's Socio-Legal Rights explore the intersections of law with women's social, cultural, and economic realities. Julie also analyses how these issues affect individuals' abilities to claim their legal and constitutional rights.

Rosalie Katsande is a senior lecturer at the Southern and Eastern African Regional Centre for Women's Law at the University of Zimbabwe, where she teaches MA courses on Theories and Perspectives in Women's Law and on Women, Commerce, and the Law in Africa. She supervises students' field work and dissertations at the postgraduate level and also teaches courses in Research Methods as well as Gender and the Law at Zimbabwe's Midlands State University. Rosalie's research centres on analysing the socio-legal aspects of women's participation in economic activities in Africa. She holds an MA in Women's Law and a PhD in Law from the University of Zimbabwe.

Olga Chisango is currently pursuing an MA in Women's Socio-Legal Studies at the Southern and Eastern African Regional Centre for Women's Law, University of Zimbabwe. She also holds an Honours Degree in English from the University of Zimbabwe, in addition to her various qualifications in Resource Mobilisation and Project Management. Olga has worked for more than 10 years with various organisations in the non-profit sector. Four of those years were spent in South Africa, where she gained experience in the fields of fundraising and project management.

Sian Maseko is a feminist development practitioner with a Masters in Violence, Conflict and Development. She worked in Southern Africa for more than 10 years specialising in women's rights. She has published widely on violence against women and health, the sexual rights of marginalised communities, and movement-building in Southern Africa. She has a particular interest in participatory research methodologies with marginalised and excluded communities. She is also a member of the Advisory Group of the Women for Global Fund (W4GF) on HIV, TB and malaria. Sian is currently working as a consultant specialising in women's rights.

Chapter 4

Manoj Bandan Balsamanta is a senior research associate at the Institute for Human Development, Delhi. His PhD dissertation focused on the intersections of caste, class, and social capital in higher education. Manoj's research interests include Indian sociology, canon formation, contemporary and unfamiliar castes, advantages and marginalities in higher education, and the political economy of inequalities and violence. He is currently engaged in studies on violence against women in rural India and caste manifestations in Indian cities.

Bhim Reddy is a Fellow at the Institute for Human Development in Delhi and an associate editor of the *Indian Journal of Human Development*. His PhD in Anthropology, from the University of Hyderabad, focused on agrarian change and rural-urban labour migration. Bhim's many research interests include agrarian political economy, contemporary manifestations of caste, and the everyday lives and politics of 'migrants' and informal workers in urban centres. He also focuses on a variety of urban issues such as recruitment practices in labour markets, spatial inequality, and social segregation. He is currently researching issues as diverse as the urban spatiality of caste and hiring practices in the formal sector.

Chapter 5

Danesh Jayatilaka is a research fellow at the International Centre for Ethnic Studies in Colombo, Sri Lanka. He is now working on a PhD in Economics, examining the impact of housing and livelihoods aid on the post-conflict recovery of resettled people. He has written a number of papers in international publications on the topic of internal displacement.

Rajith W. D. Lakshman is a research officer in the Cities Cluster at the Institute of Development Studies, University of Sussex, UK. A financial economist by training, he focuses mainly on the topics of migration, poverty, nutrition, and development. He leads the IDRC-funded project on urban violence, on which the material in this chapter is based.

Iresha M. Lakshman is a senior lecturer at the Department of Sociology, University of Colombo, Sri Lanka. Her fields of interest include education, urban studies, international migration, and forced migration.

Chapter 6

Rodolfo Calderón Umaña is a sociologist, professor, and researcher at the School of Sociology, University of Costa Rica. He holds a PhD in Social Sciences, and his current fields of interest are the sociologies of violence and inequalities. In 2012, Rodolfo won the Latin American Prize offered by the United Nations Office on Drugs and Crime (Mexico) for his book *Crime and Social Change in Costa Rica*. His most recent publication was a collaboration with Pérez Sáinz and Brenes (2016) in *Population Papers Review*, entitled "Social Exclusion, Violence, and the Domestic Sphere: Evidence and Reflections from Central America".

Chapter 7

Enrique Desmond Arias is an associate professor in the Schar School of Policy and Government at George Mason University in Fairfax, Virginia. His research focuses on security and politics in Latin America and the Caribbean. He is the author of several scholarly books, most notably *Criminal Enterprises and Governance in Latin America and the Caribbean* and *Drugs and Democracy in Rio de Janeiro: Trafficking, Social Networks, and Public Security*. Enrique is also the co-editor of *Violent Democracies in Latin America*, published by Duke University Press.

Ximena Tocornal Montt is an associate professor in the Department of Social Sciences at the University of Los Lagos, Osorno, Chile. She previously held positions with the Faculty of Psychology at the Universidad Diego Portales, and the Institute of Public Affairs at the University of Chile. She holds a PhD from Loughborough University in the UK, where her Social Sciences dissertation (2006) examined Chileans' memories of Pinochet's dictatorship. Ximena has investigated many forms of violence, such as urban conflict and crime in poor neighbourhoods, in addition to the Chilean government's response to this phenomenon since the 1990s. Her particular focus is on community-level strategies that can make a difference in preventing crime and violence.

Chapter 8

Roberto Briceño-León is professor of sociology at the Central University of Venezuela and Director of the Social Science Laboratory, where, since 2005, he has coordinated the Venezuelan Violence Observatory. He has held positions at the Sorbonne in Paris and at the National Autonomous University of Mexico, and has been a research fellow at Oxford and the Woodrow Wilson International Center for Scholars in Washington, DC. Roberto served on the International Sociological Association Executive Committee, was Global Secretary of the International Forum for Social

Science and Health, and directed the World Health Organization's Small Grants Program for young researchers. He has published (or edited) 24 books in several different languages and more than 200 scholarly articles.

Chapter 9

Francis Akindès is professor of political and economic sociology, and programme director of the UNESCO Chair in Bioethics at Université Alassane Ouattara in Bouaké, Côte d'Ivoire. His research covers diverse aspects of African politics, economy, and the social transformation of society, with a particular focus on different aspects of violence. Francis is a visiting professor at several other universities, and a subject-matter expert for many international institutions. He is the author of many scientific articles and books, including *Côte d'Ivoire: Self-Reinvention in Violence*.

Chapter 10

Sam Lloyd is a PhD student at the Institute of Science Technology and Policy at the Swiss Federal Institute of Technology in Zurich. His current research seeks to identify effective strategies for violence prevention in the urban settings of Bogotá, Colombia, and Cape Town, South Africa. Formerly, he was a researcher at the Centre for Justice and Crime Prevention in Cape Town and at the University of Cape Town's School of Public Health and Family Medicine. Sam completed his Master of Public Health at that university's School of Public Health and Family Medicine with a specialisation in Epidemiology and Biostatistics.

Richard Matzopoulos is a chief specialist scientist and deputy director at the Medical Research Council's Burden of Disease Research Unit. He is also an Honorary Research Associate at the University of Cape Town's School of Public Health and Family Medicine, where he coordinates its Violence and Injury Research programme. He advises the Western Cape Government on alcohol harm reduction, and interpersonal violence and injury prevention and surveillance. He is a South African focal point for the international Violence Prevention Alliance, and serves on the Steering Committee of the International Collaborative Effort on Injury Statistics and Methods.

Foreword

Caroline Moser

For more than 20 years now, academics and practitioners alike have considered urban violence—with its dynamics of poverty and inequality—a critical constraint on development for cities in the Global South. In 1997, when I completed the first study on urban violence and poverty in Jamaica for the World Bank, urban violence was most often considered a problem of individual criminal pathology. This was despite the fact that rapes, thefts, threats to personal safety, and politically motivated killings all dominated the pages of the local Jamaican press—as did "the erosion of local community social capital".

By the early 2000s, some researchers—many rooted in the realities of Latin American cities—had begun to use terms such as "ubiquitous", "endemic", or "banalised" to describe urban violence. They first defined the phenomenon, and then broadened its meaning to include wider contexts. Criminal violence was no longer merely an individual matter, it could also be a political one. The state itself could be, and was, viewed as a dominant perpetrator of violence, as its institutions penetrated the lives of people and communities. The boundaries between everyday violence and actual war and conflict became blurred, especially when urban warfare was associated with attacks on civilian populations.

Despite impressive advances in our understanding of urban violence, a mere two decades is indisputably a very short time frame to create theories, evolve policies, recommend changes, and implement plans. During this same period, dramatic increases in urbanisation in the Global South have intensified overall levels of crime, violence, insecurity, and fear. One disconcerting outcome of this is the widespread normalisation of "ordinary" violence, which is now almost an accepted part of everyday life—and which particularly affects the livelihoods, mobility, and well-being of the most excluded and marginalised populations. This often includes a continuum of violence between private and public spaces.

For scholars and policymakers alike, one consequence of rising urban violence has been the tendency to focus either on micro-level local details or on macro-level broad generalisations. The latter tend to identify sweeping recommendations that encompass both the Global North and South. For instance, the New Urban Agenda—created by Habitat III, and endorsed by national governments in Quito in October 2016—includes this generic commitment (Clause 39): "to promote a safe, healthy, inclusive, and secure environment in cities and human settlements for all to live, work, and participate in urban life, without fear of violence and intimidation." This is followed by specific considerations for women and girls, for children and youth, and for other persons in vulnerable situations who are most often affected by violence.

Both micro- and macro-level approaches miss the middle ground, the meso-level focus, which calls for broader comparative perspectives. This approach identifies similarities, as well as diversities, across cities with different levels of determining characteristics: degree of urbanisation, politico-economic situation, sociocultural context, and so on. This critical gap in our knowledge of those issues has now been ably filled by the recent Safe and Inclusive Cities initiative (SAIC) of Canada's International Development Research Centre (IDRC), jointly funded with the United Kingdom's Department for International Development. Since 2012, 15 research teams in 16 countries have studied more than 40 cities in Latin America, South Asia, and sub-Saharan Africa. Their dedicated work has contributed fundamentally to the body of scholarship on this urgent topic: the interactions between the key drivers of urban violence, and their relationship with poverty and inequalities.

From the initial design of the project through its successful implementation, this initiative had two unique features. The first is its specific focus on the Global South, privileging evidence and theory-building from there—and, when necessary, challenging established Global North–developed theory. The second feature is the project's inclusion of space for the researchers to document the evolution of their processes—the methodology of how they built and adapted their theories. I discuss both of these in more detail below.

The first feature, the Global South focus, was critical to the selection criteria for the project. It received more than 300 research proposals from around the globe—a real testament to the widespread recognition of the importance of studying the problems of urban violence. This challenge has involved Southern researchers testing their existing theory against new empirical data—and, frequently, having to adapt the theory. Some scholars have studied the Latin American cities of Bogotá, Lima, and Santiago; others have examined the failure of urban services in India, resulting in contesting theories of the state and its responsibilities. In Zimbabwe, the researchers' focus shifted from structural to infrastructural violence; in Central America, the change was from structural violence to social exclusion; and in Sri Lanka, the adaptation was from post-conflict theory to a humanitarian approach.

The larger challenge for the contributors was to develop theoretical and conceptual frameworks that were specifically grounded in a Southern perspective. In Pakistan, for instance, the project rejected theories of spectacular public violence linked to terrorism, introducing instead a framework to focus on "normalised" everyday violence. In Mozambique, the outcome of research on men and masculinities was to transcend feminist theory on gender-based violence, with its women-only focus, and to develop a more inclusive gendered framework. In all cases, the perspectives of these studies from the Global South can make valuable contributions to Northern debates and practices—both in terms of theory construction and of policy recommendations.

The second unique project feature is its inclusion of space to document the evolution of the actual processes of building and adapting theories. This required the researchers to create narratives of their initial conceptual frameworks, to reflect on how these frameworks were applied, to consider their adaptations for fieldwork methodologies, and, finally, to analyse the adjustments to their frameworks, based on the empirical evidence. Again, important questions underlie the implications of how such theoretical frameworks have evolved to understand urban violence from many different perspectives.

This research process not only gives researchers the opportunity to contest or adapt their ideas, it also gives them room to reflect on their research context. Critical reflexivity emphasises the testing of theory against practice, requiring researchers to question "objective" social reality. This can often be an unsettling task for the practitioner, who must be prepared to explore new possibilities and alternative explanations of reality (as well as to respond to others' perceptions of personal and professional identity). As the authors of the chapter on Zimbabwe so aptly demonstrate: Research projects tend to develop a life of their own, driven by the ever-increasing findings, and by the perspectives that develop from them. They are also deeply influenced by the personal situations of both the researchers and their subjects.

In many of the studies, gender roles and relations were particularly pertinent to reflexivity. In Pakistan, for instance, researchers came to recognise that while urban spaces shaped the people who live in them, the reverse could also be true. The problems women experienced with mobility in Karachi, for example, inspired them to challenge traditional gender roles. In Côte d'Ivoire, stereotypes around gang masculinity were challenged by the contradictory roles of women in such groups.

Researching the subject of violence was also recognised to have particular challenges. In Venezuela, a double methodology was developed to capture qualitative diversity along with the quantified measurements. In South Africa, counter-intuitive findings on levels of mental depression led the team to reposition the indicators it used to measure the multi-faced nature of violence.

The fact that IDRC's Safe and Inclusive Cities initiative provided space for reflexivity about the process itself—and that the researchers were confident enough to incorporate those components, along with their final results and recommendations—is in itself an indicator of the project's achievement. After two decades of empirical case studies, and the documentation of homicide statistics, a study that was merely "more of the same" would have had a limited ability to contribute to either theory or practice. Instead, this initiative is an important step forward in addressing the complex phenomenon that is urban violence. And, in a donor world, where most funders focus primarily on outcomes and policy implications, this project and book can definitely be viewed as exceptional.

Accordingly, as a strategic advisor to IDRC on this initiative, it gives me profound pleasure to provide this preface to the first of the two books that will present the research results. And, in the project's own spirit of reflection and collectivity, I would like to recognise all the people involved in achieving this successful endeavour. This includes the IDRC team, headed by Jennifer Salahub and ably supported by Markus Gottsbacher and John de Boer; the co-funders, the International Development Research Centre and the United Kingdom's Department for International Development, both of which had the vision to support the project; and the almost two dozen researchers on three continents, who showed such perseverance and astuteness in their ability to complete local, city-level, and cross-city studies. Above all, we should remember the hundreds of women and men—the citizens of those diverse urban environments—who willingly shared with the researchers the detailed information about their daily lives, on which the entire initiative is grounded.

Caroline Moser
Emeritus Professor
University of Manchester

Acknowledgements

While three names appear on the cover or this book, it is the result of hard work and dedication by many more than its co-editors. To that end, we offer our sincere thanks to the many contributors to the book and to the Safe and Inclusive Cities initiative. Authors and co-authors of individual chapters maintained an exceptional level of enthusiasm and engagement throughout the process. They took on the challenge of thinking about their research and research process in a different way and together, we drafted, reviewed, revised, and discussed ideas that, at many times, pushed us to think creatively and dynamically. In that process, the team benefited enormously from a write-shop hosted by the Rockefeller Bellagio Center.

Our particular thanks go to Professor Caroline Moser who immersed herself in our project and offered patient, careful, and essential advice throughout the writing and revision in addition to providing detailed comments on draft chapters. Numerous colleagues at the International Development Research Centre also provided crucial support including Barbara Alves, Patricia Alves, Florencio Ceballos, Adrian di Giovanni, Cam Do, Roula El-Rifai, Kristin Farr, Nola Haddadian, Njeri Karuru, Veronique McKinnon, Martha Mutisi, Marie Renaud, Navsharan Singh, and Ramata Thioune. Routledge's Helena Hurd guided us through the publication process with care and purpose. Antonia Morton took on the challenge of copyediting a volume with a diverse range of voices, writing styles, and approaches to citations.

As anyone who has edited a book knows, it can easily become an all-consuming task. We thank our families for their patience and support when we spent evenings bent over computer screens and dominated dinnertime conversation with talking through ideas, in particular Jahel Garfias, James McCrea, and Wynn McCrea.

Finally, Safe and Inclusive Cities would not have been possible without the financial support of Canada's International Development Research Centre and the United Kingdom's Department for International Development. The opinions expressed in this work do not necessarily reflect those of IDRC or DFID.

Acronyms and abbreviations

ARENA	Alianza Republicana Nacionalista (Republican Nationalist Alliance, El Salvador)
CE	collective efficacy (hypothesis)
CELADE	Centro Latinoamericano y Caribeño de Demografía (Latin American and Caribbean Demographic Centre)
CEPAL	Comisión Económica para América Latina (Economic Commission for Latin America)
CHS	community household survey
CID	conflict-induced displacement
CLACSO	Consejo Latinoamericano de Ciencias Sociales (Latin Amercian Council for Social Sciences)
CPTED	Crime Prevention Through Environmental Design
DFDR	development-forced displacement and relocation
DFID	Department for International Development (UK)
DRC	Democratic Republic of Congo
FGD	focus group discussion
FLACSO	Facultad Latinoamericana de Ciencias Sociales (Latin American Faculty for the Social Sciences)
FPS	Forensic Pathology Service (South Africa)
GDP	gross domestic product
GIS	geographic information systems
HOPEM	Rede Homens pela Mudança (Men for Change Network, Mozambique)
IDB	Inter-American Development Bank
IDPs	internally displaced persons
IDRC	International Development Research Centre
IMAGES	International Men and Gender Equality Survey
IOM	International Organization for Migration
IRLR	impoverishment risk and livelihood reconstruction
KII	key informant interview
MCD	Municipal Corporation of Delhi
NGO	non-governmental organisation

NSI	North-South Institute
RCT	randomised controlled trial
R-I	Rawalpindi-Islamabad
SAIC	Safe and Inclusive Cities (programme)
SAIMD	South African Indices of Multiple Deprivation
SASPRI	South African Social Policy Research Institute
SES	socioeconomic status
SGBV	sexual and gender-based violence
SN	Sarojini Nagar (market, New Delhi)
UN	United Nations
UNESCO	United Nations Educational, Scientific and Cultural Organization
UNODC	United Nations Office on Drugs and Crime
VC	Viklang Colony (New Delhi)
VPUU	Violence Prevention through Urban Upgrading (programme, Cape Town)
WHO	World Health Organization
ZANU(PF)	Zimbabwe African National Union (Patriotic Front)

Introduction

Global South theories of urban violence, poverty, and inequalities

Jennifer Erin Salahub, John de Boer, and Markus Gottsbacher

We live in an urban world, which brings both benefits and challenges. The benefits of more than half the world's population living in urban centres (UN DESA 2007) are easily visible: cities are where jobs, education, health services, and cultural activities are concentrated. Urban populations also tend to live longer and healthier lives compared to their rural counterparts (Singh 2014). Cities are often the engine of a country's economic growth, generating some 80 per cent of global GDP (World Bank 2016). For this reason, rural populations often migrate to cities—either in search of economic opportunities, or to seek refuge from war, poverty, and disaster.

Whatever their motivation, every week some 3 million people move to cities in low- and middle-income countries of the Global South—particularly in Africa and Asia, which are least equipped to deal with such growing populations (UN-Habitat 2008). From this fact come the challenges that offset the benefits of urbanisation, since many such countries must struggle to accommodate these new city dwellers. Infrastructures, both physical and social (Simone 2004), are often strained to the breaking point, and, without a conventional space designated for them, new arrivals are often forced into overcrowded informal settlements such as slums, shantytowns, and *favelas*. In these areas, there is little, if any, access to basic public services such as water, electricity, and sanitation; and these services are often neither reliable nor affordable (IOM 2015). Nor are the residents able to access social infrastructure such as education, justice, and employment. Sadly, violence in all its forms is a regular experience in many of these areas; in some cases, it even becomes normalised.[1] The structural, infrastructural, physical, and exclusionary forms of violence reflect the complexity of the phenomenon. We must emphasise that there is no single form, type, or manifestation of violence, but many different-but-equal *violences*. Given such problems to contend with, living conditions are often unsustainable.

As pressure mounts on city authorities to deal with these challenges, they have only a few empirical studies to rely on for guidance—especially ones grounded in the realities of the Global South. International conversations (whether academic, policy-focused, or practice-related) tend to be dominated by authors from the Global North. Most of their attempts to theorise the causes of urban inequality, poverty, and violence draw on experiences from the Global North, notably historic inner-city studies in the United States.[2] While these studies have often guided interventions in American cities such as Boston (Operation Ceasefire), Los Angeles (Safe Streets Program), and New York (Zero Tolerance), few have any direct relevance to the Global South. These Northern interventions, from very different urban contexts, are of limited use to Southern authorities and practitioners who want to understand and cope with the drivers of urban violence in their communities. One reason for this is that they tend to be resource-intensive and costly. This makes them challenging to implement, particularly in environments that must cope with multiple ongoing and interlocking crises, such as extreme poverty and inequalities, health emergencies, and armed conflict. These conditions are frequently combined with historical legacies of racism, sexism, and segregation, and are further exacerbated by environmental degradation and disaster. These multi-layered problems of many cities of the Global South require new approaches that are better suited to their local realities, resources, and capacities (Muggah 2012).

That is the rationale of this essay collection, which shares perspectives from three regions: Latin America, South Asia, and sub-Saharan Africa. It seeks to help fill the knowledge gap by bringing together exciting original research developed and implemented *by* Global South researchers, *for* Global South challenges. This book is based on three years of rigorous data collection and analysis in numerous urban areas of the Global South, under the auspices of the Safe and Inclusive Cities (SAIC) initiative. Jointly funded by the United Kingdom's Department for International Development, and Canada's International Development Research Centre, the SAIC programme sought to identify the drivers of urban violence, and examine how they relate to poverty and inequalities. To that end, it also supported Southern researchers in the task of theorising and conceptualising the intersections of urban violence, poverty, and inequalities—including their causes and possible explanations for these dynamics.

To our knowledge, this is a unique initiative, and, as a result, this book is also unique. Its 10 chapters describe what happens when Global North theories and conceptual frameworks meet the reality of life in some of the most dangerous cities of the Global South. It is important to note that this book does not *develop* new theories or *criticise* Northern theories; rather, it *challenges* their application to Southern contexts, and attempts to *adapt* them to new concepts and innovations. Our co-authors test and challenge conventional theories from their Southern perspectives. In the process, several themes emerge, which we explore below.

Northern theory, Southern theory

Some of the research presented here explicitly tests the relevance of Northern theory to Southern contexts. In Chapter 7, Enrique Desmond Arias and

Ximena Tocornal Montt consider the work done by Robert Sampson and his colleagues on the social bonds that hold communities together. Sampson's concept of "collective efficacy" examines what it takes to motivate communities to take action for the common good. Tested in urban Chicago since 1995, it suggests that strong social bonds contribute to collective efficacy, and act as a bulwark against crime and violence in urban neighbourhoods (Sampson and Wilson 1995). Arias, Tocornal, and their research teams sought to understand what drives violence in Latin American neighbourhoods with high levels of inequality by applying Sampson's ideas to three Latin American cities: Bogota (Colombia), Lima (Peru), and Santiago (Chile). In doing so, they found the concept wanting in such settings. Their chapter points out the important implications for security policy—particularly with respect to policing—and for interventions based on social control and social disorganisation.

Chapters 6 and 8, by Rodolfo Calderón Umaña and Roberto Briceño-León, also test Northern theory in Southern realities, applying them in Costa Rica and El Salvador (Calderón) and Venezuela (Briceño-León). The latter chapter examines our understanding of formal and informal institutions and norms, as well as the rule of law. Briceño-León describes social institutions and norms in the slums of Caracas, Venezuela, and the interactions there between poverty, inequality, and urban violence. He finds that those interactions bring about results that, from a Northern perspective, seem counter-intuitive. Particularly important is the prominent role of women in local peace-building processes. Calderón, on the other hand, challenges the idea of structural violence in Costa Rica and El Salvador. Instead, he suggests that the concept of social exclusion offers greater clarity about the economic and identity-based sources of violence among criminals, particularly young men.

Other authors construct theory inductively through their work. In contrast to the top-down manner described in the last two chapters, this bottom-up approach is best reflected in Francis Akindès' research on the relatively new phenomenon of the child and youth gangs (known as the "Microbes") in three cities of Côte d'Ivoire. In Chapter 9, Akindès assesses the personal experiences of the youth to understand the moral basis, as well as the political economy, of the gang members when they commit their crimes. He finds that—as in Central America—it is the social dimension that counts most, giving meaning to the lives the children must lead outside of mainstream society. That desire for some kind of social inclusion plays a crucial role in their decisions to join a criminal gang.

Dealing with a very different context, but with a similar approach, in Chapter 5, Danesh Jayatilaka, Rajith W. D. Lakshman, and Iresha M. Lakshman challenge the dominance of post-conflict theory in their analysis of urban environments in a country recovering from civil war, Sri Lanka. Finding these theories lacking in their explanation of what they observed in Colombo and Jaffna, the authors bring a humanitarian approach to understanding violence in those cities. The community responses to displacement they document are characterised by resilience, at both the individual and community level.

Research in Pakistan by Nausheen H. Anwar, Sarwat Viqar, and Daanish Mustafa, presented in Chapter 1, focuses on the "normalised" violence of everyday urban life experienced by the female residents of Karachi and Rawalpindi-Islamabad. Women face a range of threats: from difficulty accessing water and sanitation services, to gendered restrictions on their movement in public places due to male domination, to the direct physical danger of getting caught in the crossfire between rival tribal factions. Their focus on *everyday* violence changes the focus away from the dominant narrative of Pakistan as a place where spectacular public violence (often caused by terrorists) is endemic. Similarly, in Chapter 2, Esmeralda Mariano, Henny Slegh, and Sílvia Roque analyse men and masculinities in Maputo, Mozambique. Their work challenges our focus on women as the only group of concern for analyses of gender-based violence in urban settings.

Urban security and safety

An important topic that we have frequently debated with our research partners is terminology: the exact meanings of urban security and urban safety. Are they largely synonyms? Our Spanish-speaking colleagues use only one term: *seguridad urbana*. Yet in English, and to a lesser degree in French, the phrases invoke different sets of ideas. As our co-authors engage with the two concepts, it is worthwhile to highlight the key differences between them. In practice, the term "safety" seems to place a slightly greater emphasis on personal protection, while "security" focuses more on the "harder" aspects of security, particularly policing.

As foreign policy and international development practice have evolved, the focus has shifted to talk of urban safety. Today, policing is viewed as only one element of the task of creating a safe city and it is at the forefront along with other elements such as urban planning, the design of public spaces, and the provision of basic services. This new focus reflects a growing awareness of a wide variety of types of violence. These range from the interpersonal public or domestic violence that results in bodily injury to individuals; to the destruction of property or livelihood by private- or public-sector agents; to more insidious forms of discrimination and structural violence. This evolution is reflected, to a certain degree, in the UN-Habitat Safer Cities Programme, which supports urban municipalities in their goal of improving both safety and security for their residents.

In this book, our goal is to further expand the definition of what it means to be safe in the city. How, for instance, do measurable evidence-based safety and security compare with residents' personal perceptions of their own safety? In Chapter 7, as mentioned earlier, Arias and Tocornal examine that issue in Latin America. They find that citizens of Santiago face lower levels of violence than residents of two similar cities, Bogota and Lima, yet they feel the least secure. What are the implications of these data for researchers, city residents, or municipal policymakers? Likewise, in New Delhi, as described by Manoj Bandan Balsamanta and Bhim Reddy in Chapter 4, how do residents interpret "safety" when the violence they most experience (evictions, extortion, and abuse of power) is perpetrated by agents of the state?

Importantly, as our co-authors analyse the dynamics of violence and exclusion they reveal different ideas about what it means to be safe and secure in various contexts. In Zimbabwe, as shown in Chapter 3 by Julie Stewart, Rosalie Katsande, Olga Chisango, and Sian Maseko, the historical realities created by colonialism influence feelings of insecurity even today. In Harare, the very fabric of the city was originally designed to exclude and control black African populations. Now it is used to exclude and control different groups—often along political and gender lines. In these contexts, women are often most at risk. In many cases, they are left with no legal right to the homes they live in or access to the state services to which they are constitutionally entitled.

Taking a different approach rooted in public health and epidemiology, in Chapter 10, Sam Lloyd and Richard Matzopoulos show the socio-economic drivers of urban insecurity in the suburban townships of Cape Town, South Africa. Their analysis points to correlations among violence, income inequality, informal housing, and access to alcohol. They also share some innovative approaches to analysing these by developing groups of indicators of urban insecurity. This type of examination can greatly increase our understanding of the factors that explain why some contexts of poverty and inequality spill over into violence, and others do not. These safety factors also help to better define Southern perspectives on the urban issues we discuss here. Still, their specificity to certain contexts makes them difficult to even measure, let alone design policies and programmes that are easily replicable.

Inclusion and exclusion

A nascent, but growing, body of evidence now links urban violence to social, economic, and political exclusion (Koonings and Kruijt 2006, 2010). While this evidence is still relatively under-researched (and still largely based on urban studies in the Global North), patterns are starting to emerge that link an increase in violence and crime with a wide range of social factors. These include income and social inequality, concentrated poverty, high levels of impunity for misbehaving officials, and high unemployment and disenfranchisement, particularly among young men.[3] A focus on the aspects of inclusion and exclusion offers a promising perspective on those who are marginalised and alienated from the benefits of the city. This approach encompasses both the material challenges that exclude individuals from full membership in urban society, and the intangible normative issues that delineate and demarcate physical, social, and political spaces.

In the following chapters, we see this problem indicated in every region. In Venezuela, for instance, Briceño-León looks at why two young men who grow up in similar conditions of poverty and material deprivation experience such different outcomes—especially in their personal use of violence. As Briceño-León explains, risk factors abound in such situations, but intangible normative aspects of inclusion or exclusion also influence individuals' lives. Incorporating these important intangibles into analyses of urban violence requires understanding social norms within a society, and also how the normalisation of violence against particular social groups reinforces exclusion.

In Central America and West Africa, respectively, Calderón and Akindès show how feelings of being excluded from society are linked to ideas of needing to be economically contributing members—of families or of society more broadly. As so much of the violence in these two places comes from young men, several authors, such as Mariano, Slegh, and Roque in Mozambique, explore the links between violence, toxic forms of masculinity, and social expectations. These links clarify the continuum of violence between private and public spaces, and how it is so easily normalised—as Anwar et al. also do from a gendered perspective.

The normalisation of violence as a form of exclusion is perhaps most clearly visible in Balsamanta and Reddy's chapter on the everyday violence experienced by the urban poor at the hands of the Indian state and its agents. Rather than the catastrophic terrorist violence or epidemic-level homicide rates experienced by other countries, for most poor Indians, the violence they experience is endemic to their lives, and merely one facet of social exclusion. Forced displacement, demolition of their homes, extortion, and harassment are all explored as the authors uncover the normative aspects of exclusion that create space for the manifestations of violence that most poor people find impossible to escape. As Balsamanta and Reddy point out, these structural, infrastructural, physical, and exclusionary violences serve to reinforce the power structures that create them.

This research presents an important counterpoint to the enduring perception, particularly in the Global North, that poverty alone causes crime and violence. As pointed out by Arias and Tocornal, many poor countries have relatively low crime levels. The determining factor is not their lack of resources, but their lack of social inclusion. In terms of their potential for generating violence, the normative aspects of exclusion play a role that is equally important, if not more so, than mere poverty.

The city

Throughout the SAIC initiative, we and our research partners frequently asked ourselves why we focused specifically on *urban* violences. Why is the city setting different from other types of violence? The result of our thinking is that the city—in all its social and structural forms—contributes to, creates space for, and amplifies or dampens violence, in ways that do not happen in rural or non-urban areas. The inevitable dynamics of new urbanisation, such as large-scale in-migration and informal settlements, create conflict and violence in sometimes unexpected or unpredictable ways, which require us to expand our ideas of urban violence.

In Sri Lanka, for example, Jayatilaka, Lakshman, and Lakshman show the changing nature of violence in a post-conflict context: urban violence is not simply about counting homicides. It also extends to experiences of inclusion and exclusion from urban society. Similarly, the pressures of migration and displacement also destabilise traditional gender roles, with violent results, as highlighted by Mariano, Slegh, and Roque's work in Mozambique.

In other contexts, violence is fed by the failures of the state to meet its "social contract" responsibilities by delivering services. In Karachi, for instance (as described by Anwar, Viqar, and Mustafa), vital services such as transportation are frequently provided by private entities. In theory, all residents should have access to urban services, and seats are reserved for women on buses. But in practice, the drivers often unceremoniously eject women from their vehicles so that they can pack the space with several more men (standing and seated), and earn more revenue. Similarly, Stewart, Katsande, Chisango, and Maseko describe how agents of the state in Zimbabwe use poor residents as pawns in a political game. As the state reneges on its obligations to provide services, the violence that results can leave Harare's most vulnerable populations homeless. This example shows how violence comes about when those in power seek to capture the state and keep it for their own benefit rather than fulfilling their responsibilities toward its citizens.

Gender and urban violence

As with the other themes in this book, we present some encouraging examples of advancements in gender relations, both in theory and in practice. Several chapters—such as those by Briceño-León; Anwar, Viqar, and Mustafa; and Balsamanta and Reddy—demonstrate changes in the ways that women are typically characterised in research on urban violence. In cities as far apart as Harare and Caracas, women are claiming their spaces in the city, and moving beyond stereotypes of women as simple victims. A good example, discussed in Chapter 1, is the young woman from a traditional Karachi family, who (like many girls alone in public places) is often taunted and mocked by young men as she walks to college. Once intimidated, she and her friends are now determined to ignore the harassment so that they can continue their education. "When boys shout at me, I ignore them," she says. "We say: If they insist on barking, let them bark."

The women of Caracas, as Briceño-León explains, are capable of taking on important leadership roles in the city's social institutions: schools, the church, and informal peace-building alliances. Mothers scolded gang members who no one else dared to confront; teachers denounced delinquents if they came to school with guns; and nuns held street processions of saints to reclaim public spaces. These women are working to help prevent the violence they, their families, and neighbours see around them and to which they are exposed. Some women are breaking out of their strict gender roles to pursue lives of their own choosing. Others are finding more subtle ways to resist and create space for themselves, either at home or in public. As Balsamanta and Reddy describe, women living in informal settlements in India are likewise taking greater responsibility for their own safety as they resist government harassment and advocate for improved services. Akindès, for his part, describes girls' roles in Côte d'Ivoire's violent youth gangs, touching on both their agency and their exploitation.

Particularly in South Asia, we see the city helping to change gender roles, particularly women's roles. There are more women in urban centres than ever before, and female-headed households are increasingly common. Women are joining the workforce, albeit more in informal sectors than formal ones. But the benefits of urbanisation do not accrue equally to men and women, as women continue to be largely responsible for household work and caring for others—in addition to their paid employment (Pozarny 2016). But, as described earlier, despite women's need to travel within cities to access economic and educational opportunities, they are still regularly harassed for being out in public spaces. The traditional perception that "a good woman remains in the home" dies hard, even among the poor who cannot afford such a luxury.

However, urban violence does not always leave men untouched. Anwar, Viqar, and Mustafa, along with Mariano, Slegh, and Roque, also examine how concepts of masculinity—ideas about what it means to be a man—frequently combine to create violence in both public and private spaces. Similar iterative processes are reflected in how men shape the city and, in turn, are shaped by it. The Mozambique narrative describes how poor men in the country's capital face serious challenges to their masculinity linked to their limitations in terms of finding employment. Often men's perceptions of a dominant or hegemonic masculinity connect the male exercise of power with the act of engaging in violence towards others, particularly women. In Maputo, as elsewhere, men may see their social selves as evolving to include different versions of masculinity. In situations of post-conflict urban violence, those are often about trying to cope with the effects of a loss of power.

The research process

Finally, these 10 chapters all reflect on the actual process of doing research in challenging environments characterised by poverty, inequality, and violence. They show the struggles, compromises, and innovations that researchers must make when trying to obtain data in difficult contexts. In countries of the Global South, the available data are often extremely limited and researchers must find proxies to measure their variables, as Lloyd and Matopoulos did in South Africa. Often the researchers tried to apply an explanatory model to their context, and found it wanting, as Arias and Tocornal did with Sampson's work when applied to Latin America. And all the writers had to grapple with theories that did not fit their contexts, data that challenged their theories, or concepts that had to be adapted to make sense. The advantage of this method is that combining different approaches can yield greater insight and explanatory power.

The diverse range of scholarship assembled here represents a variety of fields, spanning criminology, sociology, economics, political science, social anthropology, health, urban studies, and women's law, to mention but a few. As a result, we hope that this book—filled with analyses of the lived realities of individuals and communities in over 40 cities across the Global South—will speak to audiences that are just as diverse.

Together, these chapters show the value of bringing together researchers from across the Global South, on the cutting edge of social science, and working with them to investigate and identify solutions to these challenging problems. For us, the privilege of working with the SAIC initiative is the opportunity it offers to support our research partners as they work to deepen and strengthen their South-to-South networks, which are helping find lasting solutions to these global problems.

Concluding thoughts

Among the many objectives of the SAIC initiative was the goal of providing resources to allow exceptional scholars in the Global South to make theoretical contributions to ongoing debates—such as on urban safety and violence, and on inclusion and exclusion—that have previously been dominated by voices from the Global North. Accordingly, this book includes chapters that directly challenge Northern-led theory, and show the futility of trying to apply it in a cookie-cutter fashion to places with very different dynamics of poverty, inequality, and violence. Some authors adapt theory inductively from the evidence, offering conceptualisations that provide greater explanatory power in the contexts of the cities they studied. Others bring analytical tools from other fields to help explain the features of their communities. All provide uniquely Southern perspectives; and all engage slightly differently with the topic of violence in urban settings, and with how gender dynamics can mould experiences of violence—for perpetrators and victims, for men and women.

Throughout, our co-authors assess how existing theories apply—or do not—to their specific contexts. They use the evidence from their original research to offer in-depth insights and analyses of these cities, and of others in the Global South. In many cases, they also offer suggestions for ways to reduce or prevent violence and exclusion—and, in the process, to make cities safer for the growing numbers of people who call them home.

Notes

1 This is the case in many informal settlements in South Africa, for example, where a significant portion of violent crimes are concentrated (Wakefield and Tait 2015).

2 Muggah (2012) provides a broad overview of the main theories that have shaped current thinking. Some of the dominant theories include the social disorganisation theories of the Chicago School of Sociology; the "broken windows" theories; the ecological model; theories about social capital and social cohesion; and studies that emphasise the impact of youth empowerment and employment. For work on social disorganisation, see Sampson and Wilson (1995). The ecological approach has been largely shaped by the health community, which promotes a preventative health approach to dealing with issues of urban violence. See, for instance, Dahlberg and Krug (2002).

Moreover, we do not intend to dismiss important research on the Global South by researchers based in the North. Our goal is simply to highlight the fact that most of the prescriptive, theory-based, and theoretical conversation has been dominated by Northern voices. For important contributions to the nexus of urban violence, poverty, and inequality in the Global South, see (for example) two special issues of *Environment and Urbanization*:

- 16(12) on "Urban Violence and Insecurity", from 2004
- 26(2) on "Conflict and Violence in 21st Century Cities", from 2014.

3 These theories are still contested. Work by Glaeser, Resseger, and Tobio (2009), for example, supports the link between inequality and violence. Roberts and Willits (2015) assessed income-inequality measures against homicide data in 208 large US cities, and concluded that the two correlated highly regardless of what measures of inequality were used. Discussions of urban unemployment rates and violence include Raphael and Winter-Ebmer (2001); Carmichael and Ward (2001); and Baron (2008). Bradford (2011) also provides some insight on impunity and police efficacy.

References

Baron, Stephen W. (2008). Street youth, unemployment, and crime: Is it that simple? Using general strain theory to untangle the relationship. *Canadian Journal of Criminology and Criminal Justice* 50(4): 399–434.

Bradford, Ben (2011). *Police numbers and crime rates: A rapid evidence review*. London: Her Majesty's Inspectorate of Constabulary. www.justiceinspectorates.gov.uk/hmic/publications/police-numbers-crime-rates-rapid.

Carmichael, Fiona, and Robert Ward (2001). Male unemployment and crime in England and Wales. *Economics Letters* 73(1): 111–115.

Dahlberg, Linda L., and Etienne G. Krug (2002). Violence: A global public health problem. In Etienne G. Krug, Linda L. Dahlberg, James A. Mercy, Anthony B. Zwi, and Rafael Lozano (Eds.), *World report on violence and health*. Geneva: World Health Organization.

Glaeser, Edward L., Matt Resseger, and Kristina Tobio (2009). Inequality in cities. *Journal of Regional Science* 49(4): 617–646.
IOM: International Organization for Migration (2015). *World migration report 2015, migrants and cities: New partnerships to manage mobility*. Geneva: Author. http://publications.iom.int/system/files/wmr2015_en.pdf.
Koonings, Kees, and Dirk Kruijt (Eds.) (2006). *Fractured cities: Social exclusion, urban violence and contested spaces in Latin America*. London: Zed Books.
——— (2010). *Megacities: The politics of exclusion and violence in the Global South*. London: Zed Books.
Muggah, Robert (2012). *Researching the urban dilemma: Urbanization, poverty and violence*. Ottawa: International Development Research Centre (IDRC). www.idrc.ca/EN/PublishingImages/Researching-the-Urban-Dilemma-Baseline-study.pdf.
Pozarny, Pamela F. (2016). *Gender roles and opportunities for women in urban environments*. Governance and Social Development Resource Centre (GSDRC) Helpdesk Research Report. Birmingham, UK: GSDRC and University of Birmingham.
Raphael, Steven, and Rudolf Winter-Ebmer (2001). Identifying the effect of unemployment on crime. *Journal of Law and Economics* 44(1): 259–283.
Roberts, Aki, and Dale Willits (2015). Income inequality and homicide in the United States: Consistency across different income inequality measures and disaggregated homicide types. *Homicide Studies* 19(1): 28–57.
Sampson, Robert J., and William Julius Wilson (1995). Toward a theory of race, crime, and urban inequality. In J. Hagan and R. D. Peterson (Eds.), *Crime and inequality*. Stanford: Stanford University Press.
Simone, AbdouMalik (2004). People as infrastructure: Intersecting fragments in Johannesburg. *Public Culture* 16(3): 407–428.
Singh, Gopal K., and Mohammad Siahpush (2014). Widening rural-urban disparities in life expectancy, US, 1969–2009. *American Journal of Preventive Medicine* 46(2): e19–e29.
UN DESA (2007). *World Urbanization Prospects. The 2007 Revision. Highlights*. New York: United Nations. www.un.org/esa/population/publications/wup2007/2007WUP_Highlights_web.pdf.
——— (2014). *World urbanization prospects: 2014*. New York: United Nations. https://esa.un.org/unpd/wup/publications/files/wup2014-highlights.Pdf.
UN-Habitat (2008). *State of the world's cities 2008/2009: Harmonious cities*. Nairobi: Author.
Wakefield, Lorenzo, and Sean Tait (2015). Crime and violence in formal and informal urban spaces in South Africa (Citizen security dialogues: Dispatches from South Africa). *Stability: International Journal of Security and Development* 4(1). doi: http://doi.org/10.5334/sta.fp.
World Bank (2016). *Urban development: Overview*. www.worldbank.org/en/topic/urbandevelopment/overview.

Part I

Gendered violences

1 Intersections of gender, mobility, and violence in urban Pakistan

Nausheen H. Anwar, Sarwat Viqar, and Daanish Mustafa

Introduction

In this chapter we explore the intersections of gender, mobility, and violence by analysing gender as a key mediator of mobility in two urban areas of Pakistan: Karachi and the twin cities of Rawalpindi-Islamabad (R-I). Karachi is the commercial hub of the country, Islamabad is the federal capital, and Rawalpindi is the headquarters of the all-powerful Pakistani military. By "mobility" we mean not only the literal physical movement of transportation, but also the contextualised activity in urban space that is imbued with meaning and power (Bondi 2005; Uteng 2009; Uteng and Cresswell 2008), and thus we also use "mobilities" to mark this plurality of meaning. The concept entails the potential for movement or the knowledge that potential trips can (or cannot) be made, due to various constraining factors. These range from poor infrastructure to cultural norms that dictate the mobility of different genders.

In particular, we situate the inhibited mobility of women within the larger context of the gendered power relations that generate and maintain a dominant masculinity, leading to claims about what is proper behaviour for men and women in public and private spaces (Srivastava 2012; Hsu 2011; Loukaitou-Sideris et al. 2009). Violence against women in public spaces often relates to ideas of "natural" claims to such spaces, following the popular perception that there are specific conditions under which men and women may access public spaces. How, then, do Pakistani women and men cope with spatial inequalities, and manage their mobility, in Karachi and R-I? How might this generate perceptions of fear and violence? How differentiated are physical and gendered mobilities between diverse neighbourhoods and across cities?

The research on which this chapter is based consists of intensive studies conducted across 12 low-income neighbourhoods in Karachi and R-I. In the course of our work, we analysed the responses to more than 2,400 questionnaires and 90 personal interviews; we also used participant photography. To present our findings, we first offer a brief sketch of our conceptual framework; this identifies the meanings of mobility and the notions of gendered processes in South Asia, and a conceptualisation of gendered violence. We then provide a summary of the city contexts. In the next section, we use quantitative and qualitative data to describe the state of access to transport in different neighbourhoods and cities. (In the poorer neighbourhoods of Karachi, access is inferior to that in R-I.) Next we discuss how the discursive and the material interact to conflate mobility and masculinity in a broader context of violence across the putative public–private divide. A key point we make is that gender-based violence is often experienced as a punishment for anyone who transgresses gender norms, with women's mobility further restricted in masculinised spaces—those deemed to be only for men—where intimidation or the threat of violence is always imminent. Finally, at the end of the chapter, we draw some conclusions based on our research.

Theoretical framework

Much journalistic, and some academic, attention has been paid to the various kinds of violence in Karachi: terrorist activity, ethnic violence, and extrajudicial killings by law-enforcement agencies (Verkaaik 2004; Gayer 2014; Chaudhry 2014; Ring 2006). However, everyday violence has not received much analysis. Scholars have identified many different forms of violence, including *structural* violence (Galtung 1969; Farmer 2004; Scheper-Hughes 1993), *symbolic* violence (Bourdieu and Wacqant 2001), *epistemic* violence (Taussig 1984), and *discursive* violence (MacKinnon 1993). However, there is no general theory of violence. We generally consider it a tactic of power involving physical coercion or the threat thereof; and, for the perpetrator, this acting-out of violence may be more the compensatory result of a loss of social power than a way to achieve it (Arendt 1969). According to various studies in Pakistan (Zulfiqar and Hasan 2012; Rozan 2007), the discourses of masculinity are deeply insecure about their control over female bodies, and hence prone to violence. This male insecurity is couched in terms of men's roles as the upholders of decency in society; therefore, violence is viewed as a necessary measure to maintain morality and tradition.

Given the power relationships inherent in gender-based violence, certain dominant ideals of manhood have an impact on women. Some scholars (Srivastava 2012) observe that gender norms and categories are directly related to the distribution of power, and that applies to control over symbolic as well as material goods—in other words, our ideas about the "appropriate" roles, capacities, and characteristics of men and women. For instance, masculinity refers to the socially produced but embodied ways of being male, and it manifests itself in speech, behaviour, gestures, social interaction, and the division of tasks thought proper for men and women in the home and in public. As a result, masculinity often stands as the binary opposite of feminine identity, being essentially an entitlement to power. The tension between that sense of entitlement, and the loss of social power, often contributes to the violence in which men and women find themselves caught up. Men in Karachi are often victims of direct state violence (Kirmani 2015) and differentiated forms of violence are interlinked across the public–private divide. Given Karachi's (and Pakistan's) lengthy and complex history of state violence, young men of a certain age and background can often simply find themselves in the wrong place at the wrong time. The fact that masculinity must be continually reinforced illustrates the tenuous and fragile nature of gender identity (Srivastava 2012).

While we envision violence as symptomatic of a loss of power, mobility can defy coercion. However, the exact way that personal mobility is actualised can either empower or disempower, depending on gender and its actualisation in urban spaces. Even though there is no strict geography of the public and private, certain behavioural norms still view the public domain as the natural preserve of men (Srivastava 2012). Men are expected to move easily between the public and private, yet women's mobility may be interpreted as transgression. In Pakistan, men generally have a greater sway over public spaces than women, and linked with this is the popular perception that men need not have any specific purpose to be in public spaces. They may loiter or hang out if they choose—but the idea of women doing so is generally inconceivable. Many feminists have questioned the relationship between masculinised places and gender inequality, including Hsu (2011), Monahan (2009), Valentine (1989), and Wesely and Gaarder (2004). Such studies show that highly masculinised spaces facilitate men's aggression towards women. When women do enter such spaces, they often rely on a set of coping strategies to negotiate the unequal treatment. This means that the relationship between mobility and space is constructed and experienced in a deeply gendered way, and this contributes to the reproduction of gender itself—as a social construct whose meanings are constantly remade and transformed within a given social context.

Since public and private spheres are not separate but intimately entwined, what happens in one always informs the other. In light of this, the dichotomy between young men's attitudes towards women within their homes, and towards women outside of their homes, makes a certain sense. Women at home are in their "proper" place, according to the gender codes. In the public sphere, they are perceived as constantly "transgressing" and hence must be policed in order to safeguard the masculinity of public spaces. For that reason, this chapter's conceptual discussion of mobility will focus on the public sphere and links between the public and private because the household scale requires different conceptual frameworks and methodologies.

We should point out that for society in Pakistan to become more socially just, a re-coding of these two spheres is required. In the urban context of our study, this is already happening to varying degrees: women are questioning their cultural relegation to the home and deliberately "transgressing" in public. This may be done out of economic compulsion: the necessity, in Pakistan's modern monetised society, for women to enter the salaried labour market. It may also happen out of political defiance, as when women engage in activism against regressive laws, such as when they seek justice for rape victims. Pakistani women might well look to the future and hope for state-supported policies to break down gender stereotypes and enhance women's ability to be mobile. It would be especially welcome if such policies could disrupt the perception that gender-based violence is merely a woman's problem. However, in this study, we focus on existing dynamics rather than potential ones.

City contexts

Pakistan has the highest annual rate of urbanisation (3.06 per cent) in South Asia and its current population (189 million) is projected to almost double by 2050, reaching 335 million. As Pakistan's largest city, and its centre of finance and commerce, Karachi is wealthy. But there are vast disparities in the distribution of its resources with 60 per cent of the population living in informal settlements and neighbourhoods (Hasan et al. 2013). These types of settlements exist in Rawalpindi, too, and the lowest-income earners live there along with ethnic and religious minorities (Mustafa 2005).

In these cities, the development of infrastructure has not kept pace with urbanisation and they have accumulated huge deficits in public services such as public transport, which adversely affect quality of life for the poorest residents (GOP 2011; Haider and Badami 2010). Most working-class residents of Karachi and R-I must rely on public transport, and R-I recently bought a very expensive state-of-the-art bus system. However, this has not helped women to increase their mobility: the issue is not the physical condition of the network, but the prevailing social attitudes. For the wealthy, private car ownership is constantly increasing. Public transport—especially in Karachi—has deteriorated rapidly to the detriment of the working classes (Hasan and Raza 2015). With continuous urban expansion, and the increase in informal settlements at the cities' peripheries, a significant disconnect now exists between the government's knowledge of its transportation networks and the mounting demands for such infrastructure in new settlements. In a recent study on the state of transport in Karachi (Hasan and Raza 2015), the authors note that, with the city's continued expansion, average commutes for the working class are now in the range of 20 to 40 kilometres.

The challenges of poor infrastructure are further exacerbated by the violent political economies. This is especially the case in Karachi, where political and state violence stems from deeply embedded historical tensions between the country's various ethnic groups (the Muhajirs and the Pakhtuns, for instance). Ethnic strife today is also driven by socioeconomic antagonisms.[1] Ethnic differences seem to be instrumental in facilitating access to power and resources and in making claims on the state. The complexity of this type of violence frequently feeds into the larger dynamic of spatial inequality in Karachi to the point that certain parts of the city have been deemed "no-go zones" for law enforcement.

Within this fractured urban context, class also plays a significant role in intensifying or mitigating the violence experienced by women and men. Rising inequality and income disparity has meant that working-class and low-income women have had to take on the role of family providers, forcing them into public spaces. Yet such women are precisely those most vulnerable to harassment and threats of violence. For them, taking public transportation is an undertaking fraught with danger—as we show in the following sections.

Physical mobility

Our analyses of the restrictions on men's and women's attitudes, perceptions, and practices of mobility in each city reveal that these depend on a combination of factors: access to transport, income levels, location of home neighbourhood, and the overall political-economic conditions. Religion was also a factor: women from some households, such as those in Karachi's Christian Colony, reported fewer restrictions on their mobility. As one female respondent explained, "We feel the difference from being more liberal." Although our respondents belonged to roughly the same income class, mobility still varied between neighbourhoods and cities. In the absence of access to private transport, most respondents depended on buses since other forms of public transport are restricted to rickshaws and taxi cabs—which are too expensive for most working-class people on a daily basis.

Since buses in urban Pakistan are always overcrowded—especially at rush hour—people are forced into close physical proximity with one another, making it impossible for women to keep the personal space necessary for modesty. For this reason, buses represent a masculinised space. The problem of male harassment of women is such that public transport is segregated, and men are not allowed in the space reserved for women in the front part of the bus (though they still manage to gain access). At best, only 10–20 per cent of the available seating is set aside for women. This means that women suffer daily intimidation and sexual harassment during their commutes. Even when the contact is not physical, women still experience the hostile gaze that objectifies them, creates fear and disgust, and affects their mobility.

This fact—that women prefer *not* to be squashed into physical contact with strange males—can make them an economic liability to the transport system. In Karachi, although the system is public, certain buses are run privately meaning that drivers may have a stake in the passenger load. One of our male respondents (Umar, 42, from Orangi Town, Karachi) explained the situation.

> The bus [driver] often does not stop for women because he knows that, instead of one woman, he can stuff four men into the same space. And sometimes if there are only one or two women in the front part of the bus and a lot of men come on board, the driver will simply make the women get off to accommodate the men because that means more money for him.

Another respondent (Sumayya, 23, from Dhok Naju, R-I) tells of her experience with using public transport: "The drivers and conductors stare at women indecently. The drivers touch us whenever they shift the gears." This situation is a common experience for women, one they also hear about from others.

Hasan and Raza's 2015 study of Karachi's public transport corroborates this dynamic and stresses the constrained choice for women. They feel uncomfortable and unwelcome on city buses, but there are no other realistic options for their daily commutes to and from work. Karachi, despite being Pakistan's main financial and commercial city, fares much worse than R-I in terms of the transportation infrastructure, as shown in Figure 1.1. (We asked respondents to rate their opinion of local transport using the Likert scale: 1 = No Access; 2 = Poor; 3 = Moderate; 4 = Good; 5 = Excellent.)

The people in our study sites mainly lived on the peripheries of Karachi, and the infrastructural disconnect there is severe. Not only are the roads generally in a state of decay, ethno-political tensions in certain parts of the city make travel problematic. For example, in Orangi Town, residents must negotiate transportation corridors that are deeply affected by Karachi's historical ethnic tensions. The five neighbourhoods of Orangi Town comprise a mixture of ethnicities. But for some Muhajir residents of Orangi Town

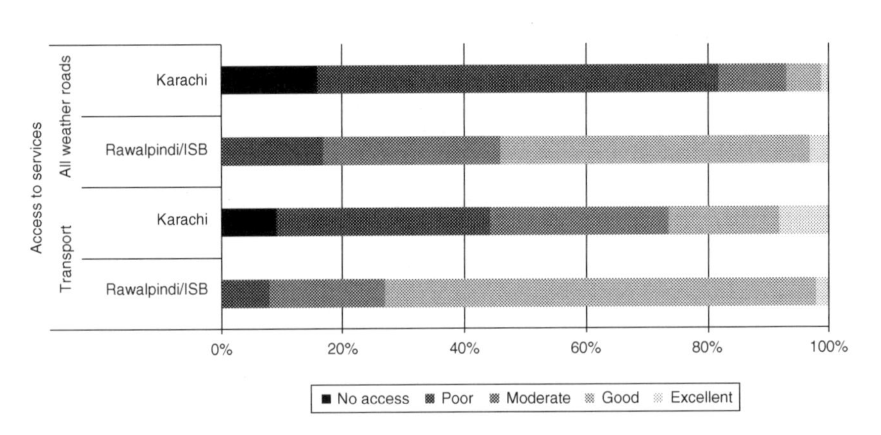

Figure 1.1 Access to transport and roads in Karachi and Rawalpindi-Islamabad
Source: Anwar et al. (2016).

to reach central Karachi, they must pass through the Pakhtun-dominated Banaras Chowk junction leading to the frequent eruption of ethnic violence between Muhajirs and Pakhtuns. Our male and female respondents from across the five neighbourhoods surveyed in Orangi Town continually emphasised that travelling via Banaras Chowk always carries a high risk of being exposed to violence. One female respondent from Orangi Town (Suneet, 25) told us of an incident she was involved in.

> My family does not allow me to go to college now. One day when I was returning home after taking an exam, the city situation changed suddenly, everything shut down in Banaras Chowk, and violence erupted along with firing [guns] and torching rubber tires. There was no public transport on the road. My friend and I were trapped on our way home, but fortunately she had a mobile phone. She immediately called her brother, who picked us [up] from Banaras and dropped me [off at] home. My family was panicked because just being at the Banaras junction poses a tremendous risk. After that incident, my family has not permitted me to study further as that would mean commuting via Banaras to another part of the city.

In contrast, such dramatic dynamics are not common in R-I. However, some residents of the Pakhtun-dominated Afghan Abadi community in Islamabad reported harassment by transport police as a major nuisance. In both cities, gender seems to be a factor in the perception of the quality of transportation. In Karachi, women were more likely to perceive access as "poor", while men perceived it as "moderate" ($p < 0.001$). In R-I, though, both genders reported access to transportation as "good" with only weak gender differences in perception.

Respondents' perceptions about transport and road accessibility across different neighbourhoods in both cities are further broken down for visual presentation in Figures 1.2 and 1.3. These figures indicate variations in perceptions across a range of income levels and types of settlements. Certain neighbourhoods—such as the poorest and highly vulnerable Afghan Abadi in R-I, and Mansoor Nagar, Ali Akbar Shah Goth, and Christian Colony in Karachi—indicate weak transport access. These patterns are associated not only with income level and settlement type, but also with factors such as location, vulnerability, and status within the city's political economy.

Figure 1.3 shows that of the seven Karachi neighbourhoods surveyed, only in the central Lines Area (Jamshed Town) do respondents report a rosy picture of transportation. Nearly all the other places are on the periphery, and, as indicated earlier, Karachi's physical expansion has happened without any concomitant upgrading of roads and transport networks. Connectivity between the new peri-urban settlements and the city centre is minimal.

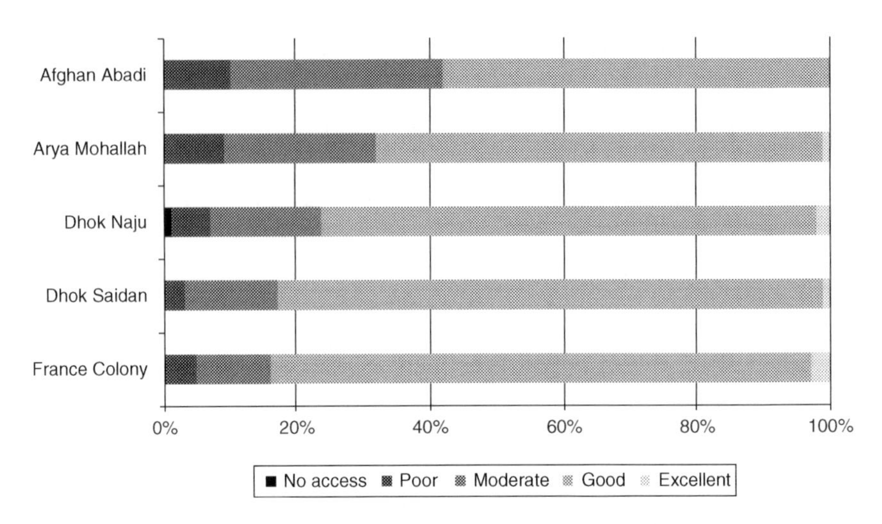

Figure 1.2 Access to transportation across neighbourhoods in Rawalpindi-Islamabad

Source: Anwar et al. (2016).

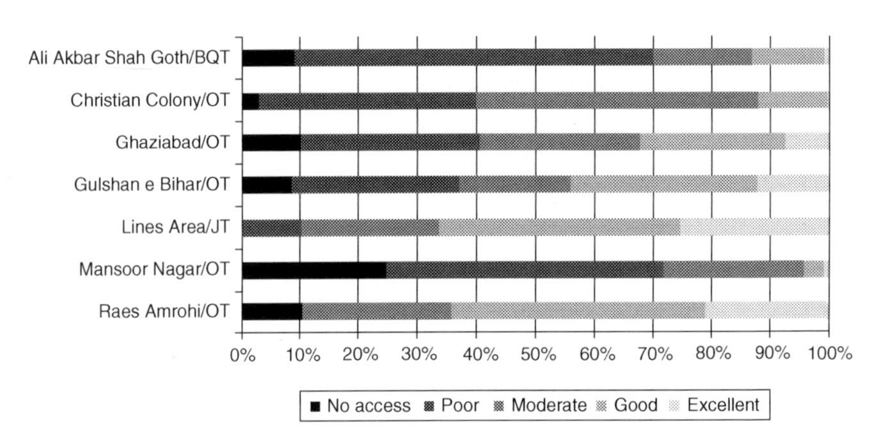

Figure 1.3 Access to transport across neighbourhoods in Karachi

Key: BQT: Bin Qasim Town; OT: Orangi Town; JT: Jamshed Town.

Source: Anwar et al. (2016).

But even within the relatively untroubled Lines Area (Jamshed Town), Karachi's violent political conditions continue to negatively affect women's mobility as Amna, 24, from Jamshed Town, explained.

> The transportation system is terrible. I had to [change buses twice] to reach college, and you know there have been bombing incidents. Whenever I enter a bus, I start reciting holy verses for my safety. I suffer

> a lot in the commute. Sometimes buses are stopped during the journey and passengers are told they can't travel any further. Buses then change their routes and sometimes we are told that the bus is not working properly and halfway through the journey we have to disembark and find another way to get to college or back home. It's really a terrible situation, especially for women.

Respondents who perceive poorer access to transportation also tend to report being victims of violence, as shown in Table 1.1. Interestingly, two communities, Christian Colony in Karachi and Dhok Naju in R-I, present a positive relationship. This indicates that households tending to be victims of violence are associated with superior perceptions of transportation. This could be partially explained by the fact that a large proportion of the violence reported in the two neighbourhoods is alcohol and drug related; it may be that good transport helps to bring in those two drivers of violence. Nevertheless, beyond the conceptual relationship between violence and mobility as inversely related, there is also statistically significant empirical evidence for that relationship.

Having described the context of uneven physical mobility within and between the various interconnected spaces of the two cities, in the next section we discuss gendered mobilities and spatial inequalities.

Gendered mobilities, masculinised spaces

As women and men move through public spaces—streets, neighbourhoods, and the larger city—they indicate different aspects of mobility. We might view different ages, sexes, and social classes in motion: a working-class woman who works as a nurse, young unemployed men loitering in the

Table 1.1 Correlation between transportation and victimisation

	Spearman's Rho statistic	*p-value (2-tailed)*	*Correlation strength*	*Relationship*
Aggregate	–0.071	0.002	Weak	Negative
Karachi	–0.138	0.000	Weak	Negative
Lines Area/Jamshed Town	–0.577	0.000	Moderate	Negative
Mansoor Nagar/ Orangi Town	–0.225	0.001	Weak	Negative
Christian Colony/ Orangi Town	0.244	0.002	Weak	Positive
Ghaziabad/Orangi Town	–0.301	0.000	Moderate	Negative
Rawalpindi-Islamabad	0.129	0.001	Weak	Positive
Dhok Naju	0.209	0.009	Weak	Positive

Source: Anwar et al. (2016).

streets, or a pair of young lovers who transgress cultural and social norms to seek freedom in the city. (Their activities there may range from walking in the park holding hands, to going to a hotel together.) Often, though, the sight of women in public places—especially young ones—produces anxiety in many people: both males and females seem to feel instinctively that women should not leave the home, travel to work, or relax or stroll in public spaces. Femininity itself may constitute a risk: a woman might fear being followed, or even threatened, by strange men. Or the men of her family might imagine this happening and fear on her behalf. They might also be afraid that she may become morally corrupt if she stays outside for too long, away from the home—which is widely viewed as the locus of moral individuals, the place of masculine dominion and feminine submission, and the space of domesticity that creates the peace and respectability men crave. Many of our respondents painted a pleasant idealised picture of family life with women forming the bedrock of social stability.

At play here is a geographic fear associated with the outside for women. Other than the obvious distinction between the home as private and the outside as public, a neighbourhood's streets can represent a transitional space where the outside world is to some degree "internalised". It is not thought improper, for example, for women to hang out on the threshold of their house, between it and the street, and talk to their neighbours. On the other hand, streets can also be "policed" by both male and female neighbours on the lookout for "transgressive" behaviours. This fact can both facilitate and curtail certain kinds of mobility. Paradoxically, of course, fear and violence are not always associated only with the outside world. The inside world—the private and domestic space—is often also a violent one for women, where they feel a lack of safety. This too relates to male domination in the form of domestic abuse. As one of our female respondents (Zainab, 51, from Afghan Abadi) pointed out, the male "is the pillar of the home and the bread earner, so that's why we have to tolerate [violence]".

In the section below, we discuss the coping strategies that women employ to manage spatial inequality in different spaces: the home, the streets of their own neighbourhoods, and lastly the big city. These strategies often include acts of self-censorship such as avoiding certain public spaces; wearing a burqa, headscarf, or hijab to veil themselves; or simply being careful to engage in non-confrontational behaviour.

Home

Constrained mobility for women, and its negative implications, is evident across all neighbourhoods in both cities. This is visible in the way women must negotiate the boundaries of home and "outside", and the coping strategies they employ. One example is the situation of Salma (20, from Orangi Town, Karachi), who attends a vocational study centre. Since her mother's death a few years ago, and her elder sisters' marriages, Salma now bears the double burden of completing her education while managing the household and looking after her father and two younger brothers. Salma's day begins early as she prepares breakfast and the rest of the day's meals for the family, including a steady stream of guests. In between these chores, she somehow finds time to study. Even though the study centre is located within walking distance of her home, Salma is not permitted to go there alone. She must be accompanied by her brother. As Salma explained, "My father says don't go alone, as the situation is not good." Her father is a community activist, and his notion of what constitutes violence guides Salma's recognition of it. But she is also guided by her female friends' perceptions, as she explained to us.

> Yes, it's dangerous ... A few days back two of my friends were walking home when some boys started following them [on motorbikes]. When my friends were nearly home, one of the boys ... snatched my friend's handbag and fled. Her [identification] documents and phone were in that bag. Boys also taunt and mock girls and shout at them. This is harassment. Sometimes I have to walk alone because my brother is unavailable. On such occasions, boys shout at me, but I have to ignore them. Now we say that if these boys insist on barking, then let them bark. If we give the boys any importance and tell our parents, we wouldn't be able to continue our education.

This scenario, which illustrates the practising of non-confrontational behaviour, shows that women's coping strategies are not shaped solely by the threat of violence itself, but also by the gender narratives that promote it. Women are taught that they are more vulnerable to crime, and that it is *their* responsibility to avoid it. Other women described behavioural tactics required to travel on local streets. Shama (26, from Arya Mohallah, R-I), for instance, told us that she always walks very fast and looks straight ahead or down at the ground because she worries that someone might snatch her cell phone, and potentially misuse her photographs. She compromises her visibility by veiling herself. Even though she talked enthusiastically about her desire to partake in leisure activities such as swimming and horse riding, her feminine body and her parents' attitude remain obstacles. The lack of power her parents feel to protect their daughter in the city causes them to circumscribe her mobility, and Shama must internalise this attitude and impose it on herself.

In the home, the social capital of having family and relatives reduces vulnerability for young women. But one facet of that protection is that they also police girls' mobility. Several female respondents told us that working outside the home—especially alongside men—was forbidden by family pressure. University-educated Amna is in that situation: she feels that the prohibition isn't right, but has to accept it. As she explained to us: "Even though this should not happen, unfortunately we have to follow our family norms and culture."

We suggest that certain mobilities, mostly masculine, impact the immobility of other genders; and that these gendered mobilities are inextricably bound with social norms, class, ethnicity, and violence.

Streets and neighbourhoods

In all neighbourhoods, we observed men and women in the streets, shopping or commuting to and from work. The most visible difference between the genders is primarily in terms of embodiment: the practice of women veiling themselves is fairly ubiquitous across both cities. And in all our conversations with female respondents, perceptions of lack of security and feelings of fear about public spaces were ever-present.

However, it is worth pointing out that in Karachi, some *male* respondents also reported feeling unsafe. Ghulam Rasool (32, a Bengali fisherman from Bin Qasim Town) told us that he fears the violent politics of his neighbourhood—the constant fighting that erupts between representatives of different religions and political parties.

> There is a group of boys that loiter in the area. They scare me because I am afraid that confronting them may make the situation worse … Threatening slogans written on walls trigger a lot of fear in me, [also] religious slogans [about] enmity and hatred. Seeing … these brings fear to my heart.

But Ghulam's feelings of fear and constrained mobility in his neighbourhood are also associated with the conflicts that arise between young men over young women.

> A few days ago, there was a serious fight in our street [about a girl. When she came] home from school … a boy was [saying] inappropriate remarks to her. When things became [too] hard for the girl to endure, she told [her family, and her] brother beat up that boy. There was firing [of guns] as well, but luckily no one got hurt.

Nevertheless, for young women like Amna, it is not so much the immediate neighbourhood that poses a threat to her mobility, but the spaces that lie beyond it, particularly in the city. In her opinion, women would feel less vulnerable if they could travel in groups.

The city

In both cities, restrictions on women's mobility are pervasive, particularly for adolescent or unmarried women, though women from Christian households report fewer restrictions. But the city is also a space where transgression is possible for young women. Generally speaking, in Pakistani society women lack power in exercising choices and making decisions about their sexuality; this includes marriage, which even today is often arranged between families.[2]

If young women ever do make independent decisions about marrying the man of their choice, it is a common custom in society to attribute her decision to abduction by the male. Newspapers regularly publish reports about young women being abducted. When we tracked such narratives, however (Sawas et al. 2014; Anwar et al. 2014), we ascertained that most are standardised: there is no indication given that the women could have exercised any choice. For instance, when women elope with their partner, they usually take some money with them suggesting that they have their parents' consent. But in order to safeguard their honour, the families must complain to police that their daughter was "kidnapped". In this way, women's marriage choices are often criminalised.

Hareem (18, a Burmi-Bengali from Bin Qasim Town, Karachi), illustrates this dynamic, and the difficulties for young women who wish to act independently. She married twice, each time against her parents' wishes. "[I] ran away [to the city] with Amin Kabeer for the court marriage. I personally [paid for our] court marriage," she explained. But the marriage ended when Amin became violent, and Hareem was able to divorce him. Then she met Fahim, who became her second husband.

> This time opposition was greater than [when] I had [a] court marriage. Even now [my father] does not like me, and does not want to see my face. Only my mother comes and visits me. My in-laws do not like me either.

Hareem's story is hardly unique. All across these cities, young men and women from diverse ethnicities and religions talked to us about their fantasies of the marriages of their choice, and how they had to circumvent socio-religious barriers to realise their aspirations. Hidden love affairs, polygamy, and civil ceremonies are not uncommon. In Hareem's case, her marriage choices facilitated her mobility. First, she left the confines of her father's home in Bin Qasim Town and moved to the upscale Defence Housing Society, where her well-to-do first husband lived with his extended family. After the divorce, she returned to her father's home until she married Fahim and went to live with him and his family. But all these movements have cast Hareem as a "rebellious" girl in the eyes of her family and neighbours—one who has transgressed the masculine rules of modesty, and behaved in a manner not befitting the feminine model of respectability. Because her actions were a source of masculine anxiety, Hareem has been slapped and beaten up by all the men in her life: her father, her younger brothers, her present husband, her ex-husband, and even her former in-laws.

The city is also where spectacular violence, represented by terrorism or political violence, can be actuated. In South Asia, for example, Appadurai (2006) outlines how fear of the unknown can drive physical violence between different groups. Political violence appears to be higher in Karachi, in large part due to the long-standing political-ethnic conflict in the city, and it impacts even the most mundane activities of the city's residents.

Conclusion

A key point we make in this chapter is that mobility—in Pakistan, and elsewhere in the Global South—is inherently gendered, and tends to disempower women within urban spaces. The larger context of dominant masculinity inhibits women's mobility, as do its claims about the appropriate and "natural" behaviours of men and women in public and private spaces (Srivastava 2012). Since masculinity is about the entitlement of power, the tension between that sense of entitlement, and any perceived loss of power, contributes to gender-based violence in public spaces. Therefore, women must not be seen to behave in any manner that incites masculine anxieties. As indicated earlier, the contradictions between men's attitudes towards women in private, in their homes, versus women in public, makes a certain sense in terms of the intimate entwinement of the two spheres.

Gender equality cannot be achieved through infrastructural changes. What is needed is to change the social institutions that create inequality (Bondi 2005; Koskela and Pain 2000). As Valentine pointed out decades ago (in 1989), women's fear of empty streets at night is not a problem of poor lighting or design, it is the symptom of a larger system of gender inequality. We emphasise this point in relation to male perceptions of public and private spaces, which play an important role in the structures of gendered power relations. Women in spaces categorised as public have certain behaviours expected of them (Srivastava 2012), whether that space is the street, the neighbourhood, the bus, or the wider city.

In conclusion, we briefly summarise below the key insights of our discussion.

- For working-class women, access to the city is made possible only by public transport; however, it is impossible for women to access that facility without exposure to sexual harassment, intimidation, or the threat of violence.
- Women use various coping strategies to help them navigate violence and harassment in the short term, such as modifying their behaviour, veiling themselves, travelling in groups, or avoiding travel altogether. However, these raise concerns about the long-term consequences for women's mobility.
- The social context for gender-based violence is the cultural assumption—the deeply embedded gender narratives—that men's behaviour is normal,

and that it is women's job to cope with it. Women's coping strategies, therefore, are not merely shaped by the threat of violence, but also by the gender narratives that promote it.
- A neighbourhood's inner lanes and streets are frequently the site of struggles to maintain social gender norms and to guard against transgression. On the one hand, this is a familiar world where neighbours know and protect each other. On the other hand, it is also a possibly claustrophobic place where anxieties about transgressing gender norms erupt into conflict.
- While the larger city represents an escape for women from this insular world, it is also a site of exposure to an impersonal world and the threatening masculine gaze of society.

Our analysis cautions against using the existence of physical transport as the sole proxy for mobility. Good-quality infrastructure services are certainly an important determinant of spatial mobility for men and women, and the state's provision of them is clearly vital. However, equally important are gendered dimensions of mobility and linkages with violences that inhibit women's mobility in the home, on the street, and in the larger city, all part of a dense urban environment.

Notes

1 Another major factor in destabilising Karachi was the Afghan jihad of the 1980s: it created an uncontainable flow of arms and drugs into the city, which gave its young males the means to cultivate a culture of ultra-violence (Gayer 2014).
2 This is also true for most young men, so this social aspect is not merely a gender imbalance; it speaks more to the tradition of families controlling individual choices—though, of course, the situation affects men and women differently.

References

Anwar, Nausheen H., Daanish Mustafa, Amiera Sawas, and Sharmeen Malik (2016). *Gender and Violence in Urban Pakistan: Final Report.* www.idrc.ca/en/article/understanding-links-between-gender-vulnerability-and-violence-urban-pakistan.

Anwar, Nausheen H., Daanish Mustafa, Sarwat Viqar, Amiera Sawas, and Humeira Iqtidar (2014). *Urbanization, gender and violence in millennial Karachi: A scoping study.* Environment, Politics and Development Working Paper Series #66, Department of Geography. London: King's College.

Appadurai, Arjun (2006). *Fear of small numbers: An essay on the geography of anger.* Durham: Duke University Press.

Arendt, Hannah (1969). Reflections on violence. *Journal of International Affairs* 23(1): 1–35.

Bondi, Liz (2005). *Gender and the reality of cities: Embodied identities, social relations and performativities.* Edinburgh: Institute of Geography, University of Edinburgh. www.era.lib.ed.ac.uk/bitstream/handle/1842/822/lbondi002.pdf?sequence=1&isAllowed=y.

Bourdieu, Pierre, and Loïc Wacquant (2001). Notes on the new planetary vulgate. *Radical Philosophy* 105: 2–5.

Chaudhry, Lubna Nazir (2014). Mohajir women survivors in postcolonial Karachi: On grief. *South Asian History and Culture* 5(3): 349–364.

Farmer, Paul (2004). An anthropology of structural violence. *Current Anthropology* 45(3): 305–325.

Galtung, Johan (1969). Violence, peace, and peace research. *Journal of Peace Research* 6(3): 167–191.

Gayer, Laurent (2014). *Karachi: Ordered disorder and the struggle for the city*. New York: Oxford University Press.

GOP: Government of Pakistan (2011). *Pakistan social and living standards measurement survey*. www.pbs.gov.pk/content/pakistan-social-and-living-standards-measurement-survey-pslm-2011-12-national-provincial.

Haider, Murtaza, and Madhav Badami (2010). Urbanization and local governance challenges in Pakistan. *Environment and Urbanization ASIA* 1(1): 81–96.

Hasan, Arif, Noman Ahmed, Mansoor Raza, and Asiya Sadiq (2013). *Land ownership, control and contestation in Karachi and implications for low-income housing*. International Institute for Environment and Development, Urbanization and Emerging Population Issues. http://pubs.iied.org/10625IIED.

Hasan, Arif, and Mansoor Raza (2015). *Karachi: The transport crisis*. Karachi: Urban Resource Centre.

Hsu, Hsin-Ping (2011). *How does fear of sexual harassment on transit affect women's use of transit?* Summary of the Fourth International Women's Issues in Transportation Conference. www.nap.edu/read/22887/chapter/10.

Kirmani, Nida (2015). Fear and the city: Negotiating everyday life as a young Baloch man in Karachi. *Journal of the Economic and Social History of the Orient* 58: 732–755.

Koskela, Hille, and Rachel Pain (2000). Revisiting fear and place: Women's fear of attack and the built environment. *Geoforum* 31(2): 269–280.

Loukaitou-Sideris, Anastasia, Amanda Bornstein, Camille Fink, Linda Samuels, and Shahin Germai (2009). *How to ease women's fear of transportation environments: Case studies and best practices*. San José: San José State University, Mineta Transportation Institute.

MacKinnon, Catharine (1993). *Only words*. Cambridge, MA: Harvard University Press.

Monahan, Torin (2009). Dreams of control at a distance: Gender, surveillance, and social control. *Cultural Studies* 9(2): 286–305.

Mustafa, Daanish (2005). The production of an urban hazardscape in Pakistan: Modernity, vulnerability, and the range of choice. *Annals of the Association of American Geographers* 95 (3): 566–586. doi: http://dx.doi.org/10.1111/j.1467-8306.2005.00475.x

Ring, Laura (2006). *Zenana: Everyday peace in a Karachi apartment building*. Bloomington: Indiana University Press.

Rozan [NGO] (2007). *Understanding masculinities: A formative research on masculinities and gender-based violence in a peri-urban area in Rawalpindi, Pakistan*. http://menengage.org/wp-content/uploads/2014/06/Understanding_Masculinities.pdf.

Sawas, Amiera, Daanish Mustafa, Nausheen H. Anwar, Humeira Iqtidar, and Sarwat Viqar (2014). *Urbanization, Gender and Violence in Rawalpindi and Islamabad: A*

Scoping Study. Environment, Politics and Development Working Paper Series #67, Department of Geography. London: King's College.

Scheper-Hughes, Nancy (1993). *Death without weeping: The violence of everyday life in Brazil*. Berkeley: University of California Press.

Srivastava, Sanjay (2012). Masculinity and its role in gender-based violence in public spaces. In Sara Pilot and Lora Prabhu (Eds.), *Fear that stalks: Gender-based violence in public spaces* (13–50). Delhi: Zubaan Books.

Taussig, Michael (1984). Culture of terror, space of death: Roger Casement's Putumayo report and the explanation of torture. *Comparative Studies in Society and History* 26(3): 467–497.

Uteng, Tanu Priya (2009). Gender, ethnicity, and constrained mobility: Insights into the resultant social exclusion. *Environment and Planning* 5: 1055–1071.

Uteng, Tanu Priya, and Tim Cresswell (Eds.) (2008). *Gendered mobilities*. Aldershot: Ashgate.

Valentine, Gill (1989). The geography of women's fear. *Area* 21(4): 385–390.

Verkaaik, Oskar (2004). *Migrants and militants: Fun and urban violence in Pakistan*. Princeton: Princeton University Press.

Wesely, Jennifer, and Emily Gaarder (2004). The gendered "nature" of the urban outdoors: Women negotiating fear of violence. *Gender and Society* 18(5): 645–663.

Zulfiqar, Humaria, and Rackham Hassan (2012). Level of awareness regarding domestic violence, a comparison between working and non-working women: A case study of Lalazar, Rawalpindi, Pakistan. *Journal of Peace, Conflict and Development* 19: 32–42.

2 Men in the city

Changing gender relations and masculinities in Maputo, Mozambique

Esmeralda Mariano, Henny Slegh, and Sílvia Roque

Introduction

> I feel very ashamed when my wife says that she is sustaining [both] our children and her husband, or when she tells me: "You are eating at my expense!"
>
> In our culture, you only count as a man when you can reproduce yourself.
>
> Money is necessary, if you are a man: to be self-sustaining, to be socially respected. Without money, [you are] discriminated against.

These are the voices of male focus group participants from the Polana Caniço neighbourhood in Maputo, the capital of Mozambique and its largest city. They were shared as part of a study on masculinities and gender relations carried out between 2013 and 2016. The men's words speak to the mutability of social categories such as "man" and "woman", and to the shifting ideologies of masculinity and femininity that are culturally and historically constructed, reconstructed, and renegotiated.

Part of the International Men and Gender Equality Survey (IMAGES), the project added a post-conflict analysis to the comprehensive, multi-country IMAGES study on men's practices and attitudes towards a range of topics such as gender norms, household dynamics, intimate partner violence, and economic stress. The study included household surveys of men and women in both high- and low-violence urban areas, as well as in-depth interviews and focus group discussions with people aged 18 to 65. In addition to providing further evidence for the shifting nature of gender identities in Maputo, as in many other parts of the world, the study shows how these reconfigurations also frequently generate uncertainty as well as conflicting representations and practices—and sometimes violent responses.

The male focus group participants' comments reveal that masculinity is constantly contested in Maputo—a city where rapid social and economic change has created an environment of social inequalities, unequal distribution of wealth, high levels of poverty, unequal access to resources, and limited social security. Another element shaping the urban environment is the fact that, shortly after the country's independence in 1975, a civil war raged for more than a decade. The post-conflict period, from 1992 to the present day, has had major effects on the national economy and culture (as we describe in more detail later). In order to grasp how gender relations and violence are shaped by different perceptions and performances of masculinity, we must first understand how men cope with their economic stress in a turbulent urban setting—one that is characterised by vast social and economic inequalities.

Marital and family relations, the ultimate locus of redistribution and social insurance, are strongly affected by economic deprivation and poverty. Men, who are considered the main providers and the heads of the families, are blamed for failing to live up to society's expectations. These dynamics result in a growing sense of powerlessness, discredit, and social discrimination among men: they fear being disrespected by their wives and children, and losing their dignity. Their lack of authority and the power to control their family are perceived as manifestations of weakness—a source of shame for them that leads to deep frustration.

In order to understand the gendered experiences of men (and women) living in Maputo, we need to look beyond the fixed social roles assigned to them. We must examine the interactions of men and women within the wider social context, exploring how they respond to complex and paradoxical situations. One way to do this is by contesting, or transforming, the social roles assigned to males and females.

It is unquestionable that women suffer the harshest consequences of unequal power relations. This has led to worldwide mobilisations to promote gender equality and to combat violence against women. However, in this process, little attention has been focused on the male aspect of gender inequality—specifically, on examining dynamics that contribute to men's use of violence against women (or, alternatively, men's non-violence). Furthermore, the standard focus on violence—on women solely as victims, and men solely as perpetrators—narrows the perspective, often excluding other factors that fuel all types of violence, not just sexual and gender-based violence (SGBV). Our objectives are to review the changing construction of masculinity in an urban post-conflict context in Mozambique, to present some of the data and qualitative findings derived from our research, and to discuss some potential drivers of violence prevention.

Conceptual framework

In this chapter, we examine the debates over the concept of masculinity and the way it is built, expressed, and signified in terms of personal identity, and of power and gender relations. Masculinities refer to the various ways of being a man—of conforming to a cultural set of norms, values, and behavioural standards that express (explicitly or implicitly) how men should act before others (Miescher and Lindsay 2003).

Theories of masculinity commonly assume that men engage in certain social behaviours and practices in order to prove their masculinity to each other, to women, and to society at large. The purpose of this gendered web of practices and rules is to assure men that they are recognised as part of a group (Barker 2005). The way men and women conduct their gendered lives defines how they perceive themselves, and how they construct their gender identities; this affects their bodily experiences, their personality, and even their culture (Connell 2005). Although men are commonly associated with a dominant or hegemonic position in societies, masculinity may still be dynamic, heterogeneous, and ambiguous. It also often intersects with other markers of identity and social status, such as class, race, religion, age, education, and sexuality (Connell 1995, 2005; Moolman 2013). For this reason, in analysing the different meanings and practices associated with being a man, we use the plural "masculinities".

Many authors have also drawn attention to the specificities of some African societies, where gender categories are not independent from age or lineage. Occasionally sex is not even the most important category in terms of the distribution of power and authority (Amadiume 1987; Oyewùmí 2006). In the case of Maputo, dominant rules of social and family relations seem to rely heavily on the meshing of the hegemonic patriarchal structure of Changana (the dominant ethno-linguistic patrilineal group in Southern Mozambique) with former Portuguese colonial cultural rules and institutions.

Perceptions and practices related to gender relations are shaped by complex hierarchies associated with masculinity. This complexity tends to be magnified in times of enduring and pervasive crisis or for marginalised urban individuals suffering the debilitating effects of poverty and inequality. Men, feeling disempowered and frustrated by their failure to live up to socially expected roles, may experience this as a crisis of masculinity (Chant 2013). Coping with feelings of failure may provoke higher levels of violence against women and against other men. However, such crises can also be peacefully navigated (Vigh 2006). In such cases, it is even possible for alternative masculinities and gender relations to emerge.

In this chapter, we identify particular elements in Maputo's post-conflict urban context that shape masculinities and influence gender relations, including gender-based violence. There are three main axes to our discussion of this topic:

- First, we explore the prevailing perceptions of gender relations and masculinity and how they affect practices of violence against women. This allows us to examine whether male power over women is considered "natural" in society. Our exploration may indeed reveal the insidious symbolic violence of male domination (Bourdieu 2002).
- Second, we highlight both the traditional and the shifting ideals of manhood. We address not only how men deal with the shifts in their

roles triggered by unemployment and poverty, but also how they respond when they do not meet the cultural perceptions of gender roles.
- Finally, we look at how men's lifetime experiences of different types of violence—such as war, urban violence, childhood traumas, and familiarity with gender-based violence—influence their own use of violence. We assume that different types of violence, at different scales and timeframes, interpenetrate one another; they are all various manifestations of a continuum of violence (Scheper-Hughes and Bourgois 2004).

Regarding the second point, an important consequence of a man's inability to meet the social and economic expectations of manhood, as the provider or breadwinner for the family, is frequently a feeling of personal failure, shame, and frustration. This stress could result in violence—not as a form of wielding power, but rather a by-product of a sense of powerlessness. That sense of disempowerment may be connected to violent practices and may also have consequences in other areas of the man's life.

For instance, several studies on masculinities in Maputo have examined risk-taking behaviours (Karlyn 2005; Cruz e Silva et al. 2007; Macia et al. 2011). A concomitant aspect is the development of sexual capital as a means to express power relations in the absence of economic capital (Groes-Green 2009). Some of these studies have contributed to a better understanding of the relationship between masculinity and the experiences of unemployment, poverty, migration, and the social impact of violence (Groes-Green 2011; Aboim 2008). Research on the lives of urban men has questioned the homogenisation of their experiences, stressing the diverse ways in which men are also structurally victimised and constrained by gender stereotypes, and how they cope with the permanent transformation and the hybridism of social norms (Aboim 2008; Groes-Green 2011; Manuel 2012).

As well, studies from other post-war African countries indicate that men who had experienced armed conflict were more likely to use violence against their female partners (Slegh et al. 2014a, 2014b). These studies also revealed that men who witnessed their fathers using violence against their mothers, or any other men doing so against their partners, were more likely to do so themselves. In many cases, too, men tried to cope with their problems and stress by using alcohol and drugs, by having sexual relations with multiple partners, and by using violence against their partners and against other men (Slegh et al. 2014a). Failure to live up to society's ideals of masculinity often resulted in alcohol abuse and violence against women. Another common result was self-directed violence, such as engaging in risk-taking behaviours, and even suicide (Dolan 2002).

This suggests that men's inability to deal with victimisation, and their perception of loss of power, may drive them to counteract feelings of failure by behaving like "super-powered" men. Men's use of violence as a strategy for responding to stress, and for coping with their problems, is a topic that has been studied less than the way women cope with violence and stress. The concept of "coping" originates from psychoanalytical psychology and refers to an individual's ability to solve problems and reduce stress. Lazerus and Folkman (1984) describe coping as a process of constantly changing cognitive and behavioural efforts to meet internal and external needs; this enhances individuals' chances of survival. Those internal and external needs are influenced by gender identity, which is shaped by the sociocultural expectations of how men and women should cope with burdensome situations.

In sum, our goal with this study was to understand men's behaviours in an urban context where violence, adversity, conflict, and poverty are rampant. Poor men, as marginalised individuals, use many different tactics in their attempts to navigate the challenges produced by adversity (Utas 2005).

Maputo: urbanisation and waves of violence

As mentioned earlier, a civil war ravaged Mozambique for 14 years. The Portuguese colonial occupation ended in 1975, after a long struggle for independence, and this was soon followed by a brutal civil war that left the country devastated. The war lasted until 1992 and caused both enormous population displacement and a rapid process of urbanisation—as many of the people driven out of rural areas by the conflict flooded into the cities. This transformed the urban landscape, especially in the capital city of Maputo. The war amplified many different forms of violence, and countless war atrocities were documented. Many innocent people were subjected to horrific experiences. Women were raped, young boys were kidnapped to become child soldiers, and many people were forced to witness (or even participate in) acts of cruelty against their loved ones. The war and its aftermath also exacerbated poverty in the country, which the government's social and economic policies could not reverse.

As often happens, the official end of the war did not mean the end of violence. Political and military tensions remained, with violent clashes taking place between opposition and government forces. Military and civilian deaths continued even after the peace agreement in 1992; people were still forced from their homes and economic activities were disrupted. The constant political instability also weakened the abilities of governmental institutions (such as the police, the justice system, and health-care services) to deal with perpetrators and victims of violence. This had the effect of making both men and women more vulnerable.

But setting aside the political instability and the long-term psychosocial effects of the war, the everyday lives of Maputo's urban poor are permeated with violence. Everyday criminality—such as car hijackings, armed assaults, and robberies of houses, banks, and stores (Shabangu 2013)—is still increasing today. Also on the rise are new forms of crime. Feeling unprotected by the authorities, citizens often resort to taking justice into their own hands: people suspected of crimes can be beaten or burned to death by vigilantes.

The population dynamics that shaped Maputo's urbanisation process evolved in a context marked by a structural crisis caused by internal and external factors. This resulted in an economic recession, which further reduced the city's capacity to absorb all the internal refugees (Espling 1999; Silva 2011). These migratory movements are still contributing to urban expansion, with all the spatial, social, cultural, economic, and environmental consequences that usually arise from such circumstances. According to the Demographic Health Survey of 2011 (the most recent such survey available), Maputo's population was then a little over 1.2 million. Nowadays, the presence of people arriving from other regions of Africa (and from all over the world) contributes to the city's heterogeneity and sociocultural diversity.

The municipality of Maputo is the country's largest, with about 70 per cent of its population living in the area that includes the city centre and its poorest periphery (Silva 2011). The city is divided into two parts, defined partly by geography and partly by architecture. The "cement city", the *bairros de cimento*, has masonry construction, asphalted streets, sewers, running water, and electricity, with a significant social infrastructure. But the "reed neighbourhoods", the *bairros de caniço*, began life mostly as informal settlements that sprang up unplanned, created by the urban poor. The houses were originally built, if not of actual reeds, with other flimsy and insubstantial building materials. Over time, these have largely been replaced with brick and zinc. Still, paved roads are rare, sanitation is practically non-existent, and most homes have no electricity or running water. There are hardly any social support services.

Today, living in the city does not necessarily mean having an actual house or home. Rather, it expresses the relationship an individual has with the urban territory (Vivet 2015). Bénard da Costa (2007) cautioned against regarding Maputo's most populous neighbourhoods, which are mostly on the peripheries, as comprising a "marginal" space around the "real" city. She emphasised the importance of understanding the city in its full complexity, since these *bairros* are very much part of its geography and economy. The preconception that the urban landscape has fixed boundaries does not reflect the actual configuration of Maputo, which is essentially a dichotomy between the "formal" and the "informal" city. The two types of spaces simply coexist. In the informal places, within the unplanned settlements, new buildings are being rapidly constructed, and urban structure is being introduced.

Today, in *bairros* like Chamankulo, Xipamanine, and Polana Caniço (where this study was carried out), there is literally no space. It is common for three or more families to share a small area of around 15 square metres (Barros and Samagaio 2014). Residents perceive these neighbourhoods as being congested, hectic, and, at times, dangerous places (Bertelsen et al. 2014). Such situations frequently drive people "to become marginal" (Vivet

2015). This is the case of the individuals—particularly young boys—who are homeless, without families or any social support to ensure their survival, and who live in the streets in a state of social exclusion. These urban youths, living in impoverished areas, are at risk of being subjected to a wide range of structural and interpersonal violence in private and public spaces.

The spiritual dimension: a holistic reality

In Southern African countries like Mozambique, the relationship between violence and spirituality is not a new phenomenon—even though it has been analysed with scepticism, as a romantic portrayal of Africa as an exotic culture (Honwana 2002). Maputo is a shifting sociocultural and religious hybrid, where many understandings of the world meet. The spiritual dimensions of Mozambican society are characterised by a cosmological worldview that entails an "explanation model" of misfortune: it is believed to be caused by imbalances between the spirits of the dead and the living. Those beliefs are integrated and adapted into "new" religions, in the form of Pentecostalism. This church experienced a worldwide revival in the 1970s and became very popular in Mozambique, especially among women. The two belief systems are closely connected in their view that spirits are intermediaries between human beings and invisible supernatural forces (van de Kamp 2012).

Throughout the history of Mozambique, religious traditions have been important in armed conflicts. People believed that the spirits of perished soldiers, and people killed during wars who were not properly buried, became angry and vengeful, tormenting the living (Honwana 2002; Lubkemann 2005; Igreja et al. 2008). The post-war scenario in Mozambique is characterised by a generally sustainable peace agreement, which prevents the country from falling into new conflicts. This fact is widely attributed to the ceremonies and rituals performed—with the help of "ancestor spirits"—to heal the "war spirits" and to restore peace. These rituals were perceived as essential in helping people to cope with the trauma and loss of war (Igreja et al. 2008; Honwana 2002; Nordstrom 1998). Traditional healers, known as *curandeiros*, work creatively to solve lingering problems from the war. They also address the individual afflictions that derive from various confrontations with "modernity" and they attempt to mitigate the harmful effects of abusive power and violence (Nordstrom 1998; Pfeiffer 2006).

Another social institution that aims to regulate and control interpersonal relations is the practice of *lovolo*. This matrimonial custom is commonly translated as "bride price", though its full range of meanings transcends a narrow commercial perspective. It essentially consists of a transfer of valuables from the husband's family to the wife's. Its purpose is to enable one of their sons, in turn, to pay the *lovolo* and acquire a wife—thus filling the place of the daughter who has married and left the family (Arnfred 2011). This pattern, enforced among the patrilineal groups of southern

Mozambique, is still practiced today in Maputo. As well as indicating the system of affinity relationships and reciprocity between individuals and families, the bride price also has a spiritual element: part of it must be "given" to the ancestral spirits, to ensure the protection of their descendants. In cases when a marriage takes place and *lovolo* is not performed (such as when a man is unable to afford it), it is widely believed to negatively affect the sexual and reproductive health of the couple. This perception of bad luck might even encourage violence against the wife, who may be accused of being possessed by evil spirits. A complex institution, *lovolo* illustrates the dynamics of the interactions between men and women and it allows us to examine the shifting ideologies of marriage and status, as discussed later.

The religious and ritual dimension of *lovolo*, and its interrelatedness with the ancestors' spirits, is a highly significant one (Bagnol 2008). But according to Agadjanian (2005) and Pfeiffer (2006), the price of "getting a woman" has now become so inflated that many men can no longer afford to pay *lovolo*, or at least not in full. This failure to fulfil the social obligation means that individuals are perceived to neglect the rules, and to exclude the ancestral spirits from their own lives and those of family members. This is felt to have a severe impact on the moral order of society (Mariano 2014).

Gender-based violence in the city

Compared to men in rural areas and in the rest of the country, men in Maputo appeared to use violence against their female partners more often (although as indicated earlier, they also seemed to suffer more from violence themselves). According to the 2011 Demographic and Health Survey, 30.7 per cent of the men in Maputo City had experienced physical violence at least once since the age of 15, the highest rate in the country. The figure for women was even higher at 38.4 per cent—the second-highest rate, after Maputo Province (INE 2011). Interestingly, the same report also indicated that women with higher incomes apparently experienced (or at least admitted to experiencing) more violence at the hands of their partners (INE 2011). While many studies have explored the situations of women exposed to power inequalities in their relationships, fewer studies have examined what drives men to use violence against their partners. Why do women with higher incomes experience more interpersonal violence? What are the main drivers causing men to behave in a violent way? How does the urban context of Maputo affect men's perceptions of manhood, gender relations, and violence—both in the private and public spheres?

Nationwide government-led initiatives have attempted to reduce violence against women; but as victims of violence (rather than as perpetrators), men usually occupy only a marginal place in such initiatives. A law to reduce violence against women was approved in 2009; and, in 2012, the government also approved a multi-sector program that aims to address SGBV, and to provide integrated care and services to survivors of SGBV. This program was adopted by the Ministry of Gender, Children and Social Action as well as the Justice, Interior, and Health ministries.

New organisations for social change in Mozambique are trying to engage men in the fight against gender violence. The Men for Change Network (in Portuguese, *Rede Homens pela Mudança*, known as HOPEM) is a coalition of human-rights activists and civil society groups, dedicated to raising men's awareness of gender and masculinity issues. It aims to promote alternative forms of non-violent masculinity and positive manhood, actively reaching out to Mozambican males through radio and television campaigns. This fact shows a growing awareness of the need to include men in the tasks of promoting gender equality and ending gender-based violence. However, deeply rooted cultural perceptions of identity cannot be effectively addressed by public awareness campaigns alone.

Shifting norms and gender relations

Mozambique's socioeconomic development has translated into increased access for women to education and jobs, but stereotypical perceptions and practices regarding gender relations still dominate the public discourse. One young man we spoke to made this statement:

> I was brought up with the idea that a woman has to be a woman in the true sense, occupying the household as housewife; also … the man is the head of the family. Though laws and policies addressing power inequality are enforced, gender equity doesn't actually exist.

"A woman is also a man": Men, power, and fragility

Despite its hazards, in some cases the city may be a space of women's emancipation—a privileged milieu that offers women opportunities to take on new family, economic, and social roles. Some women may even become the de facto heads of their families, even if they are not always recognised as such. When women become employed outside of the home and begin earning an income, no matter how small, they obtain economic power—which is a way for individuals to position themselves in relation to others, both in their immediate family and in the larger society. Economic power can redefine the meaning of being a woman or a man. As one of our Maputo informants pointed out: "A woman can also be a man, because there are women who also have their own homes, where they live with unemployed husbands." Such women may provide for their husbands, their children, and their elders. As such, she is "a man". This illustrates the fluid and overlapping notions of masculinity and femininity.

Despite this new fluidity, overall we found that social expectations, structures, and roles with respect to gender remain relatively fixed. It is almost always agreed between men and women, younger as well as older, that the man should be the economic provider and the head of the family. However, some nuances must also be addressed. For instance, older women frequently told us that it is not enough for men to just be the providers; they must also behave decently and respect their wives. And, this decent behaviour is not exclusive to men; women who perform the new role of provider also earn the respect of their children and communities.

The converse of women's new respect is that men tend to feel the lack of it. Their unemployment may then touch the significance of personhood, manhood, and identity. If husbands cannot provide for their families, they tend to feel stigmatised by their wives, family, and society. They may even feel ostracised if their salary or income is lower than that of their wife. Although men's economic stress may be connected to a rise in partner violence, it is worth pointing out that some of the older women we interviewed considered that their relationship with their husband actually *improved* when the man was unemployed. They felt that the men became friendlier with them, paid them more attention, and provided emotional space to talk and to make decisions about family life. However, this aspect was never mentioned by younger women.

Nevertheless, the projection of authority and power remains intimately tied to a personal sense of masculinity. Even when a man is unemployed, our respondents told us, he is expected to be the head of the family, and to contribute to the household—even with a lower sum. It might be said that poverty and unemployment have fragmented the traditional relationships between men and women. Nevertheless, men's power is still the norm in theory, even when it is frequently challenged in practice. For this reason, it is a fragile power.

The meanings of lovolo

As we indicated earlier, *lovolo* marriage practice is still quite pervasive—even though today's urban, young, and educated people regard it as "backward". There are certainly differences in the ways it is currently performed, and how it is perceived by individuals and by society. As a social institution, *lovolo* illustrates the relationship between power and gender. Because commonly the man "gets" a woman and "brings" her to his home, he is entitled to consider himself "the family head". Marriage represents the chief social marker of adulthood for males, the way to become a "true man": capable of owning a house, having a wife, raising children, and taking responsibility for the whole family.

In our discussion groups, both men and women defended this kind of traditional practice, perceiving "tradition" neither as static nor as opposed to modernity. For instance, many view the Catholic and Pentecostal religions as an important tool to overcome more traditional forms of oppression. Women, especially, believe that the Christian church has, to a certain extent, simplified the former impositions of tradition on them, and has given them a voice. In conversation with some women in Maputo, one observed: "The church purified what harmed us, and what does not help us to evolve." Many people, in fact, seem to assume that traditional cultural values and identities may be preserved alongside more modern ideas, rather than the latter replacing the former. Our findings suggest that men attribute different meanings to *lovolo* depending on their age. Older men mostly view it positively, as a way to formalise a marital union and make it "real". Males are assigned responsibility for the family, and gain the "right" to their children. *Lovolo* puts pressure on the woman to stay and endure even a bad marriage (Arnfred 2011). One male informant spoke emotionally to us about the wisdom of such practices: "These things are part of tradition. They are ancient things and they are very hard to change."

> When a man and a woman decide to live together without going through *lovolo* first, this union has no [meaning at all]. *Lovolo* existed long before our grandfathers. When there is a conflict between the couple, the woman has the legitimacy to say, "These are my children, because we did not go through *lovolo*." And she can leave with them.

Yet the younger generation now tends to view *lovolo* as merely an increasingly expensive business, with little personal meaning for them. Most young men do not perform the ceremony due to the lack of financial resources, while others refuse it on ideological grounds. Generally, though, most find it an acceptable way to show respect for their ancestors and their culture.

Another element that disrupts young Mozambican men's social expectations is the tension and rivalry they feel for foreign (mostly white) men. In a discussion in Mafalala, local men accused the better-skilled foreigners of taking advantage of the scarcity of technical and professional skills among Mozambicans, and of securing all the best jobs—leaving none for the locals. And since the foreigners have a higher economic and social status, some of the young men complained that they also have control over "their" women. This is the kind of situation that can lead young unemployed men to feel themselves the victims of social injustice. Without jobs or income, they cannot marry and achieve the status of manhood. To deal with their deprivation, their anxieties, and their low self-esteem, they may turn to delinquency, petty theft, abuse of alcohol or drugs, acting out aggressively, or behaving violently to women and children. The *curandeiros*, the traditional healers, may try to negotiate with the ancestors' world on their behalf, to deal with their difficulties, frustrations, and psychological discomfort.

Male violence, spiritual husbands

While urban violence, poverty, and multiple forms of disempowerment affect both men and women in Maputo, the two sexes have different psychosocial and mental-health needs, and different responses to stress and traumatic experiences. The dominant social environment, including its norms of gender inequality, shapes individuals' self-perceptions; and this affects not only their attitudes, but also their coping strategies. In Mozambique, as explained above, people's ancestors' spirits still play a crucial role in their everyday lives: they are widely perceived as still being present in some manner, and are viewed as the main sources of restoring health and well-being.

This spiritual dimension may help to explain the discomfort that individuals feel when they have difficulty getting jobs, earning money, and "living decently". For many years, all over the country, these cultural practices were accommodated in different circumstances and periods in history, and they still strongly influence the general view of social issues and mental-health problems. Quite often during our conversations, interviewees would refer to the spirits of the dead that interact with the lives of the living, either to help or harm them. For instance, an evil male spirit might possess men and lure them to drink so much alcohol that they end up being dismissed from their employment.

We were puzzled by the frank and open discussions of both spirits and sexual violence, since explicit information on these intimate domains is not usually accessible to researchers. Such private topics are frequently silenced, and require meticulous ethnographic studies and time-consuming methodologies to be grasped fully. We understood, however, that both women and men may be "possessed" by vengeful male spirits. These spirits may harm conjugal stability by manifestations of jealousy, tension, quarrels, and violent acts, and it is commonly understood that forms of gender-based violence (especially against women) are actually provoked by spirits. For this reason, they are considered not to be fully the responsibility of the "possessed" person.

It was generally felt that women are more vulnerable to being possessed by evil male spirits. Men we interviewed attributed this to the fact that women had less education than men, and were more likely to be illiterate. This made females more likely to host a "spiritual husband"—an invisible agent that governs the woman's life. Men assume that this interfering spirit is responsible whenever a woman rejects her husband's sexual advances, shows little desire during intercourse, or becomes sexually aroused while asleep, or otherwise without any male intervention. If a woman either refuses to have sex, or too obviously shows sexual desire, her partner can place the blame on her "marriage" with a spiritual husband. One solution to this problem may be to call in a traditional healer to chase away the spirit of the "rival husband". However, what may also happen is that the actual husband becomes violent towards his wife.

Masculinity: from hegemonic to fragile to more equitable

The conceptual framework of this study regards men as social navigators, using coping strategies that are informed by their gendered identities. Losing male power is perceived as traumatic and elicits coping responses in an attempt to protect the hurt self. As mentioned by Eriksson Baaz and Stern (2010), men's victimisation contradicts the prevailing norm of men as holding power. Some men would rather self-identify as perpetrators than as victims; for them, violent behaviour creates emotions that counteract feelings of vulnerability. For this reason, the perpetration of violence could be considered a negative way of coping, a destructive response to managing stress.

The division of power in relationships between men and women is politicised, with power almost invariably ascribed to men and their masculine dominance. But power dynamics also exist among men, described by Connell (2005: 22) as "hegemonic masculinities"—a cultural dynamic in which some men claim the leading positions in life and marginalise other men who are not able to fulfil those roles. As a result, men's privileged positions as leaders are intertwined with the risk of failure, making men also subject to a form of inequality. Among the men we spoke to, accounts of feeling marginalised and stigmatised were common and even included reporting themselves as victims of other men's violence.

Generally, government interventions do not tend to perceive men as active agents in terms of reducing violence against women, and they do not usually consider the specific cultural factors that construct Mozambican urban masculinity. These interventions tend to mirror the universal approaches of gender equality and gender constructions—apparently taking it for granted that these are the same in Mozambique as elsewhere in the world. This approach ignores the socioeconomic dimensions of the problem, as well as the local epistemologies that are inherent in the interrelationship between violence and spirituality.

While traditionally the domestic space and the home were strictly women's territory, today it is necessary to rethink the position occupied by men in urban housekeeping. In a discussion with some military wives from Machava, several women shared a similar opinion of ideal modern masculinity: true men spend their time at home, share their salary, and care about household expenses and ensuring the family's needs. "Real" men are faithful, talk to their wives, and get along in all matters concerning the home.

These women still view ideal husbands as providers for their families, and as responsible men who would not be unfaithful. Nevertheless, whenever men do assume social roles usually thought of as women's, they are stigmatised by other men. Additionally, men who are economically dependent on women's income and perform women's traditional tasks in the home are often regarded as bewitched. The widely used expression "to put men in a bottle" describes men who are considered to be dominated by their wives. Many people explain this as the working of women's witchcraft, aimed at gaining control over their partners. In Mozambican culture, this phrase references "women's magic powers to make men fall in love with them, or to make a man impotent if he tries to have sex with other women" (Groes-Green 2013:107). On the other hand, such perceptions of magic powers do provide women with some (very limited) sense of control in their partner relations.

Potential drivers of violence prevention

It is important to note that masculinity constructions, men's use of violence, and power dynamics in gender relations exist within a broader sociocultural context of cultural notions of manhood, exposure to war-related violence, and urban socioeconomic conditions. While targeted responses to these challenges must be implemented as violence prevention strategies, even under the negative conditions of unemployment, marginalisation, and violence, much may be done to improve men's well-being in terms of "opening alternative economic paths" and moving towards "multi-optional masculinities" (Connell 2005: 1813). We should therefore also pay particular attention to embedded social strategies that can prevent violence.

Our research on gender inequalities and violence in Mozambique reveals a deep-rooted perpetuation of gender hierarchies through traditional rites and beliefs. However, these practices may also be valuable in terms of the strategies they offer people for social transformation and spiritual coping. Our preliminary findings from this study suggest that the way men and women in Maputo cope with hardship and stress is strongly connected to their cosmological worldview and these should be further explored for their violence-prevention potential.

Conclusion

When we interviewed our subjects in Maputo, our research questions were adapted to help us, and them, make sense of Mozambican realities and dynamics—both at the public level and in terms of the individual experiences of men and women. We examined their cultural practices, their social logic, and their explanatory models with the goal of identifying the links between the sociocultural and the spiritual dimensions, and between violent and non-violent masculinities. We described men in Maputo as social navigators, socialised to be in control and to exercise power over women. But they might also be conceptualised as victims of structural violence, forced to adopt coping strategies (such as violence) that are themselves informed by their gendered identities.

Our findings entail a dynamic approach towards the universal images of manhood, and the ideology of "men as the head of women". Nevertheless, there is a mismatch between the dominant ideal of the male "breadwinner" and their frequent inability today to attain this ideal. Women, on the other hand, perceive the current changes in their social roles, and consequently the changes in masculinities and gender relations, as new opportunities for their own empowerment, which have a positive effect on gender imbalance.

As mentioned earlier, men's experiences in coping with stress and violence are less explored than women's from a gender perspective. We hope that this study, with its urban ecological perspective, will open up new opportunities for examining the links between gender-based violence and masculinity constructions. Rather than reflecting generalised assumptions of gender power relations and inequality as causes of violence, this study searched for the underlying dynamics that produce both violent and non-violent masculinities.

References

Aboim, Sofia (2008). Masculinidades na encruzilhada: Hegemonia, dominação e hibridismo em Maputo [Masculinities at the crossroads: Hegemony, domination and hybridity in Maputo]. *Análise Social* [*Social Analysis*] 43(2): 273–295.

Agadjanian, Victor (2005). Men doing "women's work": Masculinity and gender relations among street vendors in Maputo, Mozambique. In Lahoucine Ouzgane and Robert Morrell (Eds.), *African Masculinities* (257–269). Scottsville, South Africa: University of KwaZulu-Natal Press.

Amadiume, Ifi (1987). *Male daughters, female husbands: Gender and sex in an African society*. London: Zed Books.

Arnfred, Signe (2011). *Sexuality and gender politics in Mozambique: Rethinking gender in Africa*. London: James Currey.

——— (2013). *Sexual violence as a weapon of war? Perceptions, prescriptions, problems in the Democratic Republic of Congo (DRC)*. London: Zed Books.

Bagnol, Brigitte (2008). Lovolo e espíritos no Sul de Moçambique [Lovolo and spirits in South Mozambique]. *Análise Social* [*Social Analysis*] 43(2): 252–272.

Barker, Gary (2005). *Dying to be men: Youth, masculinity and social exclusion*. New York: Routledge.

Barros, Carlos, and Antonio Samagaio (2014). Urban dynamics in Maputo. *Cities* 36: 74–82.

Bénard da Costa, Ana (2007). *O preço da sombra: Sobrevivência e reprodução social entre famílias de Maputo* [*The price of the shadow: Survival and reproduction among Maputo's families*]. Lisbon: Livros Horizonte.

Bertelsen, Bjørn Enge, Inge Tvedten, and Sandra Roque (2014). Engaging, transcending and subverting dichotomies: Discursive dynamics of Maputo's urban space. *Urban Studies* 51(13): 2752–2769. www.cmi.no/publications/publication/?5012=engaging-transcending-and-subverting-dichotomies.

Bourdieu, Pierre (2002). *La domination masculine* [*Male domination*]. Paris: Éditions du Seuil.

Chant, Sylvia (2013). Cities through a "gender lens": A golden "urban age" for women in the Global South? *Environment and Urbanization* 25(9): 19–44.

Connell, Robert (1995). *Masculinities*. Cambridge: Polity Press.

——— (2005). Change among the gatekeepers: Men, masculinities, and gender equality in the global arena. *Signs: Journal of Women in Culture and Society* 30(3): 1801–1825.

Cruz e Silva, Teresa, Ximena Andrade, Conceição Osório, and Maria Arthur (2007). *Representações e práticas da sexualidade entre os jovens e a feminização do SIDA em Moçambique: Relatório de pesquisa* [*Representations and practices of sexuality among young people and the feminisation of AIDS in Mozambique: Research report*]. Maputo: Women and Law in Southern Africa (WLSA).

Dolan, Chris (2002). Collapsing masculinities and weak states: A case study of Northern Uganda. In Frances Cleaver (Ed.), *Masculinities matter! Men, gender, and development* (57–84). New York: Zed Books.

Eriksson Baaz, Maria, and Maria Stern (2010). *The complexity of violence: A critical analysis of sexual violence in the Democratic Republic of Congo (DRC)*. Working paper on gender-based violence. Stockholm: Swedish International Development Cooperation Agency.

Espling, Margareta (1999). *Women's livelihood strategies in processes of change: Cases from urban Mozambique* (unpublished doctoral dissertation). Department of Geography, University of Göteborg, Germany.

Groes-Green, Christian (2009). Hegemonic and subordinated masculinities: Class, violence and sexual performance among young Mozambican men. *Nordic Journal of African Studies* 18(4): 286–304.

——— (2011). *Transgressive sexualities: Reconfiguring gender, power and (un) safe sexual cultures in urban Mozambique* (unpublished doctoral dissertation). Institute of Public Health, University of Copenhagen, Denmark.

——— (2013). To put men in a bottle: Eroticism, kinship, female power and transactional sex in Maputo, Mozambique. *American Ethnologist* 40(1): 102–115.

Honwana, Alcinda (2002). *Espíritos vivos, tradições modernas* [*Living spirits, modern traditions*]. Maputo: Pomédia.

Igreja, Victor, Béatrice Dias-Lambranca, and Annemiek Richters (2008). Gamba spirits, gender relations, and healing in post-civil war Gorongosa, Mozambique. *Journal of the Royal Anthropological Institute* 14: 353–371.

INE: Instituto Nacional de Estatística [National Institute of Statistics] (2011). *Inquérito Demográfico e de Saúde* [*Demographic and Health Survey*] (247). Maputo: Author.

Karlyn, Andrew (2005). Intimacy revealed: Sexual experimentation and the construction of risk among young people in Mozambique. *Culture, Health and Sexuality* 7(3): 279–292.

Lazerus, Richard, and Susan Folkman (1984). *Stress, appraisal and coping*. New York: Spring Publishing.

Lubkemann, Stephen (2005). Migratory coping in wartime Mozambique: An anthropology of violence and displacement in "fragmented wars". *Journal of Peace Research* 42(4): 493–508. doi: https://doi.org/10.1177/0022343305054093.

Macia, Manuel, Pranitha Maharaj, and Ashley Gresh (2011). Masculinity and male sexual behaviour in Mozambique. *Culture, Health and Sexuality* 13(10): 1181–1192.

Manuel, Sandra (2012). *Sexuality in cosmopolitan Maputo: The aesthetics of gendered practice through the lenses of class*. Paper presented at the international conference of the Institute of Economics and Social Studies, Maputo, Mozambique. goo.gl/pLDXOp.

Mariano, Esmeralda (2014). *Understanding experiences of reproductive inability in various medical systems in Southern Mozambique* (unpublished doctoral dissertation). Faculty of Social Sciences, Institute for Anthopological Research in Africa, Catholic University of Leuven, Belgium.

Miescher, Stephan, and Lisa Lindsay (2003). Introduction: Men and masculinities in modern African history. In Stephan Miescher and Lisa Lindsay (Eds.), *Men and masculinities in modern Africa* (1–29). Portsmouth, NH: Heinemann.

Moolman, Benita (2013). Rethinking "masculinities in transition" in South Africa considering the "intersectionality" of race, class, and sexuality with gender. *African Identities* 11(1): 93–105.

Nordstrom, Carolyn (1998). Terror warfare and the medicine of peace. *Medical Anthropology Quarterly* 12(1): 103–112.

Oyewùmí, Oyeronke (2006). The invention of women. In Henrietta L. Moore and Todd Sanders (Eds.), *Anthropology in Theory: Issues in Epistemology* (540–545). Hoboken, NJ: Wiley Blackwell.

Pfeiffer, James (2006). Money, modernity and morality: Traditional healing and the expansion of the holy spirit in Mozambique. In Tracy J. Luedke and Harry G. West (Eds.), *Borders and healers: Brokering therapeutic resources in Southeast Africa* (81–100). Bloomington, IN: Indiana University Press.

Scheper-Hughes, Nancy, and Philippe Bourgois (2004). Introduction: Making sense of violence. In Nancy Scheper-Hughes and Philippe Bourgois (Eds.), *Violence in war and peace: An anthology* (1–27). Oxford: Blackwell.

Shabangu, Themba (2013). *A comparative inquiry into the nature of violence and crime in Mozambique and South Africa*. Pretoria: Institute for Democracy in South Africa.

Silva, Armenio da (2011). *Dinâmica sócioespacial e produção habitacional na periferia de Maputo-Moçambique a partir da década de 1970: Destaque para os bairros Polana Caniço A e B [Socio-spatial dynamics and housing production in the suburbs of Maputo, Mozambique, from the 1970s: Highlight of the Polana Caniço neighbourhoods A and B]* (doctoral dissertation). Centre for Philosophy and Human Sciences, University of Santa Catarina, Brazil. https://repositorio.ufsc.br/handle/123456789/95099.

Slegh, Henny, Gary Barker, and Ruti Levtov (2014a). *Gender relations, sexual and gender-based violence and the effects of conflict on women and men in North Kivu, Eastern Democratic Republic of the Congo*. International Men and Gender Equality Survey (IMAGES), Final Report. Cape Town: Promundo.

Slegh, Henny, Angela Jansen, Gary Barker, and Kate Doyle (2014b). *A study of gender, masculinities and reintegration of former combatants in Rwanda*. Washington, DC: World Bank.

Utas, Mats (2005). Victimcy, girlfriending, soldiering: Tactic agency in a young woman's social navigation of the Liberian war zone. *Anthropological Quarterly* 78(2): 403–430.

van de Kamp, Linda (2012). Violent conversion: Brazilian Pentecostalism and the urban pioneering of women in Mozambique. *Compare: A Journal of Comparative and International Education* 42(3): 559–560. doi: http://dx.doi.org/10.1080/03057925.2012.657925.

Vigh, Henrik (2006). *Navigating terrains of war: Youth and soldiering in Guinea-Bissau*. Oxford: Berghahn Books.

Vivet, Jeanne (2015). *Deslocados de guerra em Maputo: Percursos migratórios, "citadinização" e transformações urbanas da capital moçambicana (1976–2010) [Displaced by war in Maputo: Migratory routes, urbanisation, and urban transformations of the Mozambique capital (1976–2010)]*. Mozambique: Alcance Editores.

3 "We don't know when the trucks will come"

The quest for safe and inclusive cities in Zimbabwe

Julie Stewart and Rosalie Katsande, with Olga Chisango and Sian Maseko

Introduction

We met the two women on the rough, badly rutted dirt road leading into the suburb of Hatcliffe, on the outskirts of Harare, Zimbabwe. We fell into conversation with them when we stopped to ask for directions, and quickly realised that these women could be important resources for our research in Zimbabwe. In fact, Nyasha and Tendai[1] would turn out to be vital to us as local guides, informants, researchers, and our links to the community. Nyasha, in particular, with her wry sense of humour, emerged as the leader of the community research team.[2] Over the course of the project, she gained confidence about speaking in public (though she remained fearful and unsure of how to engage with state and municipal officials to tackle her own problems).

When we first met, our team was driving back to our home base, and they were walking around their home suburb of Hatcliffe at work on their usual task: selling small amounts of red floor polish to women in the area. The polish usually comes in big tins, and many women cannot afford to buy a whole one, so this enterprise provided a needed service, and earned Nyasha and Tendai a small income.

The two women talked to us frankly about their living conditions in the suburb.[3] Hatcliffe is a post-Independence mixed neighbourhood, dating from 1980, that includes both government-initiated housing schemes—intended to rehouse people who had been forcibly relocated—and self-build cooperatives. There are some substantial well-built houses in the older parts; the newly built areas began as cooperatives, and are now being converted (by government edict) into large-scale developer-led projects. There were also "wet core" houses, supposedly provided with running water and toilets.

The initial arrangement with the local municipality was that potential homeowners had to complete their buildings by 2009, to the value of a million Zimbabwe dollars (roughly US$16,000), before they could acquire full title. At that time, in 2004–2005, employment was still fairly readily available in the area, so this seemed a feasible arrangement. Unfortunately, the economic situation quickly changed. Most people failed to meet the 2009 deadline, and new terms were negotiated: a building worth US$30,000 had to be completed by 2016. However, many people did not renegotiate—and those who did quickly fell into default again. Meanwhile residents were paying rent to a suburban council and rates (property taxes) to the municipality.[4]

Nyasha and her husband had married in the traditional manner, and—when their marriage did not work out—had divorced in the customary way, too. She and her former husband were still sharing the home they had been building, living in separate parts of it. Neither could afford to move out, nor could they afford to complete the building, as required by their agreement. Electricity was supposed to be connected, but it was not; so, like the other women in the suburb, Nyasha had to source fuel for cooking and heating.[5] When we visited her home, we realised that she shared one room and a simple kitchen with her daughter and grandchildren. Water was not connected to the house, so it had to be drawn from a well shared with the next-door neighbour. The sewers were connected, but the toilet had to be flushed periodically with a bucket of well water.

Both women shared their fears for their security in their incomplete homes, which added to their stress about providing for their families. These were not idle worries. Occasionally in the past, when they had lived in informal settlements, the police and the army would descend on the community in trucks (often at night) and evict people. Those settlements, mostly little more than shacks, had been built in high-density suburbs by people just trying to put a roof over their heads when low-cost housing was unavailable. These settlements were a long-standing feature of the Zimbabwean urban landscape (as, indeed, they are in many cities in the Global South, even relatively wealthy ones). And, although the overcrowding and slum-like conditions certainly violated housing standards, the central and municipal governments[6] had chosen to ignore what was happening to the extent of being complicit in it. However, at certain times the authorities decided to stop looking the other way, and enforced a policy of demolition and eviction.[7]

Like many others in such suburbs, Tendai and Nyasha had been shuffled four or more times to different sites—sometimes even back and forth to the same site. In these summary removals, they had lost household goods, their sources of income, their shacks, and the wood used to build them. Although there might have been legal remedies to challenge the authorities and to seek restoration of their property, at that juncture few of those affected would have dared to make such an audacious move.

After the two women had told us their story on that first day, and we had agreed to stay in touch, we took their phone numbers. (The cellphone is ubiquitous in Zimbabwe, so in theory one can always contact people; but airtime is not always affordable.) When we said goodbye to Tendai and Nyasha, their parting remark was: "We don't know when the trucks will come." These intelligent, hard-working women went about their daily lives with the constant fear that the government would deprive them and their families of their home.

Our research trajectory

The Safe and Inclusive Cities research project in Zimbabwe began with the assumption that—despite significant legal and social change in the country since Independence in 1980—women's and girls' access to city facilities was still limited primarily by constitutional inadequacies in addition to sociocultural practices and attitudes. Our research goal was to study the Zimbabwean situation using the approach of women's law. Simply put, this considers what the law provides in theory, and compares it to the lived realities of those affected by it (Dahl 2001). An exploratory process, women's law recognises that multiple forces determine how individuals (particularly women) experience the intersections of many elements of society: the law, social and cultural norms, and religious and political dynamics (Stewart 2011; Bentzon et al. 1998).

We planned to explore how the country's laws and policies were currently applied, and the role that law can play in regulating the safety of a city and the lives of its inhabitants. We also wanted to examine how indigenous Zimbabweans—especially women—had been excluded from full participation, as equal citizens, during the colonial era.[8] By Independence, this had led to the lack of affordable housing in urban areas for low-income individuals.

For our study area, we selected two suburbs in each of three cities: Harare (the capital and largest city), Bulawayo, and Kadoma. Each of the six suburbs chosen reflects the various initiatives taken over the years to provide accommodation for lower-income groups. (Formerly, it used to be race that determined where and how individuals could enjoy the benefits of the city; now it is mostly class and economic status.) In each city, influenced by historical considerations, we chose two suburbs to investigate.[9]

- In Harare, we selected Hatcliffe, which we have already described, and Mbare, the city's oldest "indigenous suburb", which dates from the early 1890s. It originally housed only men, in single-room hostels; now, in a space meant for one person, it accommodates whole families of four or more. Sanitary and bathing facilities are grossly overburdened and often dysfunctional. The now-appalling toilets were designed for males; the particular needs of women are not addressed at all.[10]
- In Bulawayo, we selected Makokoba, the oldest indigenous suburb, dating from the early 1900s, and Nketa, a newer (post-1980) suburb.
- In Kadoma, we chose Rimuka, the oldest indigenous suburb (established in the 1890s to accommodate mine workers and male domestic servants), and Ngezi, a relatively new (post-1980) suburb.

Both Nketa and Ngezi (in Bulawayo and Kadoma, respectively) have both older and newer sections, which reflect different policy regimes over the decades. These include state provision of housing, employer-financed and "tied" housing, self-financing, self-builds, and cooperative housing schemes. Conditions there are a very mixed bag of arrangements, similar to those in comparable Harare suburbs. Homes and rooms are subject to multiple occupancies, with several people crowding in and splitting the rental cost between them; "hot bedding" (sharing sleeping quarters in shifts) is common; and all available space is put to whatever economic use it can yield. As in Harare, violations of the building codes and occupation density laws are rife—and extremely profitable for developers and owners, who openly flout the building regulations. (The city is also complicit in such situations.) These conditions leave lessees, tenants, and occupiers vulnerable to the risk of lawful and unlawful evictions, threats of eviction, bribery, and corrupt practices (Muggah 2012).

Our early fieldwork raised some fundamental questions against which to test the adequacy of the law:

- In a city, what is "safe" in a general sense?
- Is it a place where residents are safe from water-borne diseases?
- Is it a place with adequate, safe, and affordable housing and basic services, allowing people a sense of security?
- Is it a space with no overcrowding, and a lower risk of theft or personal insecurity?
- Is it a place where families can live as autonomous and separate units, protected from unexpected and unwanted intrusions?
- Is it characterised by personal privacy?
- Is there is adequate supply of electricity, including streets that are well lit at night?
- Do women, in particular, feel free to move about their normal activities, by night as well as day?
- Is policing adequate, non-corrupt, and responsive to the different needs of women and men?

We would answer all such questions in the affirmative. Those are all the hallmarks of a safe and inclusive city.

From a perspective of the law and its operation, the key question now becomes: how does the law facilitate such a city? This highlights a fundamental problem. While law is the "official" organising framework for rights and entitlements, and while it defines *in the abstract* how societies, spaces, and individuals should function—it is not self-defining or self-implementing. No matter what its form, law requires human agency to develop, devise, interpret, implement, and enforce its provisions. And that agency is affected by political, social, and economic forces that determine how effective a law will be in delivering and protecting rights and entitlements.

Paper versus reality

The law may define the parameters of interactions between individuals and the state, and between individuals and one another; but in itself, law has limited power to actively affect human lives. This is especially the case when there is no political will on the part of the authorities to enforce obedience or inadequate sanctions to deter violations. In such cases, even if the courts decide in favour of citizens' rights, the law effectively becomes a *brutem fulmen* (empty threat). If the authorities, or those with political clout and protection, choose not to follow laws, statutes, regulations, and court rulings, if they continue to flout the law, then no amount of judicial pronouncement will bring relief to the affected individuals.

Even lawyers can be little help to those in adverse circumstances. While their task *may* be to defend citizens' rights and pursue their entitlements, the law also constrains what they can accomplish. Mainstream lawyers, by their nature, are locked into a very limited conceptual framework for litigation, bound by existing laws. Before Independence in Zimbabwe, the white minority-rule government used strict regulatory systems to control and limit the indigenous population's access to the city and its resources. For black Zimbabweans, the matter of who could enter Harare was heavily regulated and controlled. The government had instituted a strict system of passes and documentation (based on individuals' being employed), which were regularly checked by police, and were absolutely required to establish their entitlement to be in the city. Since Independence, the old pass laws are gone, but the principle of regulation continues. The regime still tries to control occupation of the inner-city suburbs to further its own political agendas. Even the evictions and removals, as described above, have facilitated a form of electoral gerrymandering. The government literally moves people into suburban areas before elections, and afterwards summarily removes them in "clean-up campaigns".

There are also gender differences in responses to such events. Men often just move on to other areas, and seek new opportunities; but women have less freedom to do this because of their socially expected roles as carers for the children, the elderly, and the sick. They are often left responsible for putting food on the table and for providing basic necessities for their families, as well as ensuring the children's care and education.

Engaging the law

During the colonial era, before 1980, racial discrimination defined cities in Zimbabwe. The law set out who could inhabit which areas, and under what conditions. It controlled access to the city, preventing the indigenous population from coming into urban areas (as described above). It defined how space in the city could be used by different racial groups and set building standards. With Independence, racial limitations on mobility were removed. But individuals' personal capacity to take advantage of the new options was still mediated by sex, economic and marital status, employment status, and capacity to engage in economic activities.

In 2013, when we began our research, Robert Mugabe's Zimbabwe African National Union (Patriotic Front) political party, known as ZANU(PF), had held power for more than 30 years. This amalgam of forces had undertaken the liberation struggle, and was primarily responsible for the country's Independence in 1980. Between 2008 and 2013, there was a short period of political compromise, when a so-called unity government—Mugabe and the Movement for Democratic Change (MDC)—shared power. Those 2008 elections were widely viewed as a dubious outcome: it was claimed that MDC had actually won, but ZANU(PF) manipulated the result. Power sharing was seen as a way to legitimise the arrangements for governing. In 2013, the same thing happened again: the general election was "won" by ZANU(PF), though in many quarters those results were challenged as rigged. Despite the election being the subject of close scrutiny, the declaration in favour of ZANU(PF) is viewed as power stolen by electoral deceit.

Before Independence, and even after, indigenous women were perceived—both by the law, and by culture and custom—as having the legal status of minors, subject to the control and guardianship of their fathers or husbands. This is probably not an accurate portrayal of the actual status of women, especially of older women who had senior status in their families, but it was the version that was channelled into formal law.[11] The Constitution of 1980 purported to remove this gender discrimination, but then re-asserted it for women (especially those assumed to be governed by customary and personal law) via claw-back clauses that permitted discrimination.[12] There was a see-saw period of 20 years, between the early 1980s and the late 1990s, when the law teetered back and forth between favouring women's rights and "preserving" their subordinate status.[13] Such institutional uncertainties exposed women and girls to the perpetuation of discriminatory and dismissive attitudes towards them. An example is the fact that, even after Independence, police would periodically round up and arrest women who were on the streets at night—often just returning home from work. The cultural assumption, based on little or no evidence, was that they had to be sex workers, loitering there for the purpose of prostitution.

Even today, the women we interviewed were frustrated that their mobility was so often constrained by antiquated attitudes about women's roles, and their legitimate "proper" place. Women needed to access public transport during the day and the evening to go places to earn a living. Yet socially and culturally, it was felt (by men, and often by women too) that "good" women should always be at home looking after their husbands and families. A modern woman in Zimbabwe who has succeeded in becoming a senior executive, for example, may openly state that she leaves that status at the door when she comes home to her husband and reverts to a subservient role.

Solutions, or just more paper?

When our research was being designed, the newest version of Zimbabwe's constitution (of 2013) was still being drafted, but it seemed to promise a way to tackle many of the problems of the "urban excluded". The cynical might have suspected that its promises would be thwarted by a government not wholly in favour of all its provisions, especially those related to human rights. Throughout the constitution-making process, ZANU(PF) tried to limit the introduction and effects of significant governance and human-rights provisions. The party eventually conceded those points, though with unarticulated reservations. But it has attempted ever since to amend (as much as constitutionally possible) sections that it would prefer not to be in place: any provisions that are not especially protected and only require a two-thirds majority in both Houses of Parliament to change. But for cynics and optimists alike, the provisions of the constitution may technically be pursued by citizens through litigation, parliamentary scrutiny, and activism and agitation.[14]

When the new national constitution came into effect on 22 May 2013, a central plank was its Declaration of Rights (the human-rights section of the constitution). It contained comprehensive provisions to protect the human rights of women and girls, and to outlaw discriminatory religious and cultural practices. Importantly, all former laws that conflicted with the new constitution were now deemed invalid.[15] The Declaration of Rights, and its provisions regarding enforcement, offered the hope of protection and change for urban citizens who had been subject to a wide variety of ills:

- depredations, demolitions, and displacements by the state (and in some cases by municipalities, too)
- violations of their rights by developers
- poor service delivery by state and municipality
- failure to provide appropriate facilities for urban living.

For them, the constitution became a beacon of hope for their rights. And for us, in our research, it became a touchstone for determining citizens' rights.

Yet when we began our research in 2013, although the "on paper" protections had been in place for two or three years, we repeatedly found that individuals and families were in precarious legal situations. They were uncertain about the validity of their contractual agreements, or whether they were still complying with their obligations, and they were often fearful of losing their dwellings or occupation rights. Some, for instance, lived in patently unsafe, overcrowded, and unsanitary conditions, in clear violation of current building regulations and provisions. All were at risk of removal—except for one element of constitutional protection.

Section 74: Freedom from arbitrary eviction

This section of the constitution states its purpose in simple but explicit terms: "No person may be evicted from their home, or have their home demolished, without an order of court made after considering all the circumstances."[16]

In the five years since the 2013 constitution was adopted, both local magistrates and High Court judges have repeatedly found evictions and demolitions unlawful, regardless of the condition of the dwelling. Many of these summary actions have received widespread publicity, which has raised national awareness; but the offending officials still apparently act with impunity. So far the constitutional challenges have all been over demolitions. But evictions—even from unauthorised, dilapidated, unsafe, and unsanitary hostels, rooms, flats, and houses—also fall within the parameters of Section 74. The practical problem is whether the people affected by such aggressive official actions are able to invoke their constitutional protection in time to save their living spaces. In some instances, determined victims may engage in after-the-fact litigation, in an attempt to gain restitution. But unless the state acts firmly to protect citizens' rights and castigates the violators, their sense of impunity will continue and such unconstitutional actions will prevail.[17]

The constitution contains other critical provisions for those living in poorly maintained or underdeveloped areas of the city and its environs. They should not, for instance, be deprived of adequate facilities, or be effectively excluded from having the same resources as other citizens. In the Declaration of Rights, specific provisions cover environmental rights. Section 73, for instance, provides (among other things) that:

- (1) Every person has the right ... to an environment that is not harmful to their health and well-being.

To be effective, such provisions require active intervention by the state, which *must* (our emphasis):

- (2) take reasonable legislative and other measures, within the limits of the resources available to it, to achieve the progressive realisation of the rights set out in this section.

Another provision, in Section 66 (2), indicates that every Zimbabwean citizen, and anyone else who is in the country legally, has the right to:

- move freely within Zimbabwe
- reside in any part of Zimbabwe.

The only limitation on residence is where it is lawfully permitted—that is, not in illegal settlements or land occupied by squatters. But even there, citizens should at least be able to count on some protection under Section 74, as outlined above. (Nor does the right to reside anywhere apply only to indigenous people. It is perfectly possible for a white person or family to live in one of the suburbs that were formerly exclusively black, if their preference or financial needs incline them to do so.) The right of residence is not an absolute one, but it is important in terms of preventing discrimination based on grounds such as religion, culture, or race. These grounds are more precisely defined in the Prevention of Discrimination Act of 1998, which addresses the issue of banks failing to grant qualified individuals financing to acquire land or a home. It is unlawful to refuse to provide women with financing, such as small housing loans, solely on the basis of their gender, race, religion, or culture, and any institution that does this may be liable to legal action for damages. But this rarely happens in fact, since women (even more than men) are likely to lack the capital to qualify for housing loans.

One constitutional provision that has not yet been tested, but which may be appropriately used as a powerful tool for political lobbying, budget allocation, and scrutiny, is contained in the National Objectives—a special class of provisions that oblige the state to act on behalf of its citizens. It concerns adequate shelter.

Section 28: Shelter

This section of the National Objectives describes the government's responsibility for ensuring that those in need are not left homeless: "The state, and all institutions and agencies of government at every level, must take reasonable legislative and other measures, within the limits of the resources available to them, to enable every person to have access to adequate shelter."

We might term this a largely aspirational provision; it is certainly not intended as a panacea for the homeless or the poorly accommodated—especially given that avoidance clause, the phrase "within the limits of its resources". The state and its agencies have an obligation to enable the provision of shelter, but what amounts to "reasonable legislative measures" remains to be tested. Probably the most effective points of intervention are the times just before elections, or when national, municipal, or local governments are deciding on their budgets.

Sex and gender on the agenda

For women and girls, the most significant provisions of the constitution are those contained in Sections 56 and 80. In theory, at least, these swept away all forms of discrimination, including those based on sex, gender, marital status, custom, culture, pregnancy, or whether they were born in or out of wedlock. According to Section 80 (3): "All laws, customs, traditions, and cultural practices that infringe on the rights of women conferred by this constitution are void to the extent of the infringement."

However, promising as all these provisions appear, they have not changed the reality that, in Zimbabwean cities, men are still the holders and primary occupiers of land; or that wives and daughters are less likely to inherit land than their husbands, brothers, male partners, or sons. Indeed, they largely do not even consider themselves entitled to do so. On paper, wives are certainly entitled to inherit, and to remain in occupation of the matrimonial home; and daughters are entitled to inherit equally with sons. Technically, husbands and wives can co-own land, and have their joint rights recorded in municipal records. But culturally, people still tend to think of land rights as passing through the male lines of descent. The social realities are such that property-holding women view men as the natural inheritors; and even if they do not, they may still abandon their rights due to family pressure. Women from the suburbs we studied, especially, do not appreciate that this is possible. All this means that to a large extent, although women's rights are comprehensively provided for in the constitution, they remain mostly dependent on men for their living space. Their own needs are poorly accommodated.

Conclusion

At the outset of our research, we expected to find that women and girls in the suburbs we studied remained largely on the margins of society, barely included. That was in fact the case. The law granted them the legitimate right of access to the city, but the cities themselves did not adequately respond to females' needs for adequate and appropriately serviced accommodation. Men and boys suffered similar disparities between their legal entitlements and what they actually experienced. But women's needs were addressed to an even lesser extent, and they were more likely to experience social, cultural, and religious discrimination than men—even though all such forms of unfair exclusion are now outlawed.

Even though the laws have changed in Zimbabwe with respect to urban accommodation, and despite the constitutional reforms, still social, economic, and infrastructural deficits mean that, in practice, many women and girls remain excluded. We had suggested that there was some element of carry-over from pre-Independence to post-Independence in terms of both laws and policies, and that these prevented women's full enjoyment of the city. If the full force of the 2013 Constitution is to be properly applied, then all laws—present and future—must be aligned with it. All human and socio-economic rights must be rigorously enforced to end the legal continuation of exclusion.

Yet for women and girls in Zimbabwe, that exclusion persists. Social, cultural, and religious norms still make them subordinate to males, and unreformed laws are still likely to be applied to citizens unaware of their legal and constitutional rights. The state continues to fail to adequately provide for the presence of females in accommodation once meant only for men with no families. The government violates its own laws, or at least fails to apply them properly. It also fails to reform laws to align them with the 2013 Constitution. This failure perpetuates discrimination against females, facilitating the kind of continuing structural, infrastructural, and institutional violence that the law no longer permits.

January 2018 addendum: There have been modest improvements in our research themes since the change in the president and government in Zimbabwe in late 2017. The new government has moved to reverse the actions of so-called "land barons". These individuals took advantage of their political clout and influence to gain and exploit for personal profit large tracts of peri-urban land for housing schemes that were not only unlawful but also highly exploitative of those desperate to become home owners. How effective this action will be in the long term is unknown, but it is a first step towards resolving some of the problems highlighted in the chapter. We can only wait and hope.

Notes

1 These are pseudonyms; the women's real names are withheld for reasons of confidentiality.

2 Zimbabweans in general are literate and write excellent English, so engaging capable local individuals as research assistants was not difficult: they were delighted to have work, and to be engaging with their own communities. With the exception of our study of Kadoma (where our Masters in Women's Law students carried out small research projects), all qualitative interviews and quantitative surveys were conducted by members of the local communities, with the assistance and supervision of the research team.

3 In this chapter, we use the term "suburb" to describe our areas of study, although historically these settlements were known by various terms: first as native locations, then as native townships, and then as black townships. They are now officially styled "high-density suburbs" or HDs.

4 Towards the end of the research, our team received a phone call from some Hatcliffe residents who were behind in the payment of their rates—in some cases by over US$1,500. When the municipality served them a final demand for payment they took no action, hoping the problem would simply go away. Again a summons was issued, and again they sat mute and failed to answer. Needless to say, this was a mistake on their part. If they had sought advice early on, they might have challenged the amount owed or negotiated a payment plan. But failing to get any response, judgement was given in their absence, they were found in default and warrants of execution were issued against their movable property. Their beds, televisions, sofas, wardrobes, and other household goods were removed by force. The goal of this, from the municipality's viewpoint, is supposedly to prompt payment from the defaulters; in the worst case, the goods can be sold at auction to cover the ever-escalating debt.

Not until two weeks after the execution against their property did the people involved call our research team—it was difficult to understand why they had not contacted us at once. We become involved only when the situation was dire. We immediately visited them and sought professional legal advice. But by this time, the storage charges far exceeded the value of the seized property, and, in some cases, even the amount of the original debt. At the time of writing, there is no resolution in sight and the saga continues. Ironically, all parties were in default: the residents for not paying for services and rent, and the municipality for not providing the contracted services to the residents. Although it is completely unprofitable for the city to seize people's goods, it continues to do so—and it also continues to fail to provide services. The two failures lock individuals into a constant spiral of escalating costs and diminishing returns.

5 Most homes had small solar panels for lighting, television, and charging mobile phones. These power sources (forms of what we call "self-inclusion") were common in all our research areas, at all socioeconomic levels; but there are always financial and practical constraints that limit their extent. In affluent suburbs, homes often have generators as well as solar panels to power electric fences and gates; they may also have septic tanks for waste and electrically powered boreholes (wells). Less affluent areas may have only hand-dug wells without pumps that are hand-operated with winches. However, other methods of providing power were difficult to afford or to locate safely in terms of pollution and access in the premises.

6 The tiers of government in Zimbabwe (defined by Section 5 of the 2013 Constitution) include the central government, the provincial government, the municipalities, and the local community-level authorities.

7 Such demolition and removal campaigns had taken place sporadically in the past, both before and after Independence in 1980. The two most prominent campaigns occurred in 1991 and 2005. The first happened before the Commonwealth Heads of Government met in Mbare, to shield the eyes of the visiting delegations (especially Queen Elizabeth) from the unsightly shantytowns constructed of wood and plastic sheets. The more widely criticised campaign was the 2005 one (known as Operation Murambatsvina in Shona, meaning "get rid of the rubbish"). It involved pulling down unauthorised structures and evicting the "illegal" lodgers (Tabaijuka 2005; Ho 2007). This exercise, which covered all Zimbabwe's cities, was generally believed to have been a political tactic to divert the public's attention from the social and economic situations in high-density suburbs, and to alter constituency membership before pending elections. All these actions were purportedly supported by existing laws.

However, the upshot of the demolitions and evictions only exacerbated the current occupation pressures—overcrowding, lack of adequate services, instability—and tensions in the existing suburbs, since space had to be found to house the displaced people. The government's nationwide attempts to provide housing in suburbs such as Hatcliffe was dubbed Operation Garikayi (in Shona; it was HlalaniKuhle in Ndebele)—"to live well" or "to lead a better life". Neither situation transpired; the initiatives largely failed and those in the greatest need still struggled to find adequate housing.

8 We used a participatory research methodology in Bulawayo to explore women's roles as active citizens in greater depth. It was too unsafe for women to participate in such an exercise in Harare or Kadoma.

9 In retrospect, perhaps our research could have been accomplished more easily if we had focused on just one city, with all its complexities. Although there were certainly differences between the suburbs we studied, any one of the three cities would still have given us a wealth of qualitative data about law, gender dynamics, and inclusion and exclusion. That single focus would still have made our in-depth exploration possible.

10 The design of most buildings, and even whole suburbs, is male-friendly. For example, when it comes to toilet facilities, most lack the privacy to allow females to maintain their dignity (especially when they are menstruating). The differing psychological and physiological needs of women are not usually taken into account, and suitable and gender-appropriate integrity facilities are not provided, leaving women feeling excluded and able only to make do as best they can.

11 However, Jeater (2007) describes how this version of women's status was cobbled together by the white Native Commissioners of Zimbabwe. It was a patchwork of several elements: their own earlier experiences in Natal, Old Testament versions of women's subordinate status, and holdovers from nineteenth-century European jurisprudence.

12 The constitution was the product of a compromise between the former white regime, and the incoming black majority government. Mediated by the British government, it contained a standard "Westminster export model" provision that excluded customary law and personal law from the non-discrimination provisions of Section 23. In fact, many of the post-Independence constitutions dispensed by Britain had an almost identical section—also numbered 23. The effect of this was to maintain the supposed subordinate status of indigenous women. Local legislation (such as the Legal Age of Majority Act of 1982) sought to confer full legal rights on all Zimbabweans, regardless of sex, at the age of 18. The impact of this legislation was first boosted by a series of supportive judicial decisions, recognising that women also achieved majority at 18. But these were then clawed back and diminished, and the full force of the "protective" provisions for customary law were re-invoked.

The main negative impact of this clawback was to affect women's rights to marry and inherit (though general contractual rights did not seem to be affected). Women's official emergence as full members of society, with equal rights to men, was delayed until 2013. The problem is that—like many long-term restrictions on rights—these have become embedded in society as the accepted practice; and this perception may even transcend the formal legal change that liberates women from the former restrictions. Still five years after the sweeping legal changes of the 2013 Constitution, even highly educated women and men remain poorly informed about what their current rights are.

13 To expand on that point: between 1982 and 1999, the law swung between favouring women's rights—under the Legal Age of Majority Act in 1982 (now Section 15 of the General Law Amendment Act Chapter 8:07)—and reverting to an interpretation of their subordinate status, as in Magaya v. Magaya 1999 (1) ZLR 100 (S).

14 Section 59 of the constitution provides for freedom to demonstrate and petition, provided that it is done peacefully. Older legislation that purports to regulate such a right still needs to be aligned with this provision, but as it stands the right is an absolute one, requiring no state authorisation.

15 That fact is explicitly stated in Section 2: "This Constitution is the supreme law of Zimbabwe, and any law, practice, custom, or conduct inconsistent with it is invalid to the extent of the inconsistency."

16 Although the determinations reached so far by lower courts (including the High Court) have not yet been confirmed by the Constitutional Court, the trend in decisions is to require that alternative accommodation be considered, and that due and proper notice of impending demolitions be served on each resident. The customary way of giving this notice (calling a meeting under a tree) is not deemed to be adequate.

17 The constitution extensively defines the roles and obligations of public servants. One provision in particular stands out—perhaps because it always seems to escape the attention of those who should be bound by it:

> Section 196, Sub-Section 1: Authority assigned to a public officer is a public trust which must be exercised in a manner which ... demonstrates respect for the people, and readiness to serve them rather than rule them.

The authors of the constitution knew that such corrective measures were needed, yet those who implement it seem not to have read this section. Other than ordinary disciplinary measures against public servants, there seem to be no sanctions available to enforce this important constitutional provision.

References

Bentzon, Agnete Weis, Anne Hellum, and Welshman Ncube (1998). *Pursuing grounded theory in law: South–North experiences in developing women's law*. Harare: Tano Aschehoug, Oslo & Mond Books.

Dahl, Tove Stang (2001). *Towards an interpretative theory of law: The argument of women's law in methodology of women's law*. Oslo: Norwegian University Press.

Ho, Kathleen (2007). Structural violence as a human rights violation. *Essex Human Rights Review* 4(2): 1–17. http://projects.essex.ac.uk/ehrr/Vol4No2.html.

Jeater, Diana (2007). *Law, language and science: The invention of the native mind in Southern Rhodesia, 1890–1930*. Portsmouth: Heinemann.

Muggah, Robert (2012). *Researching the urban dilemma: Urbanisation, poverty and violence*. Ottawa: International Development Research Centre (IDRC). www.idrc.ca/EN/PublishingImages/Researching-the-Urban-Dilemma-Baseline-study.pdf.

Stewart, Julie E. (2011). Breaking the mould: Research methodologies and methods. In A. S. Tsanga and J. E. Stewart (Eds.), *Women and law: Innovative approaches to teaching*. Harare: Weaver Press.

Tabaijuka, Anna K. (2005). Report of the fact-finding mission to Zimbabwe to assess the scope and impact of Operation Murambatsvina. Geneva: United Nations.

Part II

State violence

4 The state, violence, and everydayness

Some insights from Delhi

Manoj Bandan Balsamanta and Bhim Reddy

Introduction

Literature on urban violence in India is scarce, except for some studies on communal violence and slum evictions or relocations. In view of this inadequacy, the Institute for Human Development in Delhi undertook exploratory research as part of its Safe and Inclusive Cities project. It sought to explore the links between poverty, inequality, and violence in Delhi, with a focus on urban planning and governance. The study's conceptual framework assumed that certain preconditions and drivers of urban violence existed in India. These included, among others, land policies and legislation, access to basic services, public finance paradigms, spaces for citizen participation, the agency of the state, the agency of civil society, and the phenomenon of social fragmentation.

The definition of violence we use here goes beyond the limited scope of direct violence identified with an agent and intent (Winter 2012); we also include "structural" and invisible violence (Galtung 1969; Farmer 1996). In the course of this study, we identified various forms of violence, focusing particularly on violence *against* the poor, and even *by* the poor. We also believed the state to be more severe in its impact on the lives of the poor—both at the top level, in terms of unequal policy implications, and at the local level, in terms of ongoing hostility by government employees (Gupta 2012). Therefore, our study probed the role of the state as the perpetrator of violence on marginalised populations.

In this chapter, we focus on state-inflicted violence in the city of Delhi. We examine how the state affects the poor in their everyday lives, and how violence is locally experienced and differentially mediated by virtue of varied spatial and material realities. Based on a survey of some 2000 households, as well as qualitative fieldwork, we explain the shifting levels of vulnerability experienced by those at the margins and the overall context of state apathy, hostility, arbitrariness, and contradictions.

Three key issues we will examine in this chapter are:

- the displacement of the poor in Delhi
- the vulnerable status of street vendors
- the infrastructure inequalities in poor areas.

The first issue is well documented by a number of urban scholars such as Bhan (2009, 2014), Dupont (2008, 2011), Kalyan (2014) and Jervis Read (2014). The liberalisation agenda and the urge for global competitiveness have invariably led to slum clearing and repeated demolitions (Dupont 2011).[1] The Commonwealth Games in 2010 (like major sports events elsewhere) acted as a catalyst for urban change. But as the government of Delhi worked to attain international recognition, this change only exacerbated the plight of the poor (Essex and Chalkey 1998). In this ever-growing climate of competitive cosmopolitanism, the poor get trapped between routine "rounds of homemaking and unmaking" (Jervis Read 2014: 197).

The second issue is the treatment of street vendors, of which Delhi has roughly half a million. These people experience daily harassment by the state, particularly by its lower functionaries: police and municipal employees. Street hawking in the city remains a largely informal institution, and it is in a perpetual state of "negotiated (im)permanence" (Schindler 2014: 2596). This informality, or failure of formal regulation, creates ample space for such harassment of hawkers.[2]

The third issue, infrastructure, stems from the lack of proper planning in the slums and the absence of functional infrastructure there.[3] This is an important issue since slum dwellers constitute about 15 per cent of the total population in Delhi (Banda and Sheikh 2014). Slum dwellers face problems with respect to the basic requirements of their lives: water, sanitation, garbage dumping, drainage, and the like. They must also compete for access to the limited amounts of these resources, resulting in tensions and conflicts. Although this dynamic is not unique to Delhi's slums, "infrastructural violence" (Rodgers and O'Neill 2012)—which includes the way poor populations and localities are discriminated against—highlights the conflict-generating attributes of unequal infrastructural practices. In brief, displacement, hawking, and infrastructure are key issues where the everyday struggles of poverty intersect with official harassment. This chapter will discuss these issues in more detail.

Violence as ordinary

Cities in developing countries (especially in Latin America, the Caribbean, and sub-Saharan Africa) are often characterised as crime-prone, and vulnerable to large-scale conflicts. Research there routinely focuses on gang activities, organised crime, and gun culture. Some cities are considered to have exceptionally high incidences of lethal violence: their homicide rates range from 30 to 120 per 100,000 population (UNODC 2011, cited in Muggah 2012). In contrast, Indian cities seem to experience less violence. From 2010 to 2014, the average homicide rate in 53 major cities was only 2.2 per 100,000 population, slightly less than the national average of 2.7.[4] This means that research on violence in Indian cities requires a different angle from that used in other developing countries. In light of this, everyday life emerges as an important contextual frame of reference in considering the roots of violence since intense *everyday* subordinations, exclusions, and conflicts are what seemingly most pervade Indian cities.

Researchers are frequently attracted by extraordinarily violent events. This is not surprising given the human attraction to the dramatic, exceptional, sensational, and remarkable—which also largely preoccupy social scientists (Malinowski 1935; Latif 2012). Meanwhile, unremarkable, inconspicuous, small-scale, and routine phenomena generally receive little attention. However, we feel that treating violence as an event puts disproportionate focus on eruptions, occurrences, and—as Tadjoeddin and Murshed (2007) describe it—"episodic violence", thereby hiding routine and everyday violence. Such event-based approaches to violence are increasingly contested. Scholars such as Schott (1995) and Cuomo (1996) have begun to see violence not as an occasional happening, but as a constant presence. Researchers are increasingly turning to everyday life as a key "site of violence" to study the interaction of the routine and the remarkable, since it reveals constitutive practices and relationships (Latif 2012).

In this chapter, we try to reframe violence within the register of the ordinary. Drawing on Das (2007), we argue that violence is best understood as something implicated in everyday life. For Das, extraordinary violence is not a disruption of the ordinary, it is entangled in it. Therefore, we focus here less on "tipping points" (Moser and Rodgers 2012; Rodgers and Satija 2012) that transform conflicts into violence, and more on how these events are locally internalised—that is, they both mediate and are mediated by people. Moreover, all tipping points may not necessarily result in violence. What prevents conflict from tipping over into violence? That is, what preempts the possibility of a full-blown crisis when the seeds of violence are persistently present? In short, we discuss here how people rebuild themselves and recreate their life possibilities amid perpetual violence (Das 2007; Chatterji and Mehta 2007).

Using the quotidian as a frame of analysis, we consider the routines of everyday life, which is not necessarily as ordinary as it may appear (Neal and Murji 2015). Rather, it is sometimes surprisingly dynamic. It embodies ambivalences, perils, puzzles, contradictions, and transformative possibilities. Although the poor and their ordinary lives do not always involve a "transformatory potential"—as is often argued by scholars like Neal and Murji (2015) and Robinson (2015)—their capacity to resist even state violence cannot be downplayed (Bourgois 2001). Their protests may not always be explicit since they may often have to employ subtle ways of resisting (Scott 1990). And they may be able to use the existing structure to their advantage, when resistance is perceived as impossible or unproductive (de Certeau 1984). They may also individualise solutions to common concerns, when collective responses fail to emerge for a variety of reasons (as proposed by Beck and Beck-Gernsheim 2002). In brief, the everyday life of the poor in Delhi involves rich nuances of experiences, struggles, and negotiations, which we discuss in the following sections.

Living violence: everyday life at Viklang Colony

They are 25 families in all. They are extremely poor, and live in makeshift structures they constructed themselves from flimsy materials like bamboo stems, wood, fabric tarpaulins, and polythene sheets. The area they call home is actually a neglected and virtually inaccessible field in the heart of the city, an uneven space filled with trees, shrubs, and grasses, situated between an open sewer and the railway lines. The area is termed a *basti* in Hindi—a common term for slums and other lower-class neighbourhoods. This particular *basti* is known as Viklang Colony (VC), named after the disabled people who used to collect alms at a nearby temple. The settlement has been here since about 2014, after the largely disabled population was evicted from their homes on the opposite side of the sewer canal. Their crime was living too close to the security wall of the Jawarharlal Nehru stadium, where the 2010 Commonwealth Games were held. As part of the renovations to the stadium and surrounding area in preparation for the Games, a flyover was built, and all the nearby residents were evicted. During the evacuation process, the authorities promised all residents land and suitable rehabilitation in the form of a house or financial compensation. Some residents did receive land, but others received no compensation at all. Absent any alternative, those luckless people chose the unused field as their place of residence.

The inhabitants of VC are often poor to the point of starvation. Before the Commonwealth Games, some were petty vendors near the stadium; however, they lost these small businesses after their forced eviction. Now the men generally make money through odd jobs in transient occupations, such as rickshaw pullers or daily labourers. The women work as domestic helpers in nearby neighbourhoods. When neither women nor men can find work, they beg. Widows, who make up a significant portion of the population, face the additional burden of being the sole income earner of the family. However, despite the social and structural disadvantages they face, the VC dwellers refuse to give up. They come together to fight for land and a roof—that ever-elusive home—and, in the course of this struggle, they try to make sense of their collective plight. Their problems include:

- a desperate urge for a feeling of belonging
- vulnerability to government action
- ongoing harassment not only by officials, but also by more affluent neighbours
- the threat of eviction
- repeated demolition of their homes
- the needlessly complex bureaucratic processes to claim their resettlement rights
- the system of dependence on the government for their livelihood.

We discuss this situation in more detail below.

Displacement

VC residents identify the shortage of land and money as their main problems, along with repeated harassment by municipal authorities. There is a pattern to this behaviour. VC sits quite close to some nearby middle-class and affluent neighbourhoods, and these people are unyielding in their hostility to VC residents, who they perceive as dirty and prone to crime. Residents of those neighbourhoods frequently complain to the Municipal Corporation of Delhi (MCD), which sends its employees to make unannounced raids on the settlement. The MCD considers VC an illegal encroachment on city property and its residents to be illegal occupants. Accordingly, its officers make occasional surprise visits to threaten, coerce, and abuse the residents. They harass women, steal belongings, and attack and demolish the residents' makeshift houses and possessions. This is all done with the goal of forcing the VC residents to leave—though they have nowhere else to go.

In response, the residents invoke their roots in the original colony from which the government first evicted them and then unjustly deprived them of resettlement. They show city employees their government identification cards, listing their former addresses on the demolished site. (Surprisingly, they can still use these cards to obtain subsidised food provisions and access voting rights—even though the place listed on the cards no longer exists.) The VC residents regularly approach various governmental agencies and political parties to beg them to stop the city from demolishing their present houses, but they have no success. Some of the authorities are indifferent to their trauma and tragedies, while others would like to assist them but are helpless.

One major complicating factor is the fractured and multi-layered nature of Delhi's governance system. As the capital city of India, Delhi comes under federal jurisdiction. It has a provincial state government and an elected chief minister. However, the police, the bureaucracy, and the control of land are all vested with the central government. The MCD, which provides civic services in the city, is an autonomous body. Political differences and frictions across these diverse structures often contribute to the troubles of the poor. As one VC resident, Sanjana,[5] puts it:

> The Chief Minister's Office has been cooperative. They genuinely want to help us. Their team has already visited our place and photographed it. They have also issued a letter in this regard. But they are helpless.... The police also sympathise with us, but there is little they can do.... The MCD people do not listen to anybody.

However, VC residents are not resigned to their fate. They understand that hostile tactics will not work for them, since they lack the numbers for aggressive protests or to force a showdown. Rather, they resist the hostile practices of the MCD through democratic means, attempting to lobby sympathetic authorities to take action in their cause. They visit government offices on a daily basis, trying to negotiate a deal. They meet with political leaders and elected representatives to lobby for a permanent settlement. They have also approached the media, and various non-governmental organisations (NGOs), to request that they publicise the plight of VC residents. All these activities are largely performed by the women of the community, while men are at work earning an income to support their families.

In their efforts to bring about change, VC residents seem to oscillate between hope and hopelessness—a situation mirrored by their impatience and perpetual waiting. They struggle for their future without any clarity about it, and their strategies regarding their interests and objectives appear to be at once coherent and incoherent. When they discuss their issues with the media and other organisations, they often appear ambivalent: they sometimes radically criticise the state, but at other times they seek to become intimate with it. This ambivalence seems to depend on what level of government is at issue. The residents mostly attack the MCD, their most direct enemy. They do not entirely blame the provincial government and police, some of whom sympathise with their plight and would help them if they could. Additionally, they actively try to befriend officials and people in positions of power to ask for specific favours and changes.[6]

In brief, VC residents live with both perpetual tension and courage. The experiences of their mundane daily lives are built around a variety of factors:

- their struggles and resistance
- their negotiations with government
- their suffering and needs
- their lobbying activities
- their critiquing of the state
- their befriending of influential persons
- their battle to create homes, and a sense of belonging, in a hostile space.

These activities and experiences bring them into more intimate contact with the state, and help them to come to terms with the violence it inflicts on them.

Street vendors

Sarojini Nagar market (known to locals simply as SN)[7] is one of Delhi's most popular markets, mainly because of its relatively cheap prices. Over the last two or three decades, it has become a hub for street vendors of all types, who fill the vacant spaces in and around the market's main shops and pedestrian pathways; they even try to find space for their stalls in the parking spaces. Some of these vendors (both male and female) were formerly employed at shops in the market, and, having learned the tricks of the trade, began to set up their own businesses. Some women, after they have sent their children to school and completed the housework, join their male family members in the morning to help with the vending.

As in so many aspects of Delhi society, there are layers of social influence at the market. *Dalals* are older vendors with more experience, who are allowed to occupy more space than is normally allotted. Due to their seniority, they act as middlemen between the regular vendors and the authorities. This go-between role is particularly important in the frequent situations when bribes must be given—since bribery is a constant aspect of business at SN market. To ensure the smooth functioning of their activity, vendors must pay the *dalals*, the police, the MCD officials, and the shopkeepers who allocate them space for their stalls. Despite the payment of bribes, though, the police and MCD routinely harass vendors over any number of petty issues. Sometimes money is extorted via the *dalals*, and it is a common occurrence for them to confiscate the vendors' goods and steal their day's earnings. These functionaries or their proxies take goods without paying, and often go so far as to reach into the vendors' pockets and snatch away their money. Occasionally, the vendors are even beaten up and physically abused, or dragged from the market into police or MCD vans. As one vendor, Raju, put it:

> They know everything. They know our secret places where we hide money. So it is difficult to escape them... They take our products, they never pay when they eat from us. Sometimes they come to us directly, sometimes they send their local proxies for extortion.... They are brutal. They beat us.

When their goods are "confiscated", vendors say, they must go and collect their seized materials from the police station. This takes them at least eight days, mostly to get together the sum they have to pay to release their property—which is at least 1,000 rupees, even for goods worth less than 100 rupees. Once the payment is made, police also routinely return only part of the goods—in order to force vendors to come back again and pay them more money. For example, one vendor who was selling fashionable eyewear had his wares confiscated. He paid the police to get the goods back, but only the cases for the eyeglasses were returned to him. For such vendors, confiscation is their biggest problem. Not only are they forced to pay the bribe, but often they lose their original investment in the goods as well.

State functionaries harass street vendors in many other ways, such as through arbitrary bureaucratic decisions. For instance, they might abruptly change the closing time for the vendors without giving them any notice or showing them a written order. Another case in point is the changing content of the *challan*, the official payment receipt issued to vendors who pay a fine after being accused of violating some government law or regulation. In the past, a *challan* contained details about the amount of the fine and the location of the alleged transgression; it also included a photo of the vendor. These former *challans* constituted an official proof of their vending activities and, therefore, could help vendors in their ongoing quest to attain a permanent market licence. Now, however, the *challan* is merely a receipt for the amount of money taken by the police without details of any kind. Vendors complain that this change is a deliberate ploy by government employees to maintain their vulnerable status as temporary and illegal merchants to ensure a perpetual source of extortion revenue.

Even the *dalals*, their fellow vendors, harass them by demanding money on a weekly basis. If vendors refuse to pay, the *dalals* complain to the authorities, who are always happy to confiscate the vendors' goods. As well as extorting money, they often also dupe vendors by pretending to help them. Sometimes, for instance, a *dalal* might take money from a vendor to bribe the police and MCD for a better spot in the market. But often the *dalal* neither helps, nor returns the money. Other enemies of the vendors include members of the market association and the major shopkeepers—either one of whom can call the police and have them removed from the streets. Despite taking rent from the vendors on a daily basis, some big shopkeepers make a point of occupying the adjacent parking spaces where vendors are allowed to set up their stalls. To eliminate vending opportunities they deliberately block the spaces by parking cars there that are old, unused, or in poor repair. Such shopkeepers also withhold the vendors' documentation when inspectors ask them for it. Yet, despite these daily hassles, vendors do not dare to complain: they know that the shopkeepers pay much larger bribes to the police than they can afford to do.

Occasionally, the street vendors come together to protest the challenges they encounter and to seek outside intervention by reaching out to the courts or some of the NGOs. However, such mobilisation is extremely rare. Collective initiatives happen only when the issue is really big, and their livelihood is at stake—since vendors know that they are always at the mercy of corrupt and vengeful authorities. Another issue that prevents vendors uniting and protesting in an organised manner is the acute state of competition between them—both for physical spaces in the market and for their share of customers (since many of the goods they sell are very similar). Despite their many problems, there is no vendors' association in the market and, in the absence of any collective activities, vendors can only search for personal solutions. Many try to build rapport with the people who matter, often using bribes and flattery as a form of "relationship management".

Infrastructure inequalities

As we indicated earlier, slum dwellers in Delhi face daily disadvantages with respect to basic requirements such as water, sanitation, drainage, and garbage disposal. While unequal access to urban infrastructure is itself a form of indirect violence, poor households are also vulnerable to specific forms of direct violence—ones that involve psychological threats or coercion, fear, and physical harm. One way such violence manifests itself is in the constant competition and disputes between residents over access to these scarce common resources. For instance, neighbours might come to blows over who gets the last gallon of water in the communal tank. Another is the highhandedness of government, with its obvious prejudice against the "culture of poverty"—which it clearly equates with criminal deviance.

Our study surveyed some 2000 Delhi households to measure their

- housing conditions
- income and expenditure
- employment opportunities
- levels of access to basic civic amenities.[8]

We also analysed the patterns of urban inequality and deprivation across social categories and localities. This analysis shows overlapping deprivations marked by the households' social status and geographic location. Using this survey and our qualitative fieldwork, we attempted to link levels of access and material conditions with reported incidences and forms of direct violence. We found that a substantial number of households suffer from lack of public water supply, toilets, drainage facilities, and subsidised cooking fuel, as well as higher-level amenities such as educational opportunities and health facilities. Such deprivation exhibits clear spatial patterns: most of the slum households we surveyed experience these disadvantages.

Conflict around these issues in poor localities manifests itself mostly in petty quarrels, verbal abuse, and, at times, physical fights. For instance, about 70 per cent of the slum households do not have running water in their homes. They must get their water either at the few communal supply points—public water taps meant for many households—or through mobile tankers, provided by the federal government, that visit the neighbourhoods to bring water. At these taps, water is often only available for short periods of time (until it runs out) and the waits can be long for the water tanker to finally arrive. With many people crowding around, jostling, arguing, jumping queues, and squabbling about how much water others are allowed to take, and who should get to it first, all the elements seem to be in place to create community stress.

Similarly, more than 60 per cent of slum households do not have private toilets. Most residents must use public toilets, and there is an insufficient number to meet demand. Quarrels often break out, especially in the morning when everyone is queuing up to use the facilities. As well, the public latrines are closed at night. A small number of residents (about 4 per cent of adults, and some children) cope with the problem by resorting to open defecation in public areas, often in empty plots of land and near rail tracks. There is also a lack of proper drainage and garbage disposal systems: the surrounding filth shows the shortage of city staff tasked to clear drains and collect garbage. Maintenance employees are infrequently found in these areas.

Between 35 per cent and 45 per cent of slum households say that the inadequacy of these basic facilities and amenities often becomes the major source of daily friction for them and in other poor localities, such as "resettlement colonies" and "unauthorised colonies". When asked if any of their household members were involved in such disputes in the previous year, a remarkably high number answered yes, in the following proportions:

- drainage: 20 per cent
- water: 17 per cent
- sanitation (toilets): 15 per cent
- garbage and solid waste removal: 11 per cent

In unauthorised colonies, which house diverse social classes with varying levels of social infrastructure, the figures were almost the same for water (18 per cent) and for garbage-related issues (12 per cent). But in authorised colonies, where populations are slightly more affluent, such disputes over basic civic services were negligible.

Other issues that cause everyday quarrels in crowded slums include

- individuals washing clothes or dishes outside their houses, or taking public baths
- residents causing the public drains to clog and overflow
- people dumping their waste into the lanes and drainage channels
- children openly defecating
- neighbours' dogs carrying garbage onto other people's premises.

These situations may appear trivial, but they constitute an ongoing frustration for the poor, especially for women and girls who are responsible for most domestic duties like fetching water, washing, and cleaning. Women and girls are also at greater risk of sexual violence when they use secluded places to defecate.

What is more, conflicts often take a collective form in slums: when quarrels break out, residents gather around and participate—some passively watching the events, others actively taking sides and joining in. In fact, this strong sense of community contributes to the larger trend of collectivisation in slums—meaning that disputes may appear to be more frequent and intense than they actually are. This can lead people from more affluent neighbourhoods, and even the police, to stigmatise these poor localities and regard them as trouble-mongering and crime-prone. Moreover, this collective participation can produce long-standing tensions and deep cleavages along lines of caste, region, and religion.[9] At times, too, politics and ideologies can also play a part in the disputes.

Our research covered nine slum locations and one resettlement colony, as well as the Viklang settlement. All these communities—long-standing settlements, established decades ago—exhibit these features to varying degrees. Such persistence of pitiable conditions, and lack of access to basic civic amenities, can only reflect apathy (or a strong class bias) on the part of the state. In addition, police presence in the slums contrasts remarkably with their practices in higher-income neighbourhoods. In more affluent areas, police patrols offer protection and security, but, in the slums, policing represents a negative factor due to their surveillance and harassment of residents. Slum dwellers are often indiscriminately picked up by the police on any pretext, and questioned and threatened. Admittedly, some slums do have a history of their youth being involved in petty crimes like pickpocketing or snatching small items like purses, mobile phones, and jewellery. Although residents claim that this is declining, the police continuously harass their youth. Meanwhile, residents' calls to the police regarding genuine criminal activities—such as gambling or illicit sales of liquor—are ignored.

Conclusion

In this chapter, we discussed a variety of issues that affect poor people's lives in various locales in Delhi: state apathy, hostility, arbitrariness, and corruption. We also examined the diverse experiences of the poor, including their concerns, vulnerabilities, and resistance strategies in the context of everyday lived violence.

In describing the experiences of the VC dwellers and the vendors of SN market, we can see a distinct difference in the strategies of the two groups as they attempt to overcome their problems. In the colony, the hostility of the lower state functionaries (police and MCD) seems immense—expressed as it is by repeated harassment and demolitions. For the residents, managing to make a living while fighting for their land and housing is a daily challenge. As we indicated earlier, VC residents work collectively, organising and strategising to tackle their problems. By contrast, SN market vendors largely tend to seek individual solutions to their common issues of harassment and subjugation. Fear of the authorities, and acute competition among themselves, prevents them from forming a union and engaging in collective action. This absence of mobilisation leaves each individual to find their own personal solutions, such as befriending and bribing influential people.

However, colony residents and market vendors—both groups that suffer daily harassment, yet fall on the extreme margins of state priorities—are becoming increasingly dependent on the government for their survival. In a corrupt system, they see their only hope as appealing to those in higher positions of authority and trying to build some rapport with them. This illustrates a larger governmentalisation of poor peoples' needs in both these situations.

The infrastructural inadequacy in Delhi slums also brings state apathy to the fore. Consequently, residents are routinely forced to fight among themselves for access to basic needs like water, drainage, toilets, and waste disposal. The state also appears apathetic about their safety and security: police rarely patrol these areas at night, unlike in affluent or middle-class parts of the city. At another level, however, these poor localities experience excessive state interference. Police generally treat slums as hotbeds of crime and frequently "round up" poor people based on nothing more than suspicion. This illustrates the contradictory view of the poor by the state: its attitudes and actions combine indifference with intrusiveness.

Moreover, like the market vendors, slum dwellers mostly seek individual solutions to their collective infrastructural problems—usually by micro-managing their lives, by way of small quarrels and fights. Sometimes residents are able to come together to fight for better infrastructure, but such instances are infrequent (and happen mainly during elections).

Finally, extreme disputes or aggression are normally rare in these contested spaces. While tensions may simmer among slum dwellers, between slum dwellers and the state, or between state and non-state actors, and although the volatile conditions appear to be fertile ground for breeding large-scale violence, a full-blown crisis rarely appears. The "tipping points" are always averted. No matter what the issue—demolition of housing, harassment of vendors, lack of basic infrastructure—big fights or riots seldom happen at these sites. Instead, more reasonable strategies and practices seem to act as safety valves. Small quarrels and everyday disputes, personal interactions between individuals, informal negotiations, and local peace-keeping practices prevent major conflicts from erupting. Other "safety valve" factors are the welfare provisions, however limited, from the government, and the positive interventions of political parties and NGOs. These allow vulnerable people to experience hope, even while hopelessness seems to surround them.

Notes

1 According to official sources, residents of 217 slums were evicted between 1990 and 2007 (Dupont 2011). Additionally, during the run-up to the 2010 Commonwealth Games, Delhi witnessed a major slum clearance. Based on reports, these operations have resulted in about 200,000 people being forcibly evicted since 2004 (Housing and Land Rights Network 2011).

2 Following lengthy campaigns and mobilisation for the rights of street vendors in the country, India's Parliament enacted a law to secure and protect their rights through *The Street Vendors (Protection of Livelihood and Regulation of Street Vending) Act, 2014*. Provincial and local governments were asked to draft rules to implement the provisions of the law. Delhi's provincial and municipal governments still have not designed a policy to put this legislation into practice. Also yet to take place is a survey of the number of designated sites for vending, and their allocation.

3 Recent definitional changes (exclusions of slum-like settlements), and the restructuring of cities, seem to produce "new spatialisations of poverty". Given such changes, official slums alone are not a "proxy for poverty" (Bhan and Jana 2013, 2015).

4 Based on National Crime Research Bureau (NCRB 2014) data, 2010–2014.

5 All names used in this chapter are pseudonyms.

6 Another negotiating strategy the VC dwellers employ is weeping, especially before people who they think can change their present status. They use tears as a political tool to try to convince others of the severity of their plight, and the justice of their

cause of rights and citizenship. However, this is not to say that their tears are not sincere: their personal sufferings and their political narratives are enmeshed. When they cry, they reveal both.

7 The market is named after the famous woman freedom fighter Sarojini Naidu, a poet and politician known as the Nightingale of India.

8 The survey used a stratified random sampling method that included all geographic categories and locations in the city; that is, it was not restricted only to the slums.

9 Such tensions are reported, in various slums in different localities, between Bangladeshi Muslims and Indians; between a group of *paswan* (lower caste) residents and others of higher caste; between Tamils and north Indian Dalits (lower caste groups); and between Muslims and Hindus (mostly Dalits).

References

Banda, Subhadra, and Shahana Sheikh (2014). *The case of Sonia Gandhi camp: The process of eviction and demolition in Delhi's Jhuggi Jhopri clusters.* New Delhi: Centre for Policy Research.

Beck, Ulrich, and Elisabeth Beck-Gernsheim (2002). *Individualization: Institutionalized individualism and its social and political consequences.* New Delhi: SAGE Publications.

Bhan, Gautam (2009). "This is no longer the city I once knew": Evictions, the urban poor, and the right to the city in millennial Delhi. *Environment and Urbanization* 21(1): 127–142.

——— (2014). The impoverishment of poverty: Reflections on urban citizenship and inequality in contemporary Delhi. *Environment and Urbanization* 26(2): 547–560.

Bhan, Gautam, and Arindam Jana (2013). Of slums or poverty: Notes of caution from Census 2011. *Economic and Political Weekly* 48(18): n.p.

——— (2015). Reading spatial inequality in urban India. *Economic and Political Weekly* 50(22): 49.

Bourgois, Philippe (2001). The power of violence in war and peace: Post–Cold War lessons from El Salvador. *Ethnography* 2(1): 5–34.

Chatterji, Roma, and Deepak Mehta (2007). *Living with violence: An anthropology of events and everyday life.* London: Routledge.

Cuomo, Chris (1996). War is not just an event: Reflections on the significance of everyday violence. *Hypatia* 11(4): 30–45.

Das, Veena (2007). *Life and words: Violence and the descent into the ordinary.* Berkeley: University of California Press.

de Certeau, Michel (1984). *The practice of everyday life* (Steven Rendall, Trans.). Berkeley: University of California Press.

Dupont, Véronique (2008). Slum demolition in Delhi since the 1990s: An appraisal. *Economic and Political Weekly* 43(28): 79–87.

——— (2011). The dream of Delhi as a global city. *International Journal of Urban and Regional Research* 35(3): 533–554.

Essex, Stephen, and Brian Chalkey (1998). Olympic Games: Catalyst of urban change. *Leisure Studies* 17(3): 187–206.

Farmer, Paul (1996). On suffering and structural violence: A view from below. *Daedalus* 125(1): 261–283.

Galtung, Johan (1969). Violence, peace, and peace research. *Journal of Peace Research* 6(3): 167–191.

Gupta, Akhil (2012). *Red tape: Bureaucracy, structural violence, and poverty in India*. Durham: Duke University Press.

Housing and Land Rights Network (2011). *Planned dispossession: Forced evictions and the 2010 Commonwealth Games*. New Delhi: Housing and Land Rights Network, and Habitat International Coalition.

Jervis Read, Cressida (2014). Un-settlement: Demolition, home remaking, and the everyday politics of citizenship in a low-income Delhi neighbourhood. *Home Cultures* 11(2): 197–218.

Kalyan, Rohan (2014). The magicians' ghetto: Moving slums and everyday life in a postcolonial city. *Theory, Culture and Society* 31(1): 49–73.

Latif, Nadia (2012). "It was better during the war": Narratives of everyday violence in a Palestinian refugee camp. *Feminist Review* 101: 24–40.

Malinowski, Bronislaw (1935). *Coral gardens and their magic: A study of the methods of tilling the soil and of agricultural rites in the Trobriand Islands*. New York: American Book Company.

Moser, Caroline, and Dennis Rodgers (2012). *Understanding the tipping point of urban conflict: Global Policy Report*. Working Paper 7. Manchester: University of Manchester.

Muggah, Robert (2012). *Researching the urban dilemma: Urbanisation, poverty and violence*. Ottawa: International Development Research Centre (IDRC). www.idrc.ca/EN/PublishingImages/Researching-the-Urban-Dilemma-Baseline-study.pdf.

NCRB: National Crime Research Bureau (2014). *Crime in India 2014: Statistics*. New Delhi: Author (Ministry of Home Affairs).

Neal, Sarah, and Karim Murji (2015). Sociologies of everyday life: Introduction to the Special Issue. *Sociology* 49(5): 1–9.

Robinson, Victoria (2015). Reconceptualizing the mundane and the extraordinary: A lens through which to explore transformation within women's everyday footwear practices. *Sociology* 49(5): 903–918.

Rodgers, Dennis, and Bruce O'Neill (2012). Infrastructural violence: Introduction to the Special Issue. *Ethnography* 13(4): 401–412.

Rodgers, Dennis, and Shivani Satija (2012). *Understanding the tipping point of urban conflict: The case of Patna, India*. Working Paper 5. Manchester: University of Manchester.

Schindler, Seth (2014). Producing and contesting the formal/informal divide: Regulating street hawking in Delhi, India. *Urban Studies* 51(12): 2596–2612.

Schott, Robin (1995). Gender and "postmodern" war. *Hypatia* 11(4): 19–29.

Scott, James (1990). *Domination and the arts of resistance: Hidden transcripts*. New Haven: Yale University Press.

Tadjoeddin, Mohammad, and Syed Murshed (2007). Socioeconomic determinants of everyday violence in Indonesia: An empirical investigation of Javanese districts, 1994–2003. *Journal of Peace Research* 44(6): 689–709.

Winter, Yves (2012). Violence and visibility. *New Political Science* 34(2): 195–202.

5 Urban community profiles

Safe relocation and resettlement in post-war Sri Lanka

Danesh Jayatilaka, Rajith W. D. Lakshman, and Iresha M. Lakshman

Introduction

For a quarter of a century, from 1983 to 2009, Sri Lanka suffered from a civil war waged by government military forces against the insurgents of the Liberation Tigers of Tamil Eelam (colloquially, the Tamil Tigers). Certain areas of the country, particularly in the north and east, were torn apart by armed conflict, and thousands of people were displaced. Such disasters are nothing new, of course: for millennia, civil conflicts—as well as natural disasters and, in more recent times, development projects—have forcibly displaced people from their homes, usually into cities. Now known as Internally Displaced Persons or IDPs (for a formal definition see Deng 1999), these people encounter gross violations of their rights during, and often far beyond, their resettlement or relocation (Davies and Jacobsen 2010; Jacobsen 2011; Jacobsen and Nichols 2011; Zetter and Deikun 2010). This often included violation of what Lefebvre (1996) described as "the right to the city". The rights violations of urban IDPs can be identified as urban violence, as defined by Moser (2004).

We also now know that post-war conditions add further layers of complexity—both to urban violence itself (Moser and McIlwaine 2001), and also to the resilience of the affected persons or communities. This resilience is defined by Hallegatte (2014) as "the ability of an economy or society to minimise welfare losses for a disaster of a given magnitude." Another definition, provided by Adger (2000), is "the ability of groups or communities to cope with external stresses and disturbances as a result of social, political and environmental change." Resilience, in the form of capabilities, is useful in the recovery process in terms of resettlement. Building this factor into existing assessment models can help to highlight the capabilities of IDPs, rather than just their vulnerabilities and their risk of impoverishment (Muggah 2000).

In this chapter, we offer some theories about how to create safer cities in post-war countries. We do this by presenting our research on the losses and gains of two relocated urban IDP communities in post-war Sri Lanka: Colombo, the national capital, and Jaffna, the capital of the country's northern province. Our community profiling approach looks at how these two communities responded with resilience to the violence and displacement that residents experienced in a post-conflict situation.

Common definitions of violence—including that proposed by the World Health Organization (WHO) in 2002—present it as the use of physical force to cause bodily hurt in order to impose one's wishes (Moser 2004). However, broader definitions of violence also include psychological hurt, material deprivation, and symbolic disadvantage (Fox 2015; Schröder and Schmidt 2001). These expanded definitions can be particularly useful in cities that have low-intensity violence, such as that documented in South Asia. Muggah (2012: 46) points out that, unlike in Latin America and the Caribbean, "South Asian cities and slums are not characterised by large-scale urban violence or criminal gangs."

For this reason, we favour Fox's broader definition of violence, which includes coercion or psychological manipulation used in a harmful or destructive way. Further, violence may not be a static factor. It can also be a dynamic process that is "constructed, negotiated, reshaped and resolved, as perpetrators and victims try to define and control the world they find themselves in" (Robben and Nordstrom 1995: 8). Violence can even be analysed into typologies, such as political, institutional, economic, social, and structural (Moser 2004).

Urban IDPs face a wide range of losses, such as chronic impoverishment, even long after they have been (often forcibly) resettled. The government may lead the recovery efforts, sometimes with the support of emergency organisations and development agencies. These perform various interventions as the victims go through the different phases of immediate relief, and intermediate and long-term development (Amirthalingam and Lakshman 2013; Brun and Lund 2008; Cornwall 2010; Gunasekara, Najab, and Munas 2015; Jaspars 2009; Romeshun, Gunasekara, and Munas 2014). A useful tool for this kind of analysis is the Impoverishment Risk and Livelihood Reconstruction (IRLR) model, developed by Cernea (1997). It identifies eight variables that increase the risk of impoverishment among IDPs:

- landlessness
- joblessness
- homelessness
- economic marginalisation
- increased morbidity
- food insecurity
- loss of access to common property
- social disintegration.

The model was originally proposed to analyse the vulnerabilities of affected communities in situations of Development-Forced Displacement and Relocation (DFDR). It was later extended to cases of Conflict-Induced

Displacement (CID) by Muggah (2000, 2003). At that time, Muggah added three other variables associated with war-related humanitarian situations:

- loss of education
- loss of political participation
- violence (since the type of violence experienced in conflict situations is different from that of development situations).

This model broadly fits the literature on the cultural and social losses incurred by displaced persons. These include loss of access to

- infrastructure services (such as public transport, water, and electricity)
- social services such as schooling, education, etc.
- common property resources and political participation
- social capital such as networks and relationships, etc. (Cernea 1999).

The new total of 11 risks and losses are clearly the result of both development and conflict, and hence easily linked with Moser's (2004) typology of urban violence. However, these variables mostly operate on a macro level, and do not take into account the IDPs' own capabilities for poverty avoidance (Muggah 2000). In terms of our theoretical and conceptual scaffolding in this chapter, it is useful to conceptualise the way IDPs negotiate the shocks of the medium-term impacts of displacement as a form of community-level resilience (Amirthalingam and Lakshman 2010; Hallegatte 2014; Schipper and Langston 2015). Measuring resilience as a response to the IRLR variables—especially in terms of outcomes to issues like social cohesion, asset accumulation, livelihood regeneration, and changes in violence experienced—allows us to understand the real potential of the resettled IDPs to avoid poverty.

Urban displacement in Sri Lanka

The 26-year war, which ended less than a decade ago, means that, for some Sri Lankans, almost an entire generation has experienced displacements. Many people have also been forced to move due to urban development projects, such as when the government evacuated a number of shantytowns and slum communities. Some individuals or groups had to move multiple times, experiencing several returns or resettlements (Brun and Lund 2008, 2009; Muggah 2008; Perera-Mubarak 2013, 2014). The development-related relocations were under the purview of the state, while conflict-related resettlements were joint interventions between the state, the United Nations (UN), various NGOs, and other multilateral entities (Godamunne and Kumarasiri 2010; Hyndman 2011; Jayatilaka 2009; Jayatilaka, Amirthalingam, and Gunasekara 2015). The government set up a number of ministries, authorities, and departments to deal with displacement.

But the complexity of the problem was such that many aspects were inappropriately or inadequately addressed: solutions were hard to find for social, psychological, and environmental adjustments (Amirthalingam and Lakshman 2010; Goodhand 2010; Jayatilaka and Amirthalingam 2015; Lakshman, Ekanayaka, and Lakshman 2016; Vithanagama et al. 2015). The latest UN data suggest that Sri Lanka is among the least urbanised countries in the world, and certainly the least in South Asia. These statistics show that the urban proportion of the population was 19 per cent in 1990, and 18 per cent in 2014; and it is projected to be just 30 per cent in 2050 (United Nations 2014). These low levels are attributed to the process of "hidden urbanisation", the result of relying on administrative boundaries to define what is (and is not) urban (Ellis and Roberts 2016).

According to the Asian Development Bank (2015), for instance, the city of Colombo was believed to have a population of 555,031 in 2012. Nearly half of these people lived in substandard conditions and lacked basic facilities such as water, sewers, and electricity. By 2014, around 900 acres of government land in and around Colombo was occupied by slum dwellers, mostly unused terrain such as railway land, canal banks, and swampy low-lying areas. Between 2010 and 2014, Sri Lanka's Urban Development Authority initiated a plan to evacuate some 68,000 families out of these slum communities, and into high-rise buildings in and around Colombo (Razick 2014). The government intended to clear away all the low-income housing units by 2020 under its Megapolis Development Plan. The government's aim in doing so was threefold:

- to free up the shantytown lands for socioeconomic development
- to help the former occupants obtain secure housing
- to pursue its vision of making Colombo a slum-free "garden city", and a commercial hub for South Asia.

The end of the war in 2009, and the return to normalcy in the country, added impetus to this plan, which is still ongoing—and is likely to increase urbanisation in the region. For example, Jaffna's metropolitan population in 2009 was only 134,134, but it is projected to reach a million by 2030 (World Bank 2012). If realised, this would mean a phenomenal 9.6 per cent annual increase in population. Part of this growth was driven by the government's mega-resettlement project, known in Sinhalese as *Uthuru Wasanthaya and Neganahira Udava* (Northern Spring and Eastern Awakening). By late 2015, the project, which included fully built and semi-built housing, had resettled 800,129 people displaced by conflict in the north and east of the country.

Methodology and locations

As indicated earlier, we took a community profiling approach with our research, drawing on existing data and using a number of methods to construct community profiles. Our goal was to make these extremely broad, in order to analyse all the resources, needs, and other issues that affect communities. Christakopoulou, Dawson, and Gari (2001), for instance, noted that neighbourhoods should be profiled in six ways:

- as part of the city
- as a place to live
- as a social community
- as an economic community
- as a political community
- as personal space.

Since different profiling methods have their advantages and disadvantages, it is worthwhile to combine methods to gain richer information and a more well-rounded view of the community (Hawtin and Percy-Smith 2007). Our studies, conducted during 2014, relied on primary, secondary, quantitative, and qualitative data to triangulate findings. They also drew on a variety of investigative techniques, including:

- interviews
- focus groups discussions
- key informant interviews
- household discussions
- ranking exercises
- seasonal calendars and timelines
- Google Earth observations
- geographic information systems (GIS) mapping
- physical exploration
- photography.

The two communities we profile here are Passaiyoor in Jaffna (Jayatilaka et al. 2015), and Sinhapura in Colombo (Lakshman et al. 2016). The latter community is in the division of Wanathamulla village, a slum area with an unsavoury reputation for violence and criminal activities. Many of the original houses there were merely small dwellings made of planks, with limited (or no) facilities such as electricity, water, or bathrooms.

The Sinhapura housing project includes Phase 1 (constructed in 2007 to house residents from Wanathamulla) and Phase 2 (constructed in 2011 to house people from Torrington, a few kilometres away). Both phases are five-storey buildings of 60 condominium-style flats each, standing next to each other; and both were constructed under the supervision of a private company, the Real Estate Exchange, and Sri Lanka's Urban Settlement Development Authority. The two groups living in the buildings, some 120 families in all, form a sharp contrast. Those in the earlier building came from the low-income Wanathamulla area, and were forced out of their own homes by the military. The Phase 2 families—a mix of blue-collar and white-collar types—formerly lived in the more high-income area of Torrington, known for its affluent lifestyle. Their displacement was less physically violent, but involved deliberate deceit on the part of politicians and officials. The residents were talked into evacuating their houses with the promise that the government would construct a new housing complex for them on the same land. In fact, that did not happen.

In Jaffna, the location we selected for the project was the small fishing village of Passaiyoor East (hereafter referred to simply as Passaiyoor). The locals there were caught in the intense fighting between government security forces, peacekeeping forces from India and the Tamil Tigers. Although no official figures are available for this turbulent time, in remote parts of the country, it is generally accepted that hundreds of people migrated out of the country; others suffered significant internal displacement and resettlement. The current population is 364 families, totalling 1,149 individuals, who live in different types of owned and rented accommodation (Jayatilaka et al. 2015). Most families earn their living by fishing, and have relational, caste, and religious ties with each other. Many people were able to return to their own houses after being displaced, and used their own labour and financial resources to repair them. Assistance for resettlement was mostly limited to some livelihood assistance provided by the government. However, one major benefit was the construction of a new anchorage and harbour by the International Organization for Migration (with aid from the Sri Lankan and Australian governments).

Colombo: Sinhapura Phases 1 and 2

In Sinhapura, people suffered physical and psychological harm as a result of the forcible evictions they experienced. The Phase 1 residents, as indicated earlier, were forced from their homes by the military. There were occasions where soldiers would physically break down the roof or walls of a house, to make it uninhabitable. As one female resident of Phase 1 explained:

> The government moved us here before they demolished our house in Wanathamulla. They removed our roof, and then we had no choice but to move. Of course they did not pull us out with our belongings. But how can one live without a roof on top of one's head?

Phase 1 residents also had to deal with problems such as paying for the new flat, coping with overflowing drainage systems in the new housing complexes, and the increased cost of living (since they now had to actually pay for their legal electricity and water supplies—rather than obtaining them illegally, as they had before). There was also the emotional stress resulting from large numbers of strangers living together. One female respondent explained the financial burden:

> We still have to pay money for this flat, which is 500 square feet. They told us that our previous house was 400 square feet, and asked us to pay for the extra 100 square feet. I have to pay 50,000 rupees [roughly US$330] more.

The psychological harm experienced by the displaced Phase 2 residents takes the form of bitterness and disappointment at the deception they experienced. During interviews, they alleged that several politicians and government officials—including the president of Sri Lanka at that time—convinced the community leaders in Torrington that the resettlement would be a beneficial outcome for the inhabitants. Now, living in Phase 2, they are essentially landless: the deeds to the new condominiums have not been given to them.

The families relocated to Sinhapura continue to face different types of issues. Phase 2 residents, for instance, are now much further from their workplaces, so they must either quit their jobs or cope with longer travel times and higher transportation costs. One man from Phase 2 said his expenses had gone up: "I have to go to Narahenpita for work. This is too far for my son to travel to work every day." The impact can be worse for women than for men. Many males have been able to secure new blue-collar casual work close by. The women, on the other hand, mostly worked as domestic helpers in houses in and around Torrington; and once they were moved away, many gave up their jobs. (Although the distance between the two communities is only a few kilometres, the distance can be an overwhelming obstacle in a place with difficult public transportation.) The impacts vary further for government employees, or people with private businesses. One woman from Phase 1 spoke wistfully of the fruit shop her daughter had in their previous house: "My daughter had a shop in our previous house. We earned about 1000 rupees per day as profit. It was a fruit shop: pawpaw, bananas, pineapple; we had all the fruits." But like many small-scale businesses, it has been shut down since the relocation. (Then again, another female resident of Phase 2 opined that things have actually improved, in terms of family income. Before, she said, "the earlier place my father worked used to give him work on one day and then no work the next. But now he goes to work every day.")

The new condominium lifestyle at Sinhapura also encouraged competition and solitude among residents. With a non-leaking roof over their heads to protect their possessions, they now felt able to buy furniture, goods, and household appliances. This created the usual effect of consumerism: everyone wanted to buy something better than their neighbour. As well as becoming competitive, they also became increasingly isolated. With private spaces came weakened interactions between families, compared to earlier times. Instead of the common public water-tap—where a lot of the neighbourhood socialisation took place—now they have water piped into their own flats.

The absence of a strong community network seemed to make residents more vulnerable to that isolation, and highlighted their lack of a sense of belonging. For Phase 2 people, the unfamiliarity of the Wanathamulla location also made fitting in very difficult. Few of them, fortunately, had first-hand experience of violence. But their perceptions of their new neighbours were clouded by Wanathamulla's notorious reputation. This promoted an "us and them" division between the Phase 1 and 2 residents, and contributed to their sense of homelessness. These "before and after" feelings are captured in comments from both sides. A woman from Phase 1 said of the old days in Wanathamulla:

> We used to be free those days. When we leave the house and meet people we know who they are. But now there are more people that we do not know. Our parents were born and raised there. So we used to know each other.

Contrast this nostalgic attitude with the former president of a community association from Torrington, a man now living in Phase 2: "[The Phase 1 residents] call us 'parachutes'—we have been dropped from above. We cannot talk about anything here; we must stay quiet. It's their rule."

The strongest grievances are about drug dealing, drug abuse, petty theft, and antisocial behaviour such as noise, shouting, and fighting. It is worth noting, however, that the perpetrators of most of these acts are not in fact residents; they are trespassers from an adjoining shanty community, who enter the Sinhapura complex to make use of its public spaces. These are the people who play loud music, use obscene language, get into fights, and steal things to meet their need for fast cash to buy drugs or alcohol. The police are reluctant to intervene, especially since the closest police post (in the adjoining Sahaspura area) is staffed by only two officers. One result of this dangerous situation is that Sinhapura residents avoid public spaces, and parents discourage their children from engaging in community activities, or even playing with their peers in the neighbourhood.

Regarding children, Sinhapura parents experience a number of difficulties. They claim that schools are reluctant to admit their children because of the negative social connotations of living in Wanathamulla. Even when children are enrolled, teachers and peers sometimes discriminate against them and stigmatise them due to their low socioeconomic standing. That said, some residents—like this Phase 2 man—also report a better social environment for their children:

> I think it is good we came to this flat. Children also like this house. We couldn't invite outsiders to our houses in the previous place. The houses were very densely located. We did not have much space in our previous house but here we have sufficient space.

In terms of aggression against women, this particular problem was not reported at Sinhapura. Most respondents agreed that it was a safe place for females, where they could move about freely in public spaces—even late in the evening. The most common issue was boys and men teasing and mocking girls.

As this description illustrates, people had mixed feelings about their new homes. In a focus group, one woman gave her opinion that: "Everything is good here, but caged. No freedom." That attitude—of seeing positive features in the physical environment, but being generally critical of the social setting—was echoed by a female resident from Phase 1 who said: "These houses are much better than where we lived earlier. But the issue is the [social] environment." Still, for them the possibility of owning a proper home—rather than a temporary or illegal house—added a dimension of social recognition and importance to their lives. That satisfaction was strongest among those Wanathamulla people who had formerly lived in plank shanties with no running water. For the sake of a better home, they were willing to adjust to the shortcomings of relocation.

Jaffna: Passaiyoor

During the war, nearly all the residents of Passaiyoor suffered high-intensity violence, including deaths, injuries, trauma, and hardships of various kinds. As IDPs, they were forced to flee their villages, land, homes, and jobs, and they encountered risk, uncertainty, and multiple and long-term displacements. Some were able to find security and shelter among friends and family; others only in various scattered welfare camps. Their survival, to a large extent, depended on relief rations; and it was hard for them to gain access to services.

With the cessation of fighting and security issues, many changes occurred in Jaffna's society:

- the restoration of freedom of movement
- the liberalisation of the economy
- the general opening up of the region
- modern changes in attitudes, and in how people behave and relate to one another.

At the time of our research, however, the residents were still experiencing different kinds of challenges. New types of social issues had begun to disrupt people's traditional culture. The older Sri Lankan population is quite conservative, and many felt that even standard modern tools, such as mobile phones and internet access, tend to corrupt the young generation. Other unwelcome elements included easy access to alcohol, cigarettes, drugs, and online pornography. Drugs (mostly marijuana) were apparently widely available: one fisherman we spoke to said that his neighbour's son was a drug addict: "they get the drug in the form of toffees while away in school."

Alcoholism, in particular, was known to have increased among IDPs. (One religious leader commented: "The consumption of alcohol is continually on the rise, and the north is known for alcoholism.") Among young males, who experienced high unemployment and disincentives to work, youth violence and gang formations emerged. In nearby parts of the region, there were also increasing concerns about various kinds of aggressive and violent behaviours, such as the sexual harassment and abuse of women, rape, and even murder. (The IDPs were not directly involved or affected by such incidents, but were naturally disturbed by them.) Property crimes such as robberies, though, seemed not to be prevalent. This was due partly to the cohesion of close-knit communities, and partly to police vigilance.

When people displaced from Passaiyoor finally returned to their own small houses, they found many of them damaged. For their process of resettlement, they relied on three main financial sources: personal savings or loans, their incomes, and support from their extended families. (This was especially the case for residents with friends and relatives who had moved away to France and Germany—as many Sri Lankans had—forming a small diaspora. One fisherman told us: "We are not struggling, thanks to [them]. The monetary assistance we received from abroad was of great use during the war.")

Many people resumed their former occupation of fishing; but even here there were anxieties and tensions. The once-rich fish stocks in the sea had been much reduced, partly due to over-fishing but also (some said) due to poaching by Indian fishers. This situation was a real concern for a community that essentially had only one source of income, and many fishermen we spoke to were troubled. One member of the Passaiyoor Fishermen's Society said: "In the future ... we may have to leave the industry. We are in a real fix." Another man explained that this had a follow-on effect. "When some fishermen leave the industry, others are also forced to leave because they do not have enough people to undertake fishing."

Other community issues that challenged resettlement included high unemployment, debt, land shortage in the village, and increasing land prices. One woman told us:

> We educate our children with the income we earn from fishing. Since the income from fishing is low, we want them to study and join other employment. Some of them like to stay on, but we want them to do better. Although the fishing industry has been good to us, it is now in decline.

That doubt over the prospects of the fishing industry caused locals to think about the future of their children. In Passaiyoor—as in much of rural Sri Lanka—there are still gendered differences in education, occupation, and income: women are not treated as equals to men, which limits their prospects. While issues such as assault, abuse, and domestic violence were not prevalent (and these were not the primary problems women faced), there were insinuations that domestic violence and assaults were on the rise.

Women, particularly widows, also struggled financially. Roughly a hundred women in this community had lost their husbands during the war, and were forced to depend on their children for income and protection. Some, however, became entrepreneurs, and successfully managed businesses of their own. Self-employed women commonly engage in small-scale commercial activities such as producing sweets or chili powder, selling firewood, preparing food parcels, etc. For instance, one member of the Passaiyoor Women's Society operates a small business that she started with the aid of loans. "I started … with the initial 10,000 rupee [loan]. I have been functioning for two years now," she said. "Next, I will get a 50,000 rupee loan from my micro-credit society and will use it to expand the business."

With the official services functioning again, and roads and buildings in fair condition, it was time to look to the future. Inspired by the new harbour, local residents—with support from the diaspora, who regularly send money home; and potentially also from the Australian government, the German government, and the British Council—were discussing plans to build a sports stadium and a library in the village. The villagers are known for their talent at football, and Passaiyoor has produced a number of Sri Lanka's best players (including a captain of the national team). They are also well known in the region for their interest in the arts, especially theatre. The village encourages many social events that strengthen engagement among locals and visitors, and it supports a number of clubs and societies for women, men, and youth.

Other features that shaped the community's socioeconomic status, and played lead roles in its activities, were the market and the church. Spirituality and religious beliefs are important for the locals, who are almost entirely Catholic (except for a few Hindus). Among the latter, caste differences are limited, since most are from the same community. One fisherman told us: "Our area is blessed by God. We have marine resources, arts, education, and music." Residents regularly expressed a significant sense of attachment and belonging towards their village, and gratitude for what it offers and what makes it unique. Most of the people who were displaced chose to return; and those who migrated away did so mainly due to the lack of other options. Diaspora relatives living in other countries (who are viewed as a type of guardian) generally keep in close touch, and visit often.

To sum up Passaiyoor's state: overall, there was a general coping attitude in the community, especially as they recollected what they had been through, and how they had adapted to those conditions by various means. The inhabitants had painful memories of witnessing violent warfare, and experiencing displacement and other losses. They tried to move forward with their lives, focusing on their religion, families, community, and work. Yet, like so many other people in the modern world, they also had to face the looming reality of issues with their livelihoods, their children's future prospects, and their housing space (not to mention the larger changes that affected their culture). They experienced a duality of attachment: to their traditional way of life on the one hand, and, on the other hand, to looking for something better—of wanting a better standard of living for themselves and their families.

Discussion and conclusions

Residents of both the communities studied here—Sinhapura and Passaiyoor—experienced displacement of different types. They coped with the events in different ways, showing their resilience in how they responded. In terms of our analysis, the 11 variables proposed in the IRLR were useful in our systematic examination of the dissimilar impacts of displacement (and subsequent resettlement) on aspects such as social cohesion, asset accumulation, and livelihood regeneration.

It is important to note those forced from their homes by development in Colombo were relocated elsewhere, while the people affected by conflict-induced displacement in Jaffna were able to return to their original site. This resulted in differences in the scale of losses, the support received, and the sense of recovery and control over life events. In Passaiyoor, the resettled CID community had experienced a greater magnitude of war-related violence, including destruction of property, psychological trauma, physical injuries, and even death. By contrast, the DFDR community in Sinhapura had experienced less harmful types and intensity of violence.

On this basis, we expected to find the Sinhapura community to be more resilient than the Passaiyoor community. However, we were surprised to find that the reverse was true. Though there are still problems in the fishing village, the residents seem to be in greater command of their experience than the inhabitants of Sinhapura. In this discussion, we will explore whether our framework can explain this finding, and whether it is able to help us accurately theorise about the resilience we encountered.

As Cernea (1997: 1575) points out, "Forced displacement tears apart the existing social fabric: it disperses and fragments communities, dismantles patterns of social organisation and interpersonal ties, [and] kinship groups become scattered as well." In order for communities to recover, that social disarticulation needs to be reversed. The evidence suggests that the Passaiyoor community may have achieved this goal relatively well. The residents endured violent conflict and were displaced for extended periods. But, when they were resettled, the community simply came back together again.

This had significant positive implications for their resilience. The ties the locals shared were deep-rooted, and encompassed many aspects of their lives. Their common occupations, interests, networks, religion, and experience of displacement played an important role in shaping their resilience. Another important factor seemed to be that donor aid was provided transparently, at the community level, rather than privately at an individual or family level. This likely reinforced the existing group ties—a fact that seems to support Moser and McIlwaine's theory (2001) that combined strategies are essential to integrate social capital.

The community dynamics and resilience we observed in Sinhapura were a sharp contrast. Displacement had indeed torn apart the social fabric, but relocation had not quite sewn it back together. We identified three reasons for this:

- The deceit and manipulation of the politicians and relocation agencies had compromised the effectiveness of existing community organisations.
- The community had been fragmented into two sets of residents, who came from different origins and locations.
- The intrusion of "outsiders", who behaved badly, into the community's public spaces, upset the community and added an extra level of stress.

Clearly (as in most urban spaces) there were issues related to living in close proximity to strangers (Franck 1980); and this was further complicated by the community's fragmentation and demoralisation. So, the experiences of past displacement and current social friction seemed to feed into each other in a downward spiral, decreasing resilience. To quote Moser (2004: 6): "Violence is linked to fear and insecurity, which pervades people's lives … [this has] serious implications for trust, well-being and social capital among communities and individuals." Perhaps Moser's terminology can help us to analyse the differences between Sinhapura and Passaiyoor. The former community seemed to have more social violence, with some political violence; whereas the latter seemed to be recovering from political violence, but had replaced it with social violence.

In Passaiyoor, with the end of the war ushering in a democratisation process, it is possible that what we saw was the democratisation of violence itself (Kruijt and Koonings 1999). People there always spoke to us of how life and survival were a struggle in the past, during the war and their displacement. And, in spite of the current economic and social woes, they appreciated their relative good fortune and were thankful to leave that past behind. They drew on various individual, family, and community capabilities for strength, which contributed to their resilience.

In Sinhapura, on the other hand, people struggled to cope, felt that they had lost more than they had gained, and longed for their past: their neighbourhoods, spaces, jobs, homes, and most of all their sense of community. This contrast highlights the difference in what the two groups considered as most meaningful and important. Both communities commonly referred to the past, "home", and "belonging" with a sense of nostalgia. In Sinhapura, residents of both phases felt that they had had much better social relationships and networks in their previous homes. Although the problems encountered in their new location were not very different from what they had been used to before, people's ability to deal with these problems had declined as a result of having to live in a neighbourhood crowded with "strangers". But in Passaiyoor, resettlement made it possible for people to reunite with the social networks they once had. This fact made it easier for them to be resilient against all kinds of threats.

The current violence encountered by the DFDR group in Sinhapura was at the extreme low end of the continuum, which was also the case for the CID group in Passaiyoor—though they had experienced high levels of violence before and the Sinhapura group had not. Therefore, the reference points with respect to violence are different for the two groups. It is also possible that the CID group, due to years of exposure to war, were already more adaptable and able to cope. After all, they had lived in various places, and engaged in assorted occupations to make ends meet. The DFDR group had not undergone such experiences, and were likely struggling as they tried to manage their situation. Further, the types and degrees of the 11 IRLR variables were different for the two locations. After their resettlement, the CID people did not experience landlessness, and they regained their social networks. For the DFDR group, their experience was the opposite. These differences affected the groups' lifestyles, well-being, and recovery times.

Hammond (2008) and Kibreab (2003) spoke of "manoeuvering freedom and space" for resettled communities to recover—especially in terms of spontaneous resettlements and planned relocations, where the settlers had different levels of choice and opportunities. The satisfaction of the beneficiaries was also affected by whether the movement was voluntary or involuntary, and by the type of resettlement programmes. These varied according to whether the displaced people were empowered enough to be able to formulate their own income-generating patterns (rather than having only restricted work opportunities), and to have a sense of ownership of the process. In the case of Passaiyoor, the locals returned of their own free will, and took up occupations according to their liking. In Sinhapura, on the other hand, residents were often compelled to change their employment, taking new jobs that were not always to their liking. This sense of mobility (or immobility) and freedom to manoeuvre affected the people's economic and psychological well-being. It also most likely contributed to reinforcing or diminishing their resilience. For example, the Passaiyoor people mentioned "space" with relish, while some in Sinhapura felt they were "in a cage".

References

Adger, W. Neil (2000). Social and ecological resilience: Are they related? *Progress in Human Geography* 24(3): 347–364.

Amirthalingam, Kopalapillai, and Rajith W. D. Lakshman (2010). Financing of internal displacement: Excerpts from the Sri Lankan experience. *Disasters* 34(2): 402–425.

——— (2013). Impact of displacement on women and female-headed households: A mixed-method analysis with a microeconomic touch. *Journal of Refugee Studies* 26(1): 26–46.

Asian Development Bank (2015). *Initial Environmental Examination: Greater Colombo Water and Wastewater Management Improvement Program*. www.adb.org/sites/default/files/project-document/172394/45148-008-iee.pdf.

Brun, Cathrine, and Ragnhild Lund (2008). Making a home during crisis: Post-tsunami recovery in a context of war, Sri Lanka. *Singapore Journal of Tropical Geography* 29: 274–287.

——— (2009). "Unpacking" the narrative of a national housing policy in Sri Lanka. *Norsk Geografisk Tidsskrift [Norwegian Journal of Geography]* 63: 10–22.

Cernea, Michael M. (1997). The risks and reconstruction model for resettling displaced populations. *World Development* 25(10): 1569–1587.

Cernea, Michael M. (Ed.). (1999). *The economics of involuntary resettlement: Questions and challenges*. Washington, DC: World Bank.

Christakopoulou, Sophia, Jon Dawson, and Aikaterini Gari (2001). The community well-being questionnaire: Theoretical context and initial assessment of its reliability and validity. *Social Indicators Research* 56(3): 319–349.

Cornwall, Andrea (2010). Introductory overview: Buzzwords and fuzzwords, deconstructing development discourse. In Andrea Cornwall and Deborah Eade (Eds.), *Deconstructing development discourse: Buzzwords and fuzzwords* (1–18). Rugby: Practical Action Publishing.

Davies, Anne, and Karen Jacobsen (2010). Profiling urban IDPs. *Forced Migration Review* 34: 13–15.

Deng, Francis (1999). Guiding principles on internal displacement. *International Migration Review* 33: 484–493.

Ellis, Peter, and Mark Roberts (2016). *Leveraging urbanization in South Asia: Managing spatial transformation for prosperity and livability*. Washington, DC: World Bank.

Fox, Michael A. (2015). Reflections on violence. In Andrew Fiala (Ed.), *The peace of nature and the nature of peace: Essays on ecology, nature, nonviolence, and peace* (31–40). Boston: Brill Rodopi.

Franck, Karen. A. (1980). Friends and strangers: The social experience of living in urban and non-urban settings. *Journal of Social Issues* 36(3): 52–71. doi: https://doi.org/10.1111/j.1540–4560.1980.tb02035.x.

Godamunne, Nayana, and Mansi Kumarasiri (2010). Development and displacement: The National Involuntary Resettlement Policy in practice. Colombo: Centre for Poverty Analysis.

Goodhand, Jonathan (2010). Stabilizing a victor's peace? Humanitarian action and reconstruction in eastern Sri Lanka. *Disasters* 34: 342–367.

Gunasekara, Vagisha, Nadhiya Najab, and Mohamed Munas (2015). *No silver bullet: An assessment of the effects of financial counselling on decision-making behaviour of housing beneficiaries in Jaffna and Kilinochchi*. Colombo: Centre for Poverty Analysis. www.cepa.lk/content_images/publications/documents/No-Silver-Bullet-english-20160224102803.pdf.

Hallegatte, Stephane (2014). Economic resilience: Definition and measurement. *World Bank Policy Research Working Paper* (6852). http://papers.ssrn.com/sol3/papers.cfm?abstract_id=2432352.

Hammond, Laura (2008). Strategies of invisibilization: How Ethiopia's resettlement programme hides the poorest of the poor. *Journal of Refugee Studies* 21(4): 517–536. doi: http://doi.org/10.1093/jrs/fen041.

Hawtin, Murray, and Janie Percy-Smith (2007). *Community profiling: A practical guide*. Maidenhead, UK: Open University Press.

Hyndman, Jennifer (2011). *Dual disasters: Humanitarian aid after the 2004 tsunami*. Sterling, VA: Kumarian Press.

Jacobsen, Karen (2011). Profiling urban IDPs: How IDPs differ from their non-IDP neighbours in three cities. In Khalid Koser and Susan Martin (Eds.), *The migration-displacement nexus: Patterns, processes, and policies* (79–95). Oxford: Berghahn.

Jacobsen, Karen, and Rebecca F. Nichols (2011). *Developing a profiling methodology for displaced people in urban areas: Final report*. Medford, MA: Tufts University.

Jaspars, Susanne (2009). *Livelihoods and protection in Sri Lanka: A review of DRC's integrated livelihoods, protection and emergency response programme in Sri Lanka*. London: Humanitarian Policy Group.

Jayatilaka, Danesh (2009). *Lessons while en route to solutions: Revisiting the IDP return and resettlement programme in the east of Sri Lanka*. Paper presented at the International Association for the Study of Forced Migration annual conference, Nicosia, Cyprus. http://repository.forcedmigration.org/show_metadata.jsp?pid=fmo:5039.

Jayatilaka, Danesh, and Kopalapillai Amirthalingam (2015). *The impact of displacement on dowries in Sri Lanka*. Brookings Institution, LSE Project on Internal Displacement. www.brookings.edu/research/the-impact-of-displacement-on-dowries-in-sri-lanka.

Jayatilaka, Danesh, Kopalapillai Amirthalingam, and Shiyana Gunasekara (2015). *Conflict, displacement, and post-war recovery: A community profile of Passaiyoor East, Sri Lanka*. Working Paper No. 8. Colombo: International Centre for Ethnic Studies. www.idrc.ca/sites/default/files/sp/Documents%20EN/Post%20Conflict%20Recovery_Community%20Profile_Passaiyoor%20Sri%20Lanka.pdf.

Kibreab, Gaim (2003). Displaced communities and the reconstruction of livelihoods in Eritrea. In Tony Addison (Ed.), *From conflict to recovery in Africa* (73–86). Oxford: Oxford University Press.

Kruijt, Dirk, and Kees Koonings (1999). *Societies of fear: The legacy of civil war, violence and terror in Latin America* (1–30). London: Zed Books.

Lakshman, Iresha M., Asela Ekanayaka, and Rajith W. D. Lakshman (2016). Going to school from a relocated urban community: Struggling for education within imposed walls. *Migration and Development* 6: 1–17. doi: http://dx.doi.org/10.1080/21632324.2016.1164941.

Lakshman, Iresha M., Dhammika Herath, Asela Ekanayaka, and Alikhan Mohammad (2016). *Experiences of a relocated community in Colombo: A community profile of Sinhapura, Wanathamulla*. Research Paper. Colombo: International Centre for Ethnic Studies.

Lefebvre, Henri (1996). The right to the city. In Eleonore Kofman and Elizabeth Lebas (Trans.), *Writings on cities* (63–181). Oxford: Blackwell.

Moser, Caroline (2004). Urban violence and insecurity: An introductory roadmap. *Environment and Urbanization* 16(2): 3–16.

Moser, Caroline, and Cathy McIlwaine (2001). *Violence in a post-conflict context: Urban poor perceptions from Guatemala*. Washington, DC: World Bank.

Muggah, Robert (2000). Through the developmentalist's looking glass: Conflict-induced displacement and involuntary resettlement in Colombia. *Journal of Refugee Studies* 13: 133–164.

——— (2003). A tale of two solitudes: Comparing conflict and development induced internal displacement and involuntary resettlement. *International Migration* 41: 5–31.

——— (2008). Protection and durable solutions: Regimes for development and conflict-induced internally displaced and resettled populations. In Katarzyna Grabska and Lyla Mehta (Eds.), *Forced displacement: Why rights matter* (26–49). New York: Springer.

——— (2012). *Researching the urban dilemma: Urbanization, poverty and violence* (46). Ottawa: International Development Research Centre (IDRC). www.idrc.ca/EN/PublishingImages/Researching-the-Urban-Dilemma-Baseline-study.pdf.

Perera-Mubarak, Kamakshi (2013). Positive responses, uneven experiences: Intersections of gender, ethnicity, and location in post-tsunami Sri Lanka. *Gender, Place and Culture* 20(5): 664–685. doi: http://doi.org/10.1080/0966369X.2012.709828.

——— (2014). Power play: Ethical dilemmas of dealing with local officials and politicians. In Jenny Lunn (Ed.), *Fieldwork in the Global South: Ethical challenges and dilemmas* (206–216). London: Routledge.

Razick, Rumana (2014). *Relocating slum dwellers and giving them new hopes.* Mirror Citizen. http://mirrorcitizen.dailymirror.lk/2014/05/06/out-of-the-pot-and-into-the-fire.

Robben, Antonius C., and Carolyn Nordstrom (1995). Introduction: The anthropology and ethnography of violence and sociopolitical conflict. In Carolyn Nordstrom and Antonius C. Robben (Eds.), *Fieldwork under fire: Contemporary studies of violence and survival* (1–24). London: University of California Press.

Romeshun, Kulasabanathan, Vagisha Gunasekara, and Mohamed Munas (2014). *Life and debt: Assessing indebtedness and socioeconomic conditions of conflict-affected housing beneficiaries in Jaffna.* Colombo: Centre for Poverty Analysis. www.cepa.lk/content_images/0d6e1cc768f1d5f53cdc8ee970a71672-2014-Romeshun-Life-and-Debt.pdf.

Schipper, E. Lisa F., and Lara Langston (2015). *A comparative overview of resilience measurement frameworks: Analysing indicators and approaches.* London: Overseas Development Institute.

Schröder, Ingo W., and Bettina E. Schmidt (2001). Introduction: Violent imaginaries and violent practices. In Bettina E. Schmidt and Ingo W. Schröder (Eds.), *Anthropology of violence and conflict* (1–24). London: Routledge.

United Nations (2014). *World urbanization prospects: The 2014 revision, highlights.* New York: Author.

Vithanagama, Ranmini, Alikhan Mohideen, Danesh Jayatilaka, and Rajith Lakshman (2015). *Planned relocations in the context of natural disasters: The case of Sri Lanka.* Washington, DC: Brookings Institution.

WHO: World Health Organization (2002). *World report on violence and health.* Geneva: Author.

World Bank (2012). *Turning Sri Lanka's Urban Vision into Policy and Action.* Colombo: Author.

Zetter, Roger, and George Deikun (2010). Meeting humanitarian challenges in urban areas. *Forced Migration Review* 34: 5–7.

Part III

Exclusion and violences

6 Violence and social exclusion in urban contexts in Central America

Rodolfo Calderón Umaña

Introduction

The social order that has emerged in Central America at the end of the twentieth century hinges on two central elements. The first is the worsening of the social inequalities that have historically characterised the region (Pérez Sáinz and Mora 2007; Pérez Sáinz 2012; Torres-Rivas 2007). The second element is the increasing violence that, unlike in wartime, is mainly carried out by civilians against civilians (Calderón 2013; Kruijt and Koonings 2001).

Several studies have analysed the link between these two phenomena and they point out three relevant aspects. First, the youth gangs, or *maras*, that have appeared in the countries of the Northern Triangle (El Salvador, Guatemala, and Honduras) emerged primarily as groups that gave their members a powerful sense of belonging socially (Cruz and Portillo 1998; ERIC et al. 2001; Fundación Arias 2006; USAID 2006; Zúñiga 2007). The strength of this benefit is such that the criminal activities they carry out are actually secondary to these social dynamics (Savenije 2012; Dudley 2012). This is a very important observation because it runs counter to the dominant discourse that these groups band together fundamentally for the purpose of committing crimes.

Second, the few studies done on "common delinquency"—defined as crimes against property rather than people and not involving organised groups—show that this form of crime not only reflects the difficulties youth face as they attempt to enter the workforce, but is also a result of their exposure to global consumerism. In the absence of legitimate job and educational opportunities, crime becomes, to them, a way to fulfil their expectations of materialistic consumption, and social recognition and prestige (Castro 2010; Calderón 2012).[1]

Third, other research has shown that in areas where the state presence is weak and ineffective—such as in border areas and marginal urban communities, for example—the absence of lawful authority fosters the emergence of groups that compete with the state for its monopoly over the use of violence. For example, drug trafficking groups gain public support either by providing people with goods and services they are otherwise unable to obtain (such as work or security) or by threatening them with violence, real or potential (UNODC 2007; CONARE 2008; UNDP 2010).[2]

In this context, the argument developed here examines the links between social exclusion and violence in cities. To do so, I draw on the results of a research project entitled "Exclusion, Violence, and Community Responses in Central American Cities: Explaining Variation to Guide Policy".[3] This work encompassed five urban areas—two in Costa Rica and three in El Salvador—that represent situations typical of Central America.

Costa Rica has lower national rates of socioeconomic inequality and violence than other Central American countries, and it shares a pattern of urbanisation similar to the most developed Latin American countries. Until the neoliberal era, this meant that the state provided public assets and services in cities, particularly health, education, and basic infrastructure (Roberts 1996). At the other socioeconomic extreme is El Salvador, a country which, like Guatemala and Honduras, historically has high rates of social inequality and violence. Its urbanisation was also delayed, meaning that its emerging cities are able to provide only scant public infrastructure assets—such as roads, sewer systems, electricity, drinkable water, etc.—and services—such as education, health, security, etc. (Roberts 1996). In both cases, neoliberal policies have exacerbated the social inequalities resulting from the poor performance of job markets and restrictions in the provision of public assets. Rising social inequalities have resulted in reduced access to health care, education, housing, pensions, and some other social rights—in other words, a contraction in the exercising of social citizenship (FLACSO 2006).

When we selected the study areas in Costa Rica and El Salvador, we chose communities located both in large metropolitan areas (El Carmen in Costa Rica and Los Palomares in El Salvador) and in smaller mid-sized cities (La Gloria in the Caribbean region of Costa Rica and San Simón and El Cocotal in the Sonsonate municipality in El Salvador). I should explain that while these five communities are real, their names have been changed in our data to protect the identities of those who participated in the work. In Costa Rica, both settlements emerged at the end of the 1980s. They are the result of state urbanisation and resettlement initiatives, which means that they have basic infrastructure and services, as well as land ownership rights.[4] By contrast, El Salvador's settlements are informal ones with a lack of basic services and infrastructure, and few property rights or home ownership.[5] To gather information in the field, our techniques included a survey of participating households we designed for the project together with general focus groups, case studies, and interviews with key informants. We then developed these into case studies.[6]

This chapter is organised into four sections. The first defines the core concepts of social exclusion and violence in urban environments and proposes a typology for analysing the forms of violence found there. The second describes the conditions of social exclusion and the forms of violence that affect the areas we studied. The third shows how both phenomena are linked. Lastly, the fourth section analyses how social exclusion promotes the rise of certain forms of violence.

Core concepts

The problem with the study of violence today is that, in our common parlance, the concept has come to mean almost anything—from an aggressive exchange of words, to manslaughter, to cheque fraud. In my opinion, this overuse has diminished the word's value as an investigative tool (Chesnais 1981). To overcome these obstacles, in this chapter, I propose to use only the original meaning of violence: the real or threatened use of force to achieve a certain purpose or goal (Keane 1996).[7] However, this conceptualisation of violence does not imply reducing the phenomenon to its immediate and palpable manifestation. Although physical confrontation—real or potential—is the bedrock of violence, we also need to understand the social processes that define the meanings that every society assigns to violence. This historic and cultural meaning is what makes it relevant from a sociological viewpoint (Hernández 2008).

However, several aspects of violence require clarification. First, the use of force, as an expression of human behaviour, is not always defined as "violent". This expression is the result of a social construct in which some people—those with relatively more resources—are able to impose their own definitions, interests, and world views on other people. Second, this capacity gives the dominant actors the power to establish and define not just what is violent and what is not, but also under what circumstances a violent act is legitimate or not. The institutionalisation of these processes, through different social mechanisms such as norms and beliefs, ends up being imposed on the dominated groups. This moulds their mental schemas and predisposes them to act in accordance with the wishes of the dominant group.

Third, as a corollary of the above, the phenomenon of violence obscures a structural and organising dimension in terms of social practice, shaped and defined by systems of cultural significance. This is different from the idea of *structural violence*, which normally refers to a set of social barriers that hinder the realisation of human potential (Galtung 1985). As such, it usually expresses an idea of social justice more than the use of force (Giddens 1993; Wieviorka 2009; Riella 2001; Winton 2004).

Fourth, in relation to that argument, if we accept the idea that violence is a meaningful social action designed to achieve a certain purpose, we must reject the idea of structural violence. This viewpoint separates the action from the actors and attributes it to the structures—which removes agency, and hence the meaning of violence in terms of social practice. Furthermore, the concept of structural violence is limited in its use. It declares the existence of barriers that prevent the development of human potential, but it does not explain how these barriers emerged in the past or how they act in the present. For this reason, I propose to use the concept of *social exclusion* here to address this dimension of the problem. Unlike the idea of structural violence, this concept does analyse and define the mechanisms that prevent a certain sector of the population from becoming members of the political community.[8]

Social exclusion—understood as an extreme form of inequality—results from a process of disempowerment experienced by certain individuals in the basic markets (a primary exclusion), as well as in regard to fundamental social policies and rights (a secondary exclusion).[9] In the first instance, it takes place in the mercantile environments where the fundamental resources circulate for the material production of society: employment, land, capital, and even knowledge (Polanyi 1992; Pérez Sáinz and Mora 2007; Pérez Sáinz 2014). In the labour market, where the struggle between capital and work takes place and the conditions for the exploitation of the workforce are created, disempowerment translates into two specific situations: unemployment and job situations in which labour rights are not respected.

In the other basic markets—credit, insurance, land, and knowledge—the conflict occurs *between* the resource owners: those with the power to hoard resources develop the capacity to accumulate capital. In contrast, those who are excluded from these resources are forced to carry out mere subsistence economic activities that rely on an unpaid workforce.[10] In this case, one form of disempowerment is manifested by small business owners, who find it almost impossible to accumulate capital (Tilly 2000; Pérez Sáinz 2014). These dynamics create the conditions for hoarding.

Thus we see that extreme disempowerment in the basic markets is caused by situations where workers are unemployed, where employees cannot exercise their labour rights, and where small business owners are excluded from opportunities for accumulation and can merely manage to subsist. However, these situations can be mitigated by the creation of citizens' social rights. These are designed to create basic equality (Marshall 1992) though their scope is limited by the economic logic of the capitalist system itself. Social rights do not aim to eliminate class inequalities, but rather to attenuate their effects (Darendorf 1959; Barbalet 1993). Also, social policies tend to segment and differentiate populations, thus making it possible for different degrees and types of citizenship to emerge (Chatterjee 2008). In this sense, the lack of access to basic goods and services such as education, health, or pensions—or the failure to offer them to others—are manifestations of *secondary exclusion*. This social policy of a state is what most engenders disempowerment and it consolidates the process of primary exclusion (Pérez Sáinz 2014).

For those on the margins of society—who lack access to institutional mechanisms such as jobs and education, but still seek to satisfy their real and perceived needs—the use of violence is one possible response.[11] In such a context of socioeconomic deprivation, violence is an effective, and hence valuable, resource for those who are socially excluded. In their hands, it becomes a tool that they can use to compete for social resources.[12] In much of the literature, the link between exclusion and criminal violence has led authors to inflate the aspect of economic gain to the point that some speak of "forced entrepreneurship". In this view, instrumental rationality predominates (Portes, Roberts, and Grimson 2005). However, other authors have highlighted the cultural and social links between violence and social exclusion (Young 2003; Sánchez 1995; Bourgois 1995; Calderón 2012). For this reason, I propose a typology (one that I originally developed in my 2013 article, *Analytical proposition for the study of violence in Central America: A look from social exclusion*) that encompasses both the financial and social dimensions of violence. Both are instrumental social actions—in effect, relationships—since they do not constitute a purpose in themselves, but aim to achieve objectives that are not reachable through institutional channels.

However, the two differ in their goals. The fact that violence is a means to achieve a purpose does not mean that the rationality behind it is of an instrumental type as some authors such as Wieviorka (2009, 2014) and Portes, Roberts, and Grimson (2005) suggest. The issue is not simply a question of maximising material or social gains, but of fighting for a place in the world. *Social violence* is carried out in order to obtain, maintain, or increase esteem, honour, and prestige. Its goal is to prevent the deprivation of social status that is generated by social exclusion (Sánchez 1995; Bourgois 1995; Calderón 2013). Some of its most common manifestations include violence in the home and neighbourhood, and among youth (ECLAC 2008; León-Escribano 2008; Sánchez 1995; IDB 2008). *Profit-seeking violence*, in contrast, stems from the need (in the absence of legal resources) for perpetrators to access, maintain, or increase material gain, in order to participate in the types of (licit or illicit) pleasure enjoyed by the dominant culture (Sperberg and Happe 2000; Zinecker 2010; Calderón 2013). This means that, at its core, the utilitarian act of criminal activity is satisfying to those who commit it precisely because it breaks the rules of the social order that humiliate and exclude those individuals (Young 2003; Calderón 2012). Theft and other property crimes are the most frequent manifestations of this principle. On the larger scale, so are criminal activities by organised groups, such as human trafficking and the international drug trade (Calderón 2012; Castro 2010; UNDP 2010).

Social exclusion and violence

In this section, I describe the conditions for social exclusion and the forms of violence identified in the areas we studied. In the following section, I analyse the links between both issues.

Social exclusion

To comprehend the degree of social inclusion or exclusion of the households in our study areas, the research team constructed an index using information from the household survey. To assess the situation, we plotted the data on three scales: *labour-market inclusion*, *educational qualifications*, and *access to public health insurance*.[13] The first captures the degree of empowerment (or lack thereof) in the labour market, a preeminent institution: disempowerment here is a primary exclusion. The second two scales approximate the concept of social citizenship, where disempowerment is a secondary exclusion.

Table 6.1 describes the different indicators of social exclusion we found in the two study areas. We classified them according to their specific disempowerment aspect: labour markets (which relate to primary exclusion) and educational qualifications and health insurance (which express secondary exclusion).

As you can see, the values differentiate the Costa Rican communities from the Salvadoran ones with the former having much greater inclusion. On the labour-market scale, for instance, El Carmen stands out both for its low percentage of workers in jobs unprotected by labour regulations, and for its relatively low incidence of small businesses unable to rise above the subsistence level (though this figure still exceeds half). Both situations can be explained by the fact that El Carmen is located in a metropolitan labour market, which is much more favourable to economic activity than the other

Table 6.1 Indicators of social exclusion in the study areas

Indicators	*Costa Rica*		*El Salvador*		
	La Gloria	*El Carmen*	*Los Palomares*	*San Simón*	*El Cocotal*
Labour-market inclusion					
% unemployment rate	8.8	6.3	6.4	5.9	5.4
% of paid workers with no labour force protections	11.0	3.7	11.1	17.7	9.9
% of small business owners in subsistence	85.3	56.6	89.4	87.7	79.4
Educational qualifications					
% of population over age 13 with no primary education	30.3	14.3	29.9	27.9	23.2
Health insurance					
% of households with no social insurance coverage	8.2	4.9	51.0	66.5	55.8

Source: FLACSO-IDRC Survey (2013).

four communities. In those, about a tenth of the paid workforce is employed in positions where labour rights are not enforced, and between 80 per cent and 90 per cent of small business owners find themselves trapped at the subsistence level. From this perspective, La Gloria appears to reflect the grim Salvadoran realities more than the relatively affluent Costa Rican ones—a situation worsened by the fact that it has the highest unemployment rate (8.8 per cent) of the five territories. This may be associated with the job instability that characterises the area's agro-industrial activities.

In terms of educational qualifications, the indicator of disempowerment we chose was the percentage of people over age 13 with no primary education.[14] In this respect, there are fewer differences between the two countries. This reflects both the unfortunate deterioration of public education in Costa Rica, and the progress made by El Salvador since generating "human capital" was a major social policy objective of the four governments of ARENA (the Alianza Republicana Nacionalista [Republican Nationalist Alliance], the political party that governed El Salvador from 1989 to 2009). The three Salvadoran communities range from 23.2 per cent to 29.9 per cent, indicating that almost a third of young individuals did not finish primary school. The highest percentage for low educational achievement corresponds to one of the Salvadoran study areas. Obviously, when some 30 per cent of the population has not finished primary school by the appropriate age, this expresses a huge social problem. By contrast, in Costa Rica, El Carmen stands out for its low percentage (14.3 per cent) of those with little education. In other words, some 85 per cent of individuals in that community had some education.

With regard to state-provided health insurance, the expected national differences stand out clearly. In Costa Rica, thanks to the Welfare State, only 8.2 per cent and 4.9 per cent of households in the two communities have no coverage. But in El Salvador, the percentage of those lacking coverage ranges from 51 per cent to 66.5 per cent. This reflects a historical situation that still persists today. However, it is important to point out that in Costa Rica the primary issue is not the lack of public services, but the deterioration of their quality. In El Salvador, the issue *is* the lack of access to public services, which is in turn a symptom of the weak institutional presence of the state. Together with the labour-market situation, this reflects processes that are characteristic of the social fragmentation experienced by disadvantaged urban groups in the neoliberal era (Portes, Roberts, and Grimson 2005).

Analysing these indicators at the household level allows us to identify which populations live in conditions of social inclusion or exclusion. Two aspects are worth pointing out, one in La Gloria and the other in El Carmen.

- In La Gloria, the inclusion group has more weight than in the Salvadoran cases, with a more consolidated inclusion status. Also, state involvement, through the provision of social services (such as health and education) and public infrastructure (such as electricity and water), ameliorates conditions for the excluded group, helping to reduce the impact of primary exclusion. Although there are similarities between this territory and the Salvadoran ones, La Gloria remains Costa Rican.

- El Carmen is the most heterogeneous territory. Although most of its households are (like La Gloria) in a zone of labour-market exclusion, this problem is offset by access to social citizenship.

In summary, in the Costa Rican study areas, unlike the Salvadoran ones, primary exclusion is mitigated by social citizenship.

Forms of violence

With regard to the forms of violence identified in the household survey, the data on victimisation shown in Table 6.2 highlight an important characteristic: the predominance of purely *social* violence, over violence for *financial* gain. Included in the former are expressions of violence, involving both adults against adults and adults against minors, that occur between people related by family ties and also between people close to them, such as neighbours.[15] These might take the form of violence against people (including verbal insults, threats, and actual physical assaults and injuries, with or without weapons of any kind) or violence against property, including total or partial destruction of a home or vehicle.[16] In all cases, the data include verbal as well as physical aggression. Surprisingly, despite the frequency, intensity, and consequences of this violence, residents do not identify social violence as a major source of fear.

With regard to profit-seeking violence, two aspects must be highlighted. The first is that more of these events are reported in Costa Rica than in El Salvador. This paradoxical fact seems to be explained by three factors.

- Costa Rican households have more assets than Salvadoran ones, and residents are more willing to report property crimes when they take place. This is particularly the case in La Gloria, where a Safety Community

Table 6.2 Violence reported by Costa Rican and Salvadoran households

Types of violence	*Costa Rican communities*	*Salvadoran communities*	*P< (chi-squared test)*
% against people	14.6	8.7	0.000
% against property	20.3	10.0	0.000
% against minors in the home	33.1	46.9	0.000
% against adults in the home	10.2	11.7	0.667
% among adults in the home	27.3	30.3	0.123

Source: FLACSO-IDRC Survey (2013).

was established to tackle the issue of insecurity. This appears to have raised awareness of the need to report such events.

- In El Salvador, the contrary tendency is to deny the existence of these crimes because residents feel that their existence creates a stigma in the community.
- In El Salvador, profit-seeking violence is monopolised by the *maras*, which reduces citizens' interest in reporting it to police. This is partly due to fear of retaliation by the gangs, and partly because people rely on the gangs to deal with local problems such as conflicts between neighbours.

The second important aspect of profit-seeking violence is the fact that these crimes are, in fact, quite rare compared to social violence. In both countries, the percentage of households surveyed who reported having been a victim of assaults and robberies in the preceding year was less than 1 per cent. This finding—that profit-seeking crimes are relatively infrequent and that other chronic forms of violence are much more damaging—is consistent with existing data, such as those provided by Muggah (2012) and Manzano (2009). In Costa Rica, we found that assaults, when they happen, mainly take place outside the community. This is consistent with reports from other Latin American cities: property crimes tend to occur in areas where wealth is concentrated[17] (Portes, Roberts, and Grimson 2005). In both countries, however, inhabitants identify profit-seeking violence as a significant source of fear and insecurity.[18]

In the study, interviews with key informants allowed us to identify other types of violence that were not captured by the survey. These are linked to two specific phenomena: small-scale drug dealing (mainly in marijuana and crack cocaine, with some powdered cocaine) in Costa Rica and the actions of the *maras* in El Salvador.

In the first case, the constant clashes between criminal groups fighting over the micro-markets frequently unleash public violence that generally ends in injury and death, often for innocent bystanders. These "collateral victims", people not involved in the use or sale of drugs, may be unintentionally wounded or murdered by drug dealers, having simply been in the wrong place at the wrong time. Or the act may be intentional but by mistake, as in when people are wrongly associated with the drug world.

As well as being endangered by the drug dealers, citizens are also at risk from the robberies, thefts, and assaults committed by drug users to finance their drug consumption. This may take place in the citizens' own homes or in the community's public spaces. Another factor, the result of the first two impacts, is the generalised fear and insecurity that people feel, which may lead them to isolate themselves both socially and physically. These actions erode the foundations of community, as people abandon public spaces such as parks, squares, and even the few convenience stores, and barricade themselves in their homes (Álvarez and Auyero 2014).

In the second case, in El Salvador, the *maras* monopolise the use of violence in the settlements where they operate.[19] Aside from controlling the sale of drugs in the community, their crimes against inhabitants include offences against property (robberies and extortion), against sexual integrity (abuse and rape), and against life (threats, assaults, and homicides). The sexual offences disproportionately affect female children and adolescents. For young girls, their greatest risk is being attacked sexually. For adolescent boys, the biggest danger is forced recruitment by the gangs, who threaten them to intimidate them into joining. If they reject the "invitation", the *maras* escalate to physical attacks in order to "persuade" these boys to become part of the gang and this might end up with the boys being injured or even murdered. The *maras* also use threats and violence to control private disputes between neighbours and family members in order to prevent the involvement of the police, since those established authorities would challenge their domination of the community.

Links between social exclusion and violence

In the previous two sections, I described both the social exclusion conditions that characterised the households of the study and the predominant forms of violence. Now, I examine the relationships between the two phenomena.

Violence in the intimate circle: family and neighbours

One aspect of personal violence we analysed was violence against minors. The results indicated that these types of episodes were most likely to occur in households in El Salvador when the parents (or heads of the family) were young and had a low level of education.[20] The last variable is an important secondary indicator of social exclusion, since education is one of the markers we use to define access, or lack thereof, to social citizenship. We also conducted a second study of violence between adults in the home, and this also found three variables that increase the probability of violence. These are a favourable demographic dependence relationship (meaning a situation where there are more adults than minors or elderly adults), low or nonexistent insurance coverage, and male unemployment.[21] The last two variables clearly express disempowerment in terms of social citizenship and the labour market. Although our survey did not allow us to determine precisely who was committing injuries and aggression in the home, and against whom, the facts of male unemployment and female victimhood allow us to infer that it is predominantly men who harm their partners. Then again, the perpetrators or victims might also be gang members, drug dealers, or other relatives, such as siblings. Those situations have different implications for policymakers.

Regarding the factors that trigger such aggression, we might propose that they are linked to the erosion of male authority in the home due to

Figure 6.1 Violence against children in the home
Source: Focus group, boys and girls aged 10 to 12, El Salvador.

the impossibility of men actually fulfilling their culturally assigned role of provider. The increase in violence against women reflects the weakening—rather than the validity—of male domination (Giddens 1993).[22] In beating up their wives, men are attempting to maintain their control of the home despite their disempowerment in the labour market.

The statistical information gathered in this survey also shows that the probability of violence occurring among neighbours is statistically associated with violence towards minors: both stem from low levels of education, a secondary exclusion. However, two other household factors are clearly linked to the social exclusion. The first is domestic overcrowding, which blurs the boundaries between private and public areas, and converts physical space into an object of constant dispute. The second is the perceived issue of honour, particularly concerning the sexual practices of women and the masculinity of men. Disputes over this last point are always more frequent in contexts where there is a lack of material goods. Lacking other sources of prestige, honour constitutes almost the only resource people have to negotiate status in their social environments (Sánchez 1995).

In Costa Rica, conflicts among neighbours are not mediated by a third party as they are in El Salvador, where the *maras* deal with these types of problems. The gangs take conflicts out of the hands of the parties concerned and effectively replace the state institutions that would otherwise be responsible for providing security and justice. This fact ensures that the *maras* maintain control of this important contribution to social order, which has the effect of legitimising their authority.

Violence in public spaces: youth

The presence of micro-markets for illegal drugs in the Costa Rican territories must be understood in the context of the "War on Drugs", promoted by the US government in the early 1990s. Since that time, Central America has become a strategic zone for international drug cartels—due both to their own need to find new routes for their product and to the fact that regional governments are too weak to control their presence (UNODC 2007). But not all of the vast cargo of drugs is shipped abroad to foreign markets. A small part always remains in the region to pay local contacts or because it was somehow stolen from the cartels. Either way, along the transport, warehousing, and supply routes, a certain amount of such substances stays trapped in the Costa Rican communities (Gurney 2014).

Our team identified the people, particularly young men, who were willing to get involved in drug dealing for two fundamental and inseparable reasons: income and social status. The occupation of selling drugs addresses the primary exclusion they experienced from the conventional working world. This is itself the result of a variety of factors: their low levels of education, the scarcity of legitimate employment in their area, their lack of access to cash or credit to start their own businesses, and the stigmatisation they suffer from living in territories considered dangerous. Drug dealing also provides valuable benefits to the young men. It gives them not just quick access to the cash resources they require to satisfy their material needs (real and perceived), but also to meet their most important symbolic needs of power and recognition.[23]

This last point is vital since it is the search for social recognition that ultimately matters most to these youth. Status symbols, such as brand-name clothing, a car, or money to spend on lavish partying, are important not only for their inherent value, but because they allow a young man to gain esteem and social recognition from his peers. The link between social exclusion and selling drugs, or between inequality and transgression, needs no further discussion, since it is well documented (both theoretically and empirically) by many others, including Merton (1968), Agnew (1998), and Calderón (2012). Rather, I intend to highlight the context that makes this activity feasible. In fact, for a few inhabitants of the communities we studied, drug dealing represents a quick and effective way to achieve some of their expectations of success, consumption, and social recognition, even in the absence of institutional resources such as education and quality jobs.

The connections between the *maras* and social exclusion can be established in at least two ways. First, as identified by several studies, most of the youths who belong to these groups are excluded not only from labour markets and the education system, but also from the majority of other social institutions. For this reason, the gangs constitute the primary source of belonging and identity for their members. These social ties enable the young men to overcome the state of economic precariousness and existential uncertainty they face in other aspects of life.

Second, the success of these groups in monopolising power in the communities where they operate stems from the weak or nonexistent presence of the state. In such places, it is almost impossible for people to exercise their citizenship. They have no basic infrastructure, such as sewers or roads, still fewer services like schools and hospitals or public justice. The situation is reinforced by the actions of the *maras*, who constitute the de facto authority. This creates an ambivalent relationship between the gangs and the residents, with the former offering protection and security to the latter. For this reason, most people rate the *maras* positively because they protect them against outside criminals and they regulate domestic and community disputes.[24] But the gangs are a double-edged sword; they also victimise residents. Therefore, the inhabitants also reject the *maras* because of their criminal acts, the increased exposure to police violence they cause, and the social isolation that comes with their control of the territory.[25]

The small-scale sale of illegal drugs in Costa Rican communities and the actions of the *maras* in Salvadoran territories illustrate significant relationships between exclusion and violence. In the first case, there is a clear connection between the disempowerment suffered by youth in the labour market and their participation in the business of prohibited drugs.[26] In the second case, the connection is not merely the primary exclusion process that drives the emergence of these groups, but also the dynamics of secondary exclusion.

Finally, it is important to point out that the forms of violence associated with the sale of drugs and the activities of the *maras* constitute a meeting point between economic and social logic. Both do more than generate economic resources; they also support the criminals' search for recognition and identity. In other words, they help overcome the lack of status generated by the social exclusion these youths experience. Therefore, it is not possible to simplify these forms of violence to mere economic rationality.

Final considerations

In this section, I highlight various aspects of the analysis that are especially useful in understanding the relationship between social exclusion and violence. Specifically, there are four points I would like to stress.

First, I note the heuristic value of social exclusion in describing the dynamics that prevent the excluded from accessing the resources they need for their material and social well-being. From this perspective, inequality originates in a process of disempowerment in the basic markets (primary exclusion), which is increased when access to the rights of social citizenship (that is, the redistributive sphere of the state) is weak or nonexistent. I propose that this is a novel concept because existing theory has always described inequality, in the context of violence, in terms either of income (the Gini coefficient)[27] or of social rights. Inequality as a disempowerment process has not previously been used to analyse the links between such inequality and violence. That shortfall ignores market relationships, and thus the social realm where the conditions for the generation of wealth are defined.[28]

This analysis suggests a major obstacle to understanding the relationship between violence and exclusion. As I argued earlier, disempowerment in the basic markets is a determining factor for the emergence of certain forms of violence, specifically that which unemployed men use against women and that originating from the small-scale drug business in Costa Rican communities. Along similar lines, my rejection of the concept of structural violence constitutes another point of contention with established theory. As I indicated earlier, one of the objectives of our study was to use the concept of social exclusion to comprehend the barriers to human potential posed by violence. In the process, we also specify and conceptualise the meaning of these practices and mechanisms, ones that prevent many thousands of people from living a decent life, according to the social, cultural, and material standards of their society.

Second, the conceptualisation of violence I have developed here achieves two major objectives. The first is to understand the meaning that people assign to the various forms of violence that they carry out. In the absence of more legitimate mechanisms, it allows them to achieve their goals of accessing the resources, whether material or symbolic, that they consider valuable. The second objective is to overcome the well-established and dominant idea that the violence brought on by social exclusion is driven primarily by utilitarian rationality aimed at material gain. Rather, such violence has as its goal the quest for respect and recognition, one of the main objectives of disempowered people. This view does not deny the existence of economic motivations; it merely gives them a subordinate place.

Third, our research has led us to rethink the traditional connection between violence and power: that the former constitutes an extreme exercise of the latter. We might also say that those subject to power use violence to break away from their subordinate condition (Fanon 1963). But my analysis here shows that disempowered subjects use violence to attempt to overturn their situations. This act is not an extreme exercise of power, nor an attempt at empowerment through political-revolutionary channels.[29]

Fourth, our field work allowed the research team to ascertain that those who live in the study areas, especially the Salvadorans, encounter serious difficulties in accessing basic government services, such as security and justice, outside of their communities, or even opportunities for work and education. There are two reasons for this lack:

- the social stigma attached to living in a community generally perceived as violent and inhabited by criminals
- the isolation imposed by the *maras*.

This aspect of our analysis shows that the link between exclusion and violence goes both ways: exclusion creates the conditions for the exercise of violence, but, at the same time, violence generates obstacles to overcoming exclusion. Residents of the areas affected by the *maras* are cut off, materially and symbolically, from the city and its opportunities.

Finally, having extensively described the dynamics of violence, I would like to offer a few thoughts on the subject of controlling and reducing it. An effective approach requires well-informed public policies, and this state intervention must address two areas. It should regulate market dynamics, mainly the labour market, to reduce primary exclusion and it should also strengthen citizenship rights to offset the negative impacts of primary exclusion and avoid secondary exclusion. These policies, if properly designed and executed, should help to reduce the impact of violence on society: if it is easier for disadvantaged populations to achieve valuable social assets in a legitimate manner, this may prevent their use of illegitimate means. Such a strategy might well neutralise the predominant source of violence in the urban context of Central America.

Notes

1 Similar results have been found in other Latin American countries. See Kessler (2002) and Portes, Roberts, and Grimson (2005).

2 For the cases of Mexico, Peru, and Colombia, see Maldonado (2010).

3 The project is part of the "Safe and Inclusive Cities" program, coordinated by Canada's International Development Research Centre (IDRC) and the United Kingdom's Department for International Development (DFID). It was conducted by a research team from the Facultad Latinoamericana de Ciencias Sociales: Costa Rica Campus and El Salvador Program. The complete results can be found in Pérez Sáinz et al. (2015).

4 Both territories were founded by migratory processes. In the first case, people moved from the country to the city; and, in the second, people moved from one urban area to another—responding to the new patterns of urbanisation that emerged during the neoliberal experiment (Portes, Roberts, and Grimson 2005).

5 Originally, the research project covered nine areas in those urban centres. However, for various reasons—safety being one of them—it was not possible to collect information from all of them in all project phases. Therefore, this analysis only includes the five communities where we were able to gather data at all stages of the project.

6 The survey involved the design of a probabilistic sample and the other techniques were applied using theoretical samples and expert criteria.

7 That goal or objective may take either of two forms: offensive or defensive. People may use violence to access valued resources they do not possess, and want to have—for example, food, alcohol and status symbols. They may also use violence to prevent the loss—real or potential—of things they already possess. See Agnew (1998, 2001).

8 In this perspective, social exclusion is not synonymous with structural violence. On the contrary, it is an alternative and competing interpretation of the same phenomenon: the barriers that prevent certain sectors of society from accessing the resources they need to develop fully. My purpose here is to underline the novelty of the way scholars have conceptualized and articulated the two categories of violence and social deprivation. This way of understanding the problem helps to improve the general body of knowledge.

9 This disempowerment is never absolute, but must be understood to be a relative and multidimensional process. See Gore (1995) and de Haan (1999).

10 When small producers operate only at the subsistence level, they characteristically are unable to pay their workers. This constitutes another expression of extreme disempowerment in the basic markets (Pérez Sàinz 2014). Normally, unpaid workers are family members, though that is not always the case. These individuals are less volunteers than conscripts: they engage in this kind of work either because they do not have the skills required to find a paying job or because, even when they do have the qualifications, it is impossible for them to find a paid position.

11 This type of action can also be carried out, as pointed out earlier, by those who perceive a threat—real or potential—to the control of the resources they own.

12 From a theoretical point of view, this connection has been dealt with by authors such as Merton (1968); Sullivan (1989); Kornhauser (1960); Toch (1965); Davies (1971); and Agnew (1998, 2001). From an empirical point of view, particularly for Latin America, the relationship between social exclusion and criminal violence has been examined by scholars such as Caldeira (2001); Riaño-Alcalá (2006); IDB (2008); Savenije and Andrade (2003); Londoño (1996); Bourguignon (1999); Arriagada and Godoy (2000); Fajnzylber, Lederman, and Loayza (1998); CONARE (2008); Hojman (2004); and Portes, Roberts, and Grimson (2005).

13 For details on the construction of this scale, see the Appendix of Pérez Sáinz et al. (2015).

14 We chose this indicator, a negative one, because the expected age for finishing primary school in Central America is 12. If a child of 13 or over has not finished primary school, that person is either out of the school system or in a situation of educational lag.

15 Although criminal actions perpetrated by strangers can be included, the case studies confirm that violence among family members and neighbours is fundamentally socially motivated.

16 The FBI's Uniform Crime Report defines larceny-theft as the unlawful taking, carrying, leading, or riding away of property from the possession of another. It also defines robbery as the taking (or attempting to take) anything of value from the care, custody, or control of a person or persons, by force, threat of force, violence, or by putting the victim in a state of fear.

17 That said, most gangs in El Salvador tend to perform their criminal activity, including extortion, in the territories they live in—and these are usually the most deprived areas of the city.

18 In this regard, Carrión (2008) has pointed out that cities with high degrees of inequality are characterised by a population that is fearful of public spaces. This leads them to seek refuge in domestic life, even though—paradoxically —this is occasionally even more dangerous and violent.

19 The role played by the *maras* in controlling the dynamics of violence in their territories is also an issue in Guatemala. See Urusquieta (2014).
20 Statistically, this exercise consisted of calculating binary logistical models with dependent variables for homes where this type of violence had occurred, and for homes where it had not. Apart from the socio-demographic characteristics of the household, the independent variables were the three social inclusion–exclusion scales (labour-market inclusion, educational qualifications, and insurance) along with male unemployment. For more details and specifics see Pérez Sáinz et al. (2015).
21 A review of the reference material showed that there is little empirical evidence to link men's socioeconomic status with violent conduct against their partners. See Vives Cases et al. (2007).
22 In our case studies, women who were victims of violence by their partners, or ex-partners, argued that the principal reason for it was consumption of legal and illegal drugs. In only a very few cases did the women identify male frustrations associated with the economic conditions of the household.
23 These results are consistent with those of Bourgois (1995); Bourgois et al. (2013); and Alvarado (2013).
24 Other authors have identified similar findings regarding the acceptance and legitimacy of gangs among residents of the areas where they operate. See Perea et al. (2014) and Alvarado (2013).
25 See also Imbusch, Misse, and Carrión (2011).
26 This primary exclusion is not sufficient to explain the problem, because there are complex processes of intermediation in its configuration. These are linked to the relational construction of expectations—a topic we did not address in this research project since there is already ample reference material about it. Some examples are Merton (1968); Agnew (1998, 2001); Bourgois (1995); and Calderón (2012).
27 The Gini coefficient (named after the Italian statistician and sociologist Corrado Gini, who first developed it in 1912) is a statistical measure that analyses the relative distribution of household income in a society. The coefficient ranges from zero (perfect equality) to one (perfect inequality). To facilitate the analysis, households are divided into 10 equal groups (deciles). This makes it possible for researchers to contrast the average income of each of the groups with the others.
28 Some examples of studies linking violence and income inequality include Fajnzylber, Lederman, and Loayza (1998); CONARE (2008); and Hojman (2004). For studies that attempt to go beyond the focus on income inequality and recognise the role of social rights, see Winton (2004).
29 Some authors have described this phenomenon as "diffused violence" in which individuals fight for social resources: no clearly defined actors come together around an institutionally recognised conflict (Blau and Blau 1982; Wieviorka 2009).

References

Agnew, Robert (1998). Foundations for a general strain theory of crime and delinquency. In Stuart Henry and Werner Einstadter (Eds.), *The criminology theory reader* (177–195). New York: New York University Press.

——— (2001). Building on the foundation of general strain theory: Specifying the types of strain most likely to lead to crime and delinquency. *Journal of Research on Crime and Delinquency* 38: 319–361.

Alvarado, Arturo (2013). La violencia juvenil en América Latina [Youth violence in Latin America]. *Estudios Sociológicos [Sociological Studies]* 31: 229–258.

Álvarez, Lucía, and Javier Auyero (2014). La ropa en el balde: Rutinas y ética popular frente a la violencia en los márgenes urbanos [Clothes in the bucket: Routines and popular ethics to cope with in front of the violence in the urban margins]. *Revista Nueva Sociedad [New Society Journal]* 251: 17–30.

Arriagada, Irma, and Lorean Godoy (2000). Prevention or repression? The false dilemma of citizen security. *CEPAL Review* 70: 111–136.

Barbalet, Jack (1993). Citizenship, class inequality and resentment. In Bryan Turner (Ed.), *Citizenship and social theory*. London: SAGE Publications.

Blau, Judith, and Peter Blau (1982). The cost of inequality: Metropolitan structure and violent crime. *American Sociological Review* 47: 114–129.

Bourgois, Philippe (1995). *In search for respect: Selling crack in el barrio*. Cambridge: Cambridge University Press.

Bourgois, Philippe, Fernando Montero-Castrillo, Laurie Hart, and George Karandinos (2013). Habitus furibundo en el gueto estadounidense [Furious habitus in the American ghetto]. *Espacio Abierto Cuaderno Venezolano de Sociología [Open Space Venezuelan Notebook of Sociology]* 22: 201–220.

Bourguignon, François (1999). *Crime, violence, and inequitable development*. Paper presented to the second annual World Bank conference on Development in Latin America and the Caribbean. Bogotá: World Bank

Caldeira, Teresa (2001). *City of walls*. Oakland: University of California Press.

Calderón, Rodolfo (2012). *Delito y cambio social en Costa Rica [Crime and social change in Costa Rica]*. San José, Costa Rica: Latin American School for Social Science (FLACSO).

——— (2013). Proposiciones analíticas para el estudio de la violencia en Centroamérica: Una mirada desde la exclusión social [Analytical propositions for the study of violence in Central America: A view from social exclusion]. *Revista Digital de la Maestría en Ciencias Penales [Digital Review of Criminal Sciences]* 5: 187–212.

Carrión, Fernando (2008). Violencia urbana: Un asunto de ciudad [Urban violence: A city affair]. *EURE: Revista Latinoamericana de Estudios Urbano Regionales [Latin American Journal of Regional Urban Studies]* 34: 111–130.

Castro, Julio (2010). *Delincuencia común y exclusión social en Honduras [Common delinquency and social exclusion in Honduras]*. San José, Costa Rica: Latin American School for Social Science (FLACSO).

Chatterjee, Partha (2008). *La nación en tiempo heterogéneo y otros estudios subalternos [The nation in heterogeneous times, and other subaltern studies]*. Buenos Aires: Siglo XXI.

Chesnais, Jean-Claude (1981). *Histoire de la violence*. Paris: Robert Laffont.

CONARE: Consejo Nacional de Rectores [National Council of Rectors] (2008). *Informe: Estado de la región [Report: State of the region]*. San José, Costa Rica: Programa de las Naciones Unidas para el Desarrollo [United Nations Development Program].

Cruz, José Miguel, and Nelson Portillo (1998). *Solidaridad y violencia en las pandillas del Gran San Salvador: Más allá de la vida loca [Solidarity and violence in the gangs of Greater San Salvador: Beyond the crazy life]*. El Salvador: UCA Editores.

Darendorf, Ralf (1959). *Class and class conflict in industrial societies.* London: Routledge and Kegan Paul PLC.

Davies, James (1971). *When men revolt and why.* New York: The Free Press.

de Haan, Arjan (1999). *Social exclusion: Towards a holistic understanding of deprivation.* London: Department for International Development.

Dudley, Steven (2012). Part II: Gangs, deportation, and violence in Central America. *InSight Crime.* www.insightcrime.org/investigations/part-ii-gangs-deportation-and-violence-in-central-america.

ECLAC: Economic Commission for Latin America and the Caribbean (2008). *Panorama social de América Latina* [*Social panorama of Latin America*]. Santiago: Economic Commission for Latin America.

ERIC (Equipo de Reflexión, Investigación y Comunicación [Reflection, Research and Communication Team]), IDESO (Instituto de Encuestas y Sondeos de Opinón [Institute of Polling and Opinion Surveys]), IDIES (Instituto de Investigaciones Económicas y Sociales [Institute for Economic and Social Research]), and IUDOP (Instituto Universitario de Opinión Pública [University Institute of Public Opinion]). (2001). *Maras y pandillas en Centroamérica* [*Maras and gangs in Central America*]. Managua, Nicaragua: Universidad Centroamericana [Central American University].

Fajnzylber, Pablo, Daniel Lederman, and Norman Loayza (1998). *Determinants of crime rates in Latin America and the world: An empirical assessment.* Washington, DC: World Bank.

Fanon, Frantz (1963). *Los condenados de la tierra* [*The wretched of the earth*]. Mexico City: Fondo de Cultura Económica [Economic Cultural Fund].

FLACSO: Facultad Latinoamericana de Ciencias Sociales [Latin American School for Social Science] (2006). *Taller regional: Exclusión social y política social en América Latina* [*Regional workshop: Social exclusion and social policy in Latin America*]. San Salvador: Author.

Fundación Arias para la Paz y el Progreso Humano [Arias Foundation for Peace and Human Progress] (2006). *La cara de la violencia urbana en América Central* [*The face of urban violence in Central America*]. San José, Costa Rica: Author.

Galtung, Johan (1985). Twenty-five years of peace research: Ten challenges and some responses. *Journal of Peace Research* 22: 141–158.

Giddens, Anthony (1993). Life in a post-traditional society. *Journal of the West* 150: 61–90.

Gore, Charles (1995). Markets, citizenship and social exclusion. In Gerry Rodgers, Charles Gore, and José Figueiredo (Eds.), *Social exclusion: Rhetoric, reality, responses.* Geneva: International Institute for Labour Studies, United Nations Development Program.

Gurney, Kyra (2014). Why are the world's most violent cities in Latin America? *InSight Crime.* www.insightcrime.org/news-analysis/why-world-most-violent-cities-latin-america.

Hernández, Tosca (2008). Descubriendo la violencia [Discovering violence]. In Roberto Briceño-León (Ed.), *Violencia, sociedad y justicia en América Latina* [*Violence, society and justice in Latin America*]. Buenos Aires: CLACSO (Consejo Latinoamericano de Ciencias Sociales [Latin Amercian Council for Social Sciences]).

Hojman, David (2004). Inequality, unemployment and crime in Latin American cities. *Crime, Law and Social Change* 1: 33–51.

IDB: International Development Bank (2008). *Outsiders: The changing patterns of exclusion in Latin America and the Caribbean.* Washington, DC: Inter-American Development Bank.

Imbusch, Peter, Michel Misse, and Fernando Carrión (2011). Violence research in Latin America and the Caribbean: A literature review. *International Journal of Conflict and Violence* 5: 87–154.

Keane, John (1996). *Reflections on violence.* London: Verso.

Kessler, Gabriel (2002). Entre fronteras desvanecidas: Lógicas de articulación de actividades legales e ilegales en los jóvenes [Blurred borders: Logics of articulation of legal and illegal activities in young people]. In Sandra Gayol and Gabriel Kessler (Eds.), *Violencias, delitos y justicias en la Argentina* [*Violence, crimes, and justice in Argentina*]. Buenos Aires: Manantial-Sarmiento National University.

Kornhauser, William (1960). *The politics of mass society.* New York: The Free Press.

Kruijt, Dirk, and Kees Koonings (2001). *Las sociedades del miedo: El legado de la guerra civil, la violencia y el terror en América Latina* [*Societies of fear: The legacy of civil war, violence and terror in Latin America*]. Salamanca: Ediciones Universidad de Salamanca.

León-Escribano, Carmen (2008). Violencia y género en América Latina [Violence and gender in Latin America]. *Pensamiento Iberoamericano* [*Ibero-American Thinking*] 2: 71–91.

Londoño, Juan Luis (1996). *Violence, psyche, and social capital.* Paper presented to the second annual World Bank conference on Development in Latin America and the Caribbean. Bogotá: World Bank.

Maldonado, Salvador (2010). Globalización, territorios y drogas ilícitas en los estados-nación: Experiencias latinoamericanas sobre México [Globalisation, territories and illicit drugs in nation states: Latin American experiences in Mexico]. *Estudios Sociológicos* [*Sociological Studies*] 83: 411–442.

Manzano, Liliana (2009). *Violencia en barrios críticos: explicaciones teóricas y estrategias de intervención basadas en el papel de la comunidad.* Santiago: Instituto de Asuntos Públicos [Institute of Public Affairs].

Marshall, Thomas H. (1992). *Ciudadanía y clase social* [*Citizenship and social class*]. Madrid: Alianza Editorial.

Merton, Robert K. (1968). Social structure and anomie. In Robert K. Merton (Ed.), *Social theory and social structure* (175–214). New York: The Free Press.

Muggah, Robert (2012). *Researching the urban dilemma: Urbanization, poverty and violence.* Ottawa: International Development Research Centre (IDRC). www.idrc.ca/EN/PublishingImages/Researching-the-Urban-Dilemma-Baseline-study.pdf.

Perea, Carlos Mario, Ana María Jaramillo, Andrés Rincón Morera, Michel Misse, César Alarcón, and Max Yuri Gil (2014). La paradoja latinoamericana: Ciudades en perspectiva comparada [The Latin American paradox: Cities in comparative perspective]. In Carlos Mario Perea and Ana María Jaramillo (Eds.), *Ciudades en la encrucijada: Violencia y poder criminal en Río de Janeiro, Medellín, Bogotá y Ciudad Juárez.* [*Cities at the crossroads: Violence and criminal power in Rio de Janeiro, Medellín, Bogotá and Ciudad Juárez*]. Medellín: International Development Research Centre, Universidad Nacional de Colombia [National University of Colombia].

Pérez Sáinz, Juan Pablo (2012). Exclusión social: Una propuesta crítica para abordar las carencias materiales en América Latina [Social exclusion: A critical proposal to address material deprivation in Latin America]. In Juan Pablo Pérez Sáinz (Ed.),

Sociedades fracturadas: La exclusión social en Centroamérica [*Fractured societies: Social exclusion in Central America*]. San José, Costa Rica: Latin American Faculty for Social Sciences (FLACSO).

——— (2014). *Mercados y bárbaros* [*Markets and barbarians*]. San José, Costa Rica: FLACSO.

Pérez Sáinz, Juan Pablo, Larissa Briosso, Rodolo Calderón, Karla Sánchez, and Mario Zetino (2015). *Exclusión social y violencias en territorios urbanos centroamericanos* [*Social exclusion and violence in Central American urban territories*]. San José, Costa Rica: Latin American Faculty for Social Sciences (FLACSO).

Pérez Sáinz, Juan Pablo, and Minor Mora (2007). *La persistencia de la miseria en Centroamérica: Una mirada desde la exclusión social* [*The persistence of misery in Central America: The view from social exclusion*]. San José, Costa Rica: Latin American Faculty for Social Sciences (FLACSO), Fundación Carolina [Carolina Foundation].

Polanyi, Karl (1992). *La gran transformación: Los orígenes políticos y económicos de nuestro tiempo* [*The great transformation: The political and economic origins of our time*]. (Eduardo L. Suárez, Trans.). Mexico City: Fondo de Cultura Económica [Economic Cultural Fund].

Portes, Alejandro, Bryan Roberts, Alejandro Grimson (2005). *Ciudades latinoamericanas: Un análisis comparativo en el umbral del nuevo siglo* [*Latin American cities: A comparative analysis on the threshold of the new century*]. Buenos Aires: Prometeo Libros.

Riaño-Alcalá, Pilar (2006). *Dwellers of memory: Youth and violence in Medellín*. New Brunswick, NJ: Transaction.

Riella, Alberto (2001). Violencia y control social: El debilitamiento del orden social de la modernidad [Violence and social control: The weakening of the social order of modernity]. *Papeles de Población* [*Population Studies*] 30: 183–204.

Roberts, Bryan (1996). The social context of citizenship in Latin America. *International Journal of Urban and Regional Research* 20: 38–65.

Sánchez, Martín (1995). Ethnography, inequality, and crime in the low-income community. In John Hagan and Ruth Peterson (Eds.), *Crime and inequality*. Redwood City: Stanford University Press.

Savenije, Wim (2012). Las pandillas callejeras o maras [Street gangs or maras]. In Mario Zetino-Duarte (Ed.), *Delincuencia, juventud y sociedad* [*Crime, youth and society*]. El Salvador: Latin American School for Social Science (FLACSO).

Savenije, Wim, and Katharine Andrade (2003). *Conviviendo en la orilla: Violencia y exclusión social en el Área Metropolitana de San Salvador* [*Living on the margins: violence and social exclusion in the metropolitan area of San Salvador*]. El Salvador: Latin American School for Social Science (FLACSO).

Sperberg, Jaime, and Barbara Happe (2000). Violencia y delincuencia en barrios pobres de Santiago de Chile y Río de Janeiro [Violence and delinquency in the shantytowns of Santiago in Chile, and Río de Janeiro]. *Revista Nueva Sociedad* [*New Society Journal*] 169: 44–60.

Sullivan, Mercer L. (1989). *Getting paid: Youth crime and work in the inner city*. New York: New York University Press.

Tilly, Charles (2000). *La desigualdad persistente* [*Durable inequality*]. Buenos Aires: Manantial.

Toch, Hans (1965). *The social psychology of social movements*. Indianapolis: Bobbs-Merrill.

Torres-Rivas, Edelberto (2007). *La piel de Centroamérica* [*The skin of Central America*]. San José, Costa Rica: Latin American School for Social Science (FLACSO).

UNDP: United Nations Development Program [Programa de las Naciones Unidas para el Desarrollo] (2010). *Informe de desarrollo humano para América Central* [*Human development report for Central America*]. Bogotá: Author.

UNODC: United Nations Office on Drugs and Crime (2007). *Crime and development in Central America: Caught in the crossfire*. New York: United Nations Publications.

Urusquieta, Ulises (2014). Urbe, violencias y jóvenes [Cities, violence and youth]. In Arturo Alvarado (Ed.), *Violencia juvenil y acceso a la justicia en América Latina* [*Juvenile violence and access to justice in Latin America*]. Mexico City: El Colegio de México [College of Mexico].

USAID: United States Agency for International Development (2006). *Central America and Mexico gang assessment*. Washington, DC: Author.

Vives Cases, Carmen, Diana Gil-González, Mercedes Carrasco-Portiño, and Carlos Álvarez-Dardet (2007). Revisión sistemática de los estudios sobre el nivel socioeconómico de los hombres que maltratan a sus parejas [Systematic review of studies on the socioeconomic status of men who mistreat their partners]. *Gaceta Sanitaria* [*Sanitary Gazette*] 21: 425–430.

Wieviorka, Michel (2009). *Violence: A new approach*. London: SAGE Publications.

——— (2014). The sociological analysis of violence: New perspectives. *Sociological Review* 62: 50–64.

Winton, Alisa (2004). Urban violence: A guide to the literature. *Environment and Urbanization* 16: 165–184.

Young, Jock (2003). Merton with energy, Katz with structure: The sociology of vindictiveness and the criminology of transgression. *Theoretical Criminology* 3: 389–414.

Zinecker, Heidrum (2010). Gewaltkriminalität in Zentralamerika: Entwurf eines erklärenden Theorie-Modells [Violent crime in Central America: Designing an explanatory model of theory]. In Kristin Seffer and Heidrum Zinecker (Eds.), *Gewaltkriminalität in Zentralamerika* [*Violent crime in Central America*]. Berlin: Nomos.

Zúñiga, Mario (2007). Las maras salvadoreñas como problema de investigación para las ciencias sociales [The Salvadoran maras as a research problem for the social sciences]. *Anuario de estudios Centroamericanos* [*Yearbook of Central American studies*] 33–34: 87–110.

7 Social disorganisation and neighbourhood effects in Latin America

Insights and limitations

Enrique Desmond Arias and Ximena Tocornal Montt

Introduction

In Latin American cities today, violence has a critical impact on the daily life of tens of millions of people. These effects are particularly acute for those living in urban areas that are characterised by high levels of social disadvantage (Sabatini, Cáceres, and Cerda 2001; Rodriguez and Sugranyes 2005). However, evidence indicates that the lack of economic resources alone does not fully explain the violence that afflicts these regions (Buvinic et al. 1999; Fay 2005). For example, some isolated rural communities are highly impoverished yet have relatively low levels of violence (Medina-Mora Icaza et al. 2005). In the urban context, particularly in Latin America, inequality and social exclusion—rather than poverty itself—are the key elements of interpersonal violence (Pérez Sáinz 2015).

To understand the determinants of violent crime in disadvantaged neighbourhoods, in 2014–2015 our team carried out comparative research in three large urban areas: Bogotá, capital of Colombia; Lima, capital of Peru; and Santiago, capital of Chile. Our project in those cities was to analyse violence in impoverished communities in order to understand the implications of social disorganisation with respect to crime. In fact, this work builds heavily on social disorganisation theory, which argues that social stresses, such as high levels of poverty and social marginalisation, produce higher levels of crime.

We focus particularly on the Collective Efficacy (CE) hypothesis, developed by Robert Sampson and his colleagues, which shows that local social ties and norms can help to control crime (Sampson and Groves 1989; Sampson, Morenoff, and Raudenbush 2005; Sampson 2008; Sampson and Graif 2009; Sampson 2012). Over the past 30 years, CE theory has emerged from masses of quantitative and qualitative data, principally from North American cities. Sampson and colleagues played a seminal role in this literature, based on their long-term research with the Project on Human Development in Chicago Neighborhoods. These data show that indicators of extreme disadvantage—factors such as a high density of poverty, low population stability, and many single-parent households—tend to correlate strongly with the presence of violent crime.

However, this social disorganisation approach emerges from the North American context and must be adapted to the particular dynamics that characterise Latin American communities. These local dynamics—particularly the two aspects of population migration and police legitimacy—are key factors in the Latin American metropolis.

Migration from rural to urban areas is a late phenomenon here compared to North America: it did not really begin until the 1960s. People coming from the countryside and looking for a place to live with no means to afford it developed an organised and collective housing strategy. Lacking any means to acquire formal lodging, they settled—usually illegally—in the interstices of the city, occupying land in the gaps and on the peripheries. These poor neighbourhoods were mostly constructed by their inhabitants, and were characterised by the absence of any public services or proper urban planning. (In recent years, such areas have to some degree become regularised: some residents—who might have lived there for more than 30 years—are now being given deeds of ownership.)

Such areas also lack effective and legitimate policing—an element that, in this region, is very different from in North America. Policing in Latin America originally emerged from a historical context of repressing and abusing the poor populations. At the same time, the police are often woefully underpaid, making the temptation to engage in corruption (for instance, by taking bribes and abusing their authority for personal gain) very difficult to resist. Even when this does not happen, inadequate resources still limit their ability to control criminal activity. This fact plays a key role in our understanding not just of why violence occurs, but also of the specific types of violence, and of the ways these are reinforced through political and social practices. These local differences place constraints on CE theory that are not adequately conceptualised in models derived from the United States.

Our project had three main phases. The first consisted of interviews with public officials and policymakers in the three cities, regarding trends in public safety. The second phase involved a battery of household interviews in two impoverished areas of each city, chosen for their different levels of violent crime. Finally, we surveyed a total of 81 neighbourhoods across the three cities to measure their levels of social capital, social disorganisation, and victimisation by crime. We used part of this survey data to illustrate the general perception of crime in each city.

To better understand the causal connections between social disorganisation, urban segregation, and violent crime, we selected the two focus neighbourhoods in each city with an eye towards finding ones with similar levels of social disadvantage, but dissimilar levels of crime. Eventually, we chose one area at the centre of each city, and one at the periphery. For comparison, we also identified three or four census zones in each city region that we felt reflected the median conditions, and then worked to develop our knowledge of those areas. These characteristics are outlined in Table 7.1.

In each of the six neighbourhoods, our research teams conducted some two dozen in-depth interviews with a variety of people: local residents, community leaders and organisers, members of the police force, and public servants. These interviews were based on standardised questionnaires. To guarantee confidentiality to those concerned, and to minimise any potential stigmatisation of the localities, in our research we refer to the communities by the pseudonyms indicated in Table 7.1.

- Bogotá: the small Santa Fé neighbourhood we studied became La Fuente and that in Ciudad Bolívar became Las Rosas.
- Lima: neighbourhoods in Independencia and Villa El Salvador became San José and El Sarmiento, respectively.
- Santiago: our Pedro Aguirre Cerda neighbourhood became Las Carmelitas and its counterpart in La Pintana became Los Copihues.

Site selection

The cities we selected for this study are all large ones, each with around eight million residents—which accounts for a sizeable portion of the population of that country: Santiago holds 45 per cent of Chile's total, Lima 29 per cent of Peru's, and Bogotá 16 per cent of Colombia's. Table 7.2 gives a "by the numbers" overview of the three communities. (Since data were drawn from different sources in different countries, they are not available for exactly the same years in all places.)

Beginning in the 1960s, each city began experiencing a rapid population increase as people migrated there from rural parts of the country. This was the result of several factors: not only the cities' own substantial economic growth, but also the economic dislocations and states of conflict prevailing in the countryside. This influx led to new neighbourhoods being created haphazardly, often via land invasions, and the burgeoning impoverished populations were displaced from the city centres to the peripheries. Since these expansions took place without any systematic urban planning, they created a number of problems with respect to transportation, water pollution, and rapidly increasing land prices.

Santiago's influx has now levelled off somewhat, but Lima and Bogotá still continue to receive considerable numbers of rural migrants: their respective annual growth rates are 1.6 per cent and 1.5 per cent, respectively. This trend reinforces residential isolation among the poorest and most needy segments, who increasingly live on the margins of the cities in a closed cycle of poverty and urban segregation. While all three cities are trying to bring their poverty levels under control, Bogotá and Santiago still have Gini coefficients that reflect significant inequalities. (Lima is among the least unequal cities in the region.)

Table 7.1 Characteristics of the neighbourhoods studied

City	*City region housing neighbourhood*	*Neighbourhood pseudonym*	*Location in city*	*Violence level*	*Origin of settlement*
Bogotá	Santa Fé	La Fuente	Centre	Moderate	Built in 1940 as homes for forestry labourers; main migration in the 1970s and 1990s; neighbourhood legalised in 1996.
	Ciudad Bolívar	Las Rosas	Periphery	High	Settled in 1993 via land invasion, as the result of a civic strike.
Lima	Independencia	San José	Centre	High	Settled in 1967 via land invasion.
	Villa El Salvador	El Sarmiento	Periphery	Low	Land was first occupied in the 1980s, and was officially invaded in 1995.
Santiago	Pedro Aguirre Cerda	Las Carmelitas	Centre	Moderate	Settled in 1957–1958 via land invasion.
	La Pintana	Los Copihues	Periphery	High	In 1992, the government constructed public housing for a population that had previously occupied another site.

Source: Arias and Tocornal (2017).

Table 7.2 Population and poverty in the three cities

Urban factors	*Bogotá*	*Lima*	*Santiago*
City population	7,878,783	8,894,412	7,092,988
Percent of national population	16.3%	28.6%	45.1%
Growth rate 2002–2012	1.5%	1.6%	0.96%
Poverty rate	31.8% (2002) 11.6% (2012)	25.1% (2007) 14.5% (2012)	15.1% (2000) 11.5% (2011)
Gini coefficient*	0.54 (2010)	0.4 (2010)	0.56 (2009)

* The Gini coefficient, an indicator of inequality, refers to distribution of income and wealth in a territory. A coefficient of 0 means complete equality, while 1 means maximum inequality—that is, all the resources are concentrated among a very few inhabitants. (Source: UN-Habitat 2014.)

Sources: Bogotá data, DANE (2016); Lima data, INEI (2015); Santiago data, INE (2016) and CASEN (2016).

Table 7.3 Victimisation and homicides in the three cities

Disadvantaged neighbourhood factors	*Bogotá*	*Lima*	*Santiago*
Rate of property crime	17.7%	16.3%	17.6%
Rate of violent property crime	19.1%	28.3%	12.7%
Rate of violent crime	38.2%	34.7%	17.8%
Rate of homicide (2011, per 100,000 inhabitants)	18.2	5.4	3.4

Sources: Arias and Tocornal (2017); UNDP (2013); INEI (2015).

In terms of the relative levels of victimisation and poverty, all three cities have similar levels of property crime; however, Bogotanos suffer more violent home burglaries than Santiaguinos do (19.1 per cent versus 12.7 per cent). Table 7.3 shows that Lima has slightly fewer burglaries overall than Bogotá, but nearly a third (28.3 per cent) of those events are accompanied by violence. Bogotá and Lima suffer markedly higher levels of violent crime than Santiago. In almost 40 per cent of the households interviewed in Bogotá, and 34.7 per cent of those in Lima, at least one member was the victim of a violent crime in the previous year; in Santiago, this occurred in only 17.8 per cent of cases. In terms of homicides, however, Bogotá has far higher rates than either of the other two cities. It reports 18.2 murders per 100,000 inhabitants compared to 5.4 in Lima and 3.4 in Santiago.

The data in Table 7.3 illustrate the varied interactions between urban poverty, inequality, and violence. Despite similar levels of poverty, homicide rates in the three cities vary. Santiago has the highest levels of inequality, but the lowest rates of homicide and general victimisation across all four categories. Lima has the least inequality and median victimisation, but the highest level of property crime—yet its homicide rate is nearly as low as Santiago's. Finally, Bogotá has inequality levels similar to Santiago's, an average amount of property crime, but the highest rate of violent crime. Before assessing what these numbers reveal, let us turn briefly to examining the background of our study.

Theoretical framework: collective efficacy

As indicated earlier, CE theory argues that socially and economically disadvantaged areas have higher levels of social disorganisation—of which violent behaviours are merely one indicator. Physical and social disorder, in the forms of delinquency and violence, are common symptoms of neighbourhoods that lack sufficient state investment in physical infrastructure (such as roads, water supply, sewers, street lighting, etc.) and social infrastructure (such as police presence), and that also lack strong social cohesion. However, in exceptional cases, the shortage of the former can be compensated for by the latter: social ties among residents can be sufficiently vigorous to control disorder.

Both these factors can be measured by assigning values to the intensity of interpersonal relationships and the degree to which local organisations have developed formal institutional structures. The first factor is an indicator of people's potential to cooperate and provide mutual aid for socially normative ends. When close enough relationships exist, we can examine the effects of CE (Sampson 2012). As a community attribute, CE results from two mechanisms: overall social cohesion and shared expectations about the exercise of informal social control. This is only possible when neighbours have mutual trust.

Ultimately, CE is a situational variable—that is, it differs according to the specific tasks needed to maintain physical and social order by regulating people's behaviour in public spaces. In any particular neighbourhood, CE depends on the vigilance and commitment required of residents to cope with threats. It also requires that they share the same tolerance thresholds for disorder and the same shared expectations about what constitutes a state of order and a common good. This, of course, varies culturally and socially.

In residential areas without any signs of physical or social disorder in their public spaces, there generally exist active mechanisms of formal or informal social control that prevent undesirable activities. The formal type is provided by the public authorities, in the form of legal restrictions, bylaws, and police presence; the informal type is usually set by normative social mores, customs, and practices, as well as by formal and informal institutions. But when public and private resources are both too limited to address basic needs, it is easy to understand that neither public officials nor community residents choose to focus primarily on physical and social disorder. Thus, in any particular geographic area, there may be a continuum of greater or lesser levels of social order. And these levels of social order or social disorganisation—the state of the social fabric—are reflected by the visible presence or absence of antisocial behaviours that undermine the security of property and persons. They are also reflected in the degree to which the community at large succeeds in maintaining order in common spaces.

At the public level (depending on the nature of political order in each country), it is national and local governments that implement policies to improve public services. In highly disadvantaged areas, where residents have few resources of their own, governments may help to provide basic necessities such as access to housing, child care, and health interventions, including treatment for addiction. In the absence of any local security resources, state interventions—such as the police responding to requests for assistance or to community disturbances—play an important role in guaranteeing basic order. This allows residents to dedicate their own limited resources to addressing what needs are most important to them. Another important factor in social organisation is the quality of the relationship between an area's residents and the local police force. Can the residents work effectively with the police to enforce law and order, or not? If that is not the case, even intelligent and well-intentioned public safety policies can fail. (In the Latin American context, these failures are intensified by the presence of powerful criminal gangs that engage in drug trafficking in disadvantaged areas.)

What are the implications of these facts for Latin America? The work of Villareal and Silva (2006) points to some significant differences from those seen in the American context. In Chicago, for instance, bonds of trust and intimacy are an important factor in CE, the positive results of neighbourhoods' mobilising their human resources to minimise disorder. But in Latin American shantytowns—such as the poor and violent neighbourhoods in Belo Horizonte, Brazil, where public goods and social services are often provided by the joint commitment of neighbours—society operates differently. The need to resolve problems collectively forges strong social ties, but also creates higher levels of crime. Another critical difference between Chicago and Bogotá, as pointed out by Escobar (2012), is the degree of police violence and abuse in Colombia. More positively, Cerda et al. (2012) have shown that neighbourhood-level policy interventions have lowered crime rates in Medellín, Colombia's second-largest city. These are some of the factors that limit the applicability of North American theory and data in explaining crime in Latin America.

Our research framework builds on these critiques, but goes beyond them to translate the principles of the Project on Human Development in Chicago Neighborhoods into a form that can be tested in disadvantaged Latin American cities (Sampson 2012). Our model gives special attention to the actions and institutions of the state, which have a fundamental role in public safety, social policy, and the administration of justice. The efficacy of this critical structure in applying the law and controlling crime is taken as a given in much of North American criminology. But in Latin America it is highly variable. In North America, the issue of policing is usually about how to understand a social problem correctly, design a well-thought-out policy, and exercise force in the right way. In Latin America, by contrast, the variation in police efficacy can be dramatic. Chronic abuse and corruption riddle the system with highly deleterious effects on the implementation of even high-quality public safety policies.

In CE theory, interpersonal relations among neighbours, including residents' associations, play an important role in producing order. Even in Latin America's most impoverished neighbourhoods, at the time of their settlement the inhabitants themselves organised and managed the housing construction and solved problems such as access to water, sanitation, and electricity (Sepulveda 2006). During the mid-to-late twentieth century, amid the great waves of migration from the countryside to the cities, the poor had increasingly little access to housing in existing neighbourhoods. As a result, these migrants—along with others who lacked housing in the city—illegally built their homes on any unused land they could find: on steep hillsides, waste land, ravine edges, or other inaccessible terrain. Under pressure, some governments tolerated these settlements or even provided construction materials. But nearly all these places lacked basic civic services to begin with and, since there was usually no systematic plan for their development, certain parts of many Latin American cities have complex, almost medieval, street patterns (Davis 2005). While many of these problems have been ameliorated over time, the original informal citizen-organised solutions have left substantial legacies in most cities in the region (Portes et al. 2005). Even today, many such neighbourhoods still exist on the very edge of legality and are under constant threat of eviction by the police.

Such self-organising efforts, autonomous tendencies, and cohesive social ties in poor neighbourhoods form a strong contrast with the United States, where the poor are so often accommodated in public housing built by government and also with more established middle- and upper-class neighbourhoods in Latin America, where services are provided by the local government. In this context, with the recent history of rapid city growth, migration into communities plays an important role in the nature of local CE.

The urban dimension and the role of migration

The United States experienced its phase of rapid urbanisation much earlier than Latin America: in the first half of the twentieth century rather than from mid-century onwards. In 1900, urban populations accounted for only 40 per cent of the US population; by 1960, the figure had risen to 69 per cent, and by 2010, 80 per cent of the US population lived in cities. (A similar pattern prevailed in New York: in 1950 it had a population of 7.8 million, and, in 2010, a population of nearly 8.5 million.) But in Chicago, the source of most of Sampson's data, the numbers rose even faster at first, then dropped. The population was around 1.7 million in 1900; by 1950, that had more than doubled to 3.6 million, and then the city's population decreased to just above 2.7 million in 2010 (US Census Bureau 1993).

The combination of rapid and unequal urbanisation in the US in the early twentieth century may have contributed to the conditions of urban social disorganisation during this period and even in subsequent generations. During this epoch, there was a great deal of public interest, among policy-makers and social reformers, in the condition of urban slums, and there was some discussion among scholars of systems of informal social control that could counter the problems (Whyte 1943). The concomitant slowing of rural-to-urban migration in the late twentieth century, and the extended process of extending public services to poor urban areas, may have contributed to the declining crime rates in US cities over the past 30 years.

Unfortunately, the contrast with Latin America in general, and with our study sites in particular, could not be starker. As indicated earlier, rural-to-urban migration began there in the middle of the twentieth century and the trend continues to have major impacts on urban dynamics to this day (Varela 1998). Between 1970 and 2010, for instance, the population of the three study cities skyrocketed:

- Bogotá went from 2.8 million to 8.5 million
- Lima went from nearly 3 million to 8.9 million
- Santiago went from 2.6 million to nearly 6 million (UN-Habitat 2012).

This rapid growth of Latin American cities in the second half of the twentieth century put immense stresses on public and social infrastructures. While urban areas are important engines of growth in the regions, they are also often characterised by a shortage of housing that meets basic standards and by inadequate public services, irregular building and planning, and poor sanitation. These disadvantaged areas—either in the hearts of urban areas or at their peripheries—also often face (among their many other challenges) high levels of inequality and high incidences of crime (UN-Habitat 2008).

Each city discussed in this study faces particular challenges associated with internal or external migration. Table 7.4 compares the rates of internal and external migration for the poor neighbourhoods of the three cities. Santiago, for instance, has a relatively high degree of residential stability: 27.7 per cent of the residents we interviewed were born in the neighbourhood where they now live. If we include those who were born within the same general city region (12.8 per cent), then more than 40 per cent of the population has remained within their area of birth, and more than 80 per cent has remained in the urban area of Santiago. Only 17 per cent of residents moved there from another city or region of the country. As a result of the relative parochialism in these neighbourhoods, the 2.3 per cent of truly foreign immigrants, from another country, have a high salience. (This fact was often commented on by residents in our interviews.)

Table 7.4 Internal and external migration in the three cities

Place of birth	*Bogotá*	*Lima*	*Santiago*	*Average*
In the same community	19.9%	19.0%	27.7%	22%
In another sector or district of the same city region	8.6%	7.1%	12.8%	9.5%
In the same city, but a different city region	23.5%	17.3%	40.2%	26.9%
In another city, or another region of the country	47.4%	56.5%	17.0%	40.5%
In another country	0.5%	0.1%	2.3%	1.0%

Source: Arias and Tocornal (2017).

In Bogotá, on the other hand, 47.4 per cent of poor inhabitants—almost half—were born in another part of the country. This fact reflects substantial and ongoing internal migration, the result of half a century of civil conflict and criminal violence in the country. In 2008, for instance, Colombia had 2.9 million internally displaced people, accounting for 7 per cent of the national population (Ibáñez and Velez 2008). Millions sought refuge from the conflict in cities, many bearing the physical, economic, and psychological scars of their experiences (Shultz et al. 2014). In Bogotá, this large-scale rural-to-urban displacement placed a particularly heavy burden on neighbourhoods, leading to real challenges in building social capital. Another ongoing factor is intra-urban displacement, when city residents flee from one neighbourhood to another; their movements have real effects on neighbourhood cohesion.

Such internal migration is often not captured by national statistics, but it has tangible effects on social cohesion within a neighbourhood. One of our interviewees, a community leader from Las Rosas, described the recently displaced as unsupportive of local collective efforts—even though national policies offer such forced migrants the kind of economic support that other residents often need but do not get. She sounded a note of resentment about the fact that the newcomers obtained government assistance:

> I mean, give them help to buy things. They suddenly give them clothes for children. They pay their rent for a certain time... So, take a girl or a young woman who is in a better situation, [but] who is going to get shot [if she stays in the neighbourhood. She does not] have that help, simply because [she] is not displaced. Then, if displacement is a terrible thing, and taking away their land and taking away their life is tough, but also... Look, people don't have to be [forcibly] displaced to need [help].

Another local leader commented that some people who were not really victims of forced migration still claimed displacement benefits and that this generated some distrust. However, he also noted that the neighbourhood he lived in was mostly made up of displaced persons, and that fact contributed to understanding and support for the displaced.

Lima, in Peru, had the highest percentage of national migration: more than half (56.5 per cent) of its population was born in another city or region of the country and moved to the city in the 1980s. There, too, conflict-induced migration has affected neighbourhood growth, though it weighs less heavily on social relations. In interviews, residents frequently indicated that such migration was an important issue in the construction of their communities. One woman from El Sarmiento spoke of the tragedy that forced her family to move to Lima: "They killed my father. They burned him... They burned my house. Why, [we] were left with only the clothes on our backs. We had no help from anyone... because everything is far away from my village: you need a car to go to Ayacucho and then it takes a week to get to Lima."

Today, however, when we asked residents about the origins of their neighbours, most merely noted that they came from diverse regions around the country. Migrants now seem to be accepted in these communities, but there is still evidence of some potentially negative effects from continued resettlement since new arrivals have little space to build homes. As a result, they tend to rent, which makes them more transient residents. They have fewer reasons to commit to collective improvements and less ability to accumulate even limited wealth. One local city councillor of El Sarmiento noted that "many young couples come here to work ... [but] they don't have enough money to buy themselves a [home]. ... so they continue to rent." He contrasted such newcomers with "those of us who are children of the founders", whose living space consists of "the second or third floor of our parents' homes".

So while migration is widely accepted in all three cities, it is evident from our interviews that migrants to established neighbourhoods tend to have different land ownership patterns. This results in a different level of engagement with the community, which affects CE.

In Santiago, Chile, the overall rate of migration is lower. The residents we spoke with referred less often to migration than in the other two cities: this subject came up in only about a third of our interviews in Santiago, but in almost all interviews in Bogotá and Lima. Their statements usually focused on the migration of other national groups from abroad, since lack of internal conflict in Chile, plus the relatively rapid growth of its domestic economy, has attracted many immigrants from other countries. For some residents and leaders, this issue creates concern. One local social leader from Los Copihues noted the increase in property crime. "We have Peruvians, which are the ones that you see most. We also have some Dominicans, if I am not mistaken. They are persons of the coloured race, Afro-Americans," she said. "[Sadly], they have already gotten into ... houses to rob them."

Another person from the municipality of Los Copihues, a local city councillor, had a different perception of the Peruvian and Colombian immigrants.

The Peruvians, he believes, are "much more educated, more prepared" to fit into Chilean society. But the Colombians, he feels, "generate problems".

> [In Colombia,] there is everything: drugs, trafficking, that is ... There is everything ... There are good people [in Colombia], but there is also prostitution, drugs, trafficking, and terrorism ... How did that wave of terrorism manifest when they come [sic] here?... I don't know. We don't know. We have not confirmed that ... but they may be involved ... in another country, with the bombs.

This perception—that some migrants are terrorists or criminals fleeing from police at home—is not an uncommon one. Neither is a tendency to look down on the nationals from other countries: one interviewee referred to them as *negritos*, a local term meaning "little black people". The data from all cities point to the very different challenges migration poses for CE. In Lima, the effects were relatively limited, but new migrants found it much harder than older residents to save money, accumulate capital, buy property, and build a place in the community. In Bogotá, significant waves of newcomers fleeing from conflict had a different vision of local life, with its obligations and solidarities, than more settled inhabitants. Government policies to support the migrants contributed to solidarity among them, but also created tensions between them and the other residents. And in Santiago a large majority of residents have lived in the city for an extended period, and a fair degree of solidarity exists among them—which results in a certain amount of animosity against the small number of recent foreign migrants, which some of the long-term inhabitants view as an alien group. In this case, strong CE coexists with a rejection of perceived outsiders.

The efficacy of policing

As already indicated, Latin American cities differ significantly from North American ones in many respects—not least in the ways these regions manage urban space and neighbourhood security (Salcedo and Dear 2012). In urban Latin America, there are serious issues with police efficiency that usually do not exist (or not to such a degree) in the Global North. In general, policing in the North has positive effects on crime control and the ability to build social control (Sampson 2012). Studies of social disorganisation tend to treat police and the justice system as a constant, an institution that can be relied on, in a way that is often not possible in Colombia, Chile, and Peru. While police inefficiency, abuse, corruption, and engagement with criminals certainly happens in every country, Latin America has historically had serious problems with those aspects. In his detailed work on Chicago, Sampson (2012) acknowledged that police corruption may play a role in neighbourhood effects in Latin America. Indeed, Escobar (2012) has shown that a higher police presence in Bogotá actually correlates with *more*

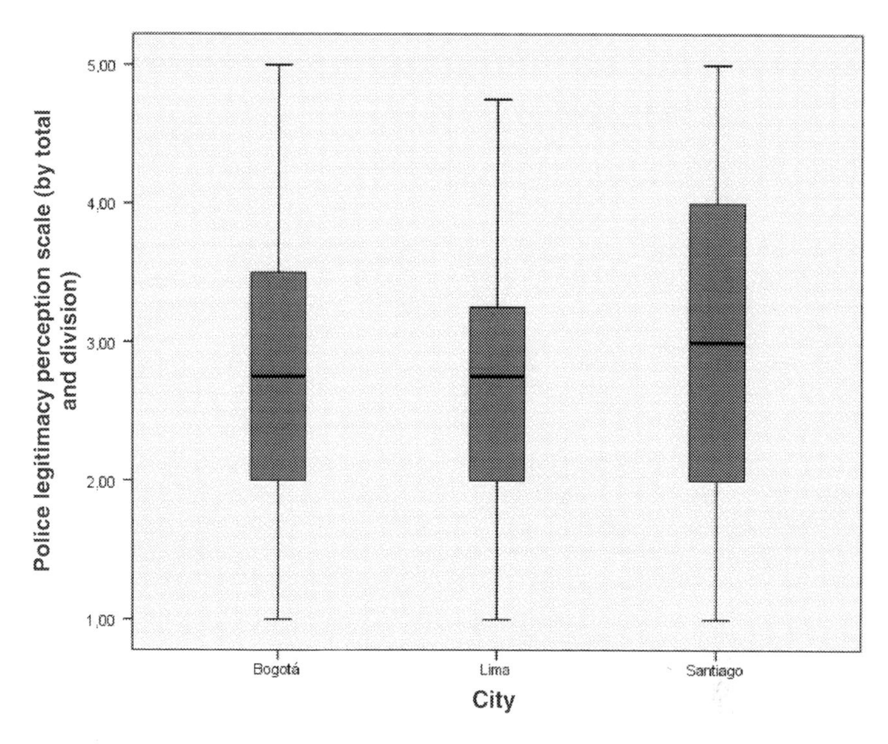

Figure 7.1 Box plot of police legitimacy
(A box plot displays the distribution of data through their quartiles.)
Source: Arias and Tocornal (2017).

homicides, rather than fewer. For this reason, to understand the implications of policing on social control, we should examine the logic of the failed efficacy of these organisations.

Our survey showed only moderate levels of respect for the police. On a scale of 1 (lowest) to 5 (highest), values in all three cities fell below 3. Figure 7.1 shows that Santiago's police had a very slightly higher level of legitimacy; the services in Bogotá and Lima received slightly lower ratings.

In our neighbourhood interviews in each city, we heard descriptions from residents of three main types of police failures. The inhabitants' array of complaints ranged from chronic inefficiency to corruption and outright abuse. Regarding inefficiency, for example, some Bogotá residents said they would file complaints about property crimes such as burglaries, but that police were useless in situations of violence (such as a fight breaking out). People also noted that police response times were consistently out of sync with the nature of the crime. A deep lack of confidence and trust in law enforcement was also expressed. Many residents were explicit in their belief that the local police were corrupt. One man from La Fuente, in Bogotá, complained that he had to pay the police to protect his business. Another, from Las Rosas, said "They always go for money, they are very easy to buy." A woman from La Fuente said she didn't trust the police, because "they themselves are accomplices of the drug addicts ... they extort money from those that sell, and those that consume." Such complicity with criminals caused most people to fear the police, a fact that raises important questions about how the police contribute to the prevailing disorder rather than combatting it.

More chillingly, many people still well remember the history of violence and abuse at the hands of both police and the military during the conflicts that tore the country apart in the 1990s. One woman from La Fuente told us that she remembered hearing about complicity between local residents and the police: the locals had a list of names of people "to keep an eye on" and, ostensibly, have jailed. But, "they didn't jail them, they had a list and with that list they went killing," she said. "There was the police behind [them]. The [local] man still lives down there ... they didn't come dressed as police, they were soldiers or police, but [the police] gave them munitions and they came here from Boyacá ... they had their assassins." As a result of such incidents, Bogotanos in general have a remarkably low opinion of the police. These negative relationships likely contribute to the poor police–citizen interactions that impede crime control efforts (Arias and Ungar 2009; Moncada 2009).

In Lima, as in Bogotá, people complained that local police responded late to calls about serious incidents and generally did little to suppress crime or create improvements in the neighbourhood. The service was most effective when victims only needed to report stolen belongings after a robbery. They did contact the police for robberies, though it didn't usually do much good. "We tell them what happened, but we still see the armed robbers walking around here!" said one person.

That said, concerns about police corruption in Lima were much more limited than in Bogotá. Even the infrequent accusation of corruption seemed to involve fairly mild forms of "shaking down" neighbourhood residents. For instance, one man from El Sarmiento grumbled that the police, when called, show up only "when everything is over", and then demand money "for gasoline, and that type of thing". Even this much was uncommon among Lima interviewees, who did not express as much fear of police abuse as people in the other two cities did.

In Santiago, inhabitants also had little confidence in police. A number complained about their limitations, and their inability to effectively enforce the law in their neighbourhoods. However, relatively few people accused the Chilean police of not responding to calls as they did in Lima and Bogotá. But there were pervasive concerns about police corruption. One non-governmental organisation worker from Los Copihues described a situation when the *carabineros*, the Chilean national police, catch someone "with kilos of coca". They don't charge people immediately, he said: "Instead they leave you in the dungeon. Then they wait for a relative to arrive and say, 'What can we do? How much does that cost [to get him out]?' " Then the relative pays the police to release the offender.

Even when drugs are not involved, the theme of legality versus illegality is a constant refrain when talking about the police. A religious leader from Los Copihues noted the distrust around the matter of alcohol.

> We know that the *carabineros* who supposedly protect us from crime, are also the ones who are consuming [illegal drugs], who go to the clandestine bars... One of the sources of funding [for neighbourhood associations] are their licenses to sell alcohol. But, you know, it's hard to sell officially if the place is full of illegal shops—and even more so if those are the ones the *carabineros* go to.

On the whole, there was extensive and sharp dissatisfaction with the Chilean police.

The foregoing tells us that the nature of police legitimacy varies significantly. In Lima, the police are detached, slow, and absent, but generally less abusive and corrupt. In Santiago, police respond to at least some calls, but are seen as very corrupt. Bogotá's police seem worst of all: they combine a poor response time with corruption and abuse. This points to different issues that need to be addressed to control crime in the three cities. In Lima, increasing police funding, and developing better training and policies, might have significant effects in improving criminal justice outcomes. In Bogotá and Santiago, on the other hand, greater funding may actually exacerbate the existing problems, since it may empower a police force that is already corrupt. In the communities we studied, at least, reforms of local police units would have to be accompanied by larger policy changes to have any real effect.

Discussion

This chapter has examined two key areas where the contemporary Latin American experience differs from the North American. One is the urban dimension and the role of migration, and the other is the efficacy and legitimacy of the police. Our analysis focused on how variation in these two areas affects social disorganisation, and the issue of formal and informal social control. Comparing results across the three cities reveals the immense differences that emerge in different national contexts. And using the concepts of social disorganisation and CE allowed us to look at both the similarities and the differences in migration patterns in Latin America and the US.

Heavy migration always tests social ties for a variety of reasons. However, the particularities vary, and, as a result, the effects on social ties can also differ. For example, relatively low levels of external migration create some very real tensions in Santiago. In Lima, significant migration generates few overt tensions, but new migrants face economic challenges with respect to property ownership, meaning that they are relegated to lower economic, social, and political positions in the community. Bogotá experiences significant and ongoing migration as a result of conflicts. For the rural migrants, this is a benefit as it provides them with a community to participate in when they move to the city. But their numbers, combined with the fact that they receive government benefits amid extensive community poverty, results in long-term tensions with their neighbours. All this confirms the general insight that a transient population contributes to strained social ties, which in turn may increase crime in urban neighbourhoods. This data provides a perspective on culturally specific vectors through which migration can affect local collective efficacy.

A further insight from this research is that the people we interviewed in the three cities demonstrate an openness to discussing police legitimacy—an openness that is not evident in existing ecological approaches to neighbourhood-level crime developed in the United States. The residents' experiences of law-enforcement failure provide us with some important insights, notably into the limitations of standard measures of formal social control. The operative question, it seems, is not so much whether police are present, but how effective they are. Having a small police station in a neighbourhood is good, but it is less beneficial if response times are slow. If the police are corrupt and abusive, their presence is counterproductive to the community. The specific nature of these failures provides important perspectives on the implications of policing policy, and on the wider application of social disorganisation and social control concepts in the Latin American context.

References

Arias, Desmond, and Ximena Tocornal (2017, unpublished). *Violence in three Latin American cities: A comparative study at the local level.*

Arias, Desmond, and Mark Ungar (2009). Community policing and policy implementation: A four-city study of police reform in Brazil and Honduras. *Comparative Politics* 41(4): 409–429.

Buvinic, Mayra, Andrew Morrison, and Michael Shifter (1999). *La violencia en América Latina y el Caribe: Un marco de referencia para la acción* [*Violence in Latin America and the Caribbean: A framework for action*]. Washington: Inter-American Development Bank.

CASEN: Encuesta de Caracterización Socio Económica Nacional [National Socioeconomic Characterisation Survey database] (2016). http://observatorio.ministeriodesarrollosocial.gob.cl/casen/casen_obj.php.

Cerda, Magdelena, Jeffrey D. Morenoff, Ben B. Hansen, Kimberley J. Tessari Hicks, Luis F. Duque, Alexandra Restrepo, and Ana V. Diez-Roux (2012). Reducing violence by transforming neighbourhoods: A natural experiment in Medellín, Colombia. *American Journal of Epidemiology* 175(10): 1045–1053. doi: doi/10.1093/aje/kwr428.

DANE: Departamento Administrativo Nacional de Estadística, Gobierno de Colombia [Government of Colombia, National Administrative Department of Statistics database] (2016). www.dane.gov.co.

Davis, Diane E. (2005) Cities in global context: A brief intellectual history. *International Journal of Urban and Regional Research* 29(1): 92–109.

Escobar, Gipsy A. (2012). El uso de la teoría de la desorganización social para comprender la distribución de homicidios en Bogotá, Colombia [Using social disorganisation theory to understand homicides distribution in Bogotá, Colombia]. *Revista INVI* [*INVI Journal*] 74(27): 21–85.

Fay, Marianne (Ed.). (2005). *The urban poor in Latin America*. Washington, DC: World Bank.

Ibáñez, Ana Maria, and Carlos Eduardo Velez (2008). Civil conflict and forced migration: The micro-determinants and welfare losses of displacement in Colombia. *World Development* 36(4): 659–676.

INE: Instituto Nacional de Estadísticas, Gobierno de Chile [Government of Chile, National Statistics Institute database] (2016). www.ine.cl.

INEI: Instituto Nacional de Estadísticas e Informática, Gobierno del Perú [Government of Peru, National Institute of Statistics and Informatics database] (2015). www.inei.gob.pe.

Medina-Mora Icaza, Maria Elena, Guilherme Borges-Guimaraes, Carmen Lara, Luciana Ramos-Lira, Joaquin Zambrano, and Clara Fleiz-Bautista (2005). Prevalencia de sucesos violentos y de trastorno por estrés postraumático en la población mexicana [Prevalence of violent events and post-traumatic stress disorder in the Mexican population]. *Salud Pública de México* [*Public Health in Mexico*] 47(1): 8–22.

Moncada, Eduardo (2009). Toward democratic policing in Colombia? Institutional accountability through lateral reform. *Comparative Politics* 41(4): 431–449.

Muggah, Robert (2012). *Researching the urban dilemma: Urbanization, poverty and violence*. Ottawa: International Development Research Centre (IDRC). www.idrc.ca/EN/PublishingImages/Researching-the-Urban-Dilemma-Baseline-study.pdf.

Pérez Sáinz, Juan Pablo (Ed.). (2015). *Exclusión social y violencias en territorios urbanos centroamericanos* [*Social exclusion and violence in Central American urban territories*]. San José, Costa Rica: Facultad Latinoamericana de Ciencias Sociales (FLACSO) [Latin American Faculty for the Social Sciences].

Portes, Alejandro, Bryan R. Roberts, and Alejandro Grimson (2005). *Ciudades latinoamericanas: Un análisis comparativo en el umbral del nuevo siglo* [*Latin American cities: A comparative analysis on the threshold of the new century*]. Mexico City: Universidad Autónoma de Zacatecas [Independent University of Zacatecas].

Rodriguez, Alfredo, and Ana Sugranyes (2005). *Los con techo: Un desafío para la política de vivienda social* [*People and roofs: A challenge for social housing policy*]. Santiago: Ediciones SUR.

Sabatini, Francisco, Gonzalo Cáceres, and Jorge Cerda (2001). Segregación residencial en las principales ciudades chilenas: Tendencias de las tres últimas décadas y posibles cursos de acción [Residential segregation in major Chilean cities: Trends of the last three decades, and possible courses of action]. *Revista EURE* 27(82): 21–42.

Salcedo, Rodrigo, and Michael Dear (2012). La escuela de Los Ángeles y las metrópolis sudamericanas [The school of Los Angeles and the South American metropolis]. *Bifurcaciones* [*Bifurcations*] 11. www.bifurcaciones.cl/2012/12/la-escuela-de-los-angeles-y-las-metropolis-sudamericanas.

Sampson, Robert (2008). Moving to inequality: Neighborhood effects and experiments meet social structure. *American Journal of Sociology* 114(1): 189–231.

Sampson, Robert (2012). Great American City: Chicago and the enduring neighborhood effect. Chicago: University of Chicago Press.

Sampson, Robert, and Corina Graif (2009). Neighborhood social capital as differential social organization: Resident and leadership dimensions. *American Behavioral Scientist* 52(11): 1579–1605.

Sampson, Robert, and W. Byron Groves (1989). Community structure and crime: Testing social disorganization theory. *American Journal of Sociology* 94(4): 774–802.

Sampson, Robert, Jeffrey D. Morenoff, and Stephen Raudenbush (2005). Social anatomy of racial and ethnic disparities in violence. *American Journal of Public Health* 95(2): 224–232.

Sepulveda, Rubén (2006). *Un análisis crítico de las políticas nacionales de vivienda en América Latina* [*A critical analysis of national housing policies in Latin America*]. San José, Costa Rica: Centro Cooperativo Sueco [Swedish Cooperative Centre].

Shultz, James M., Dana Rose Garfin, Zelde Espinel, Ricardo Araya, Maria A. Oquendo, Milton L. Wainberg, Roberto Chaskel, Silvia L. Gaviria, Anna E. Ordóñez, Maria Espinola, Fiona E. Wilson, Natalia Muñoz García, Ángela Milena Gómez Ceballos, Yanira Garcia-Barcena, Helen Verdeliand, and Yuval Neria (2014). Internally displaced victims of armed conflict in Colombia: The trajectory and trauma signature of forced migration. *Current Psychiatry Reports* 16(10): 1–16.

UN-Habitat (2008). *The state of the world's cities 2010/2011: Bridging the urban divide*. London: Earthscan.

——— (2012). *The state of Latin American and Caribbean cities 2012: Towards a new urban transition*. Nairobi: Author.

——— (2014). *Construcción de ciudades mas equitativas: Políticas públicas para la inclusión en América Latina* [*Building more equitable cities: Public policies for inclusion in Latin America*]. Bogotá: Programa de la Naciones Unidas para los Asentamientos Humanos [United Nations Program for Human Settlements].

UNDP: United Nations Development Program [Programa de las Naciones Unidas para el Desarrollo] (2013). *Informe regional de desarrollo humano 2013–2014. Seguridad ciudadana con rostro humano: Diagnóstico y propuestas para América Latina* [*Regional human development report 2013–2014. Citizen security with a human face: Diagnosis and proposals for Latin America*]. New York: Author.

US Census Bureau (1993). *1990 census of population and housing population and housing unit counts*. Washington, DC: United States Department of Commerce.

Varela, Carmen (1998). La ciudad latinoamericana en nuestros días [The Latin American city today]. *Revista Austral de Ciencias Sociales* [*Southern Journal of Social Sciences*] 2: 19–26.

Villareal, Andrés, and Bráulio F. A. da Silva (2006). Social cohesion, criminal victimization and perceived risk of crime in Brazilian neighbourhoods. *Social Forces* 84(3): 1725–1753.

Whyte, William Foote (1943). Social disorganization in the slums. *American Sociological Review* 8(1): 34–39.

8 Urban poverty and institutions in Venezuela

Roberto Briceño-León

Introduction

The neighbourhoods where the poor of Caracas have built their homes sit on the slopes of the mountains or are sunk into the ditches carved by the rivers that flow through the city. The flat spaces of the three valleys that make up Caracas are occupied by formal urban scenery: homes, high-rises, and commercial buildings—all legally constructed, with official permits to occupy the land and build on it. But the areas where the poor live have no such authorisation. Their settlements were built in the interstices of private property, on rocky and difficult public land on mountains, or on the riverbeds where construction is hazardous and expressly prohibited.

On one of those mountain slopes lives 17-year-old Jonathan, whose house has a beautiful view of the city's towers and buildings. But the house's foundations are so fragile that it is in danger of collapsing. His mother had no money for repairs, so Jonathan decided to help her. He left school, joined a neighbourhood gang, and began stealing. Now, he unabashedly tells of having already killed two people.

Not far from there, at the edge of one of the mountain gullies, lives Ederson, another 17-year-old. When he was a boy, the rising river destroyed his family's home. They lost almost everything. But despite the danger, Ederson's father decided to rebuild the house in the same spot. The location may be illegal, but it's convenient for everyone in a central area of the city, near where the parents work and the children go to school. Ederson packed groceries at a nearby supermarket to help pay for the repairs and for his own education. He currently dreams of attending university.

Here are two poor yet ambitious young men, who grew up in the same conditions of urban poverty and exclusion. Why does one enter the world of crime and violence, and the other hope for higher education? This chapter will examine the results of research into criminal violence in three Venezuelan cities. With the evidence gathered here, I aim to establish a critical and constructive dialogue on the theories of urban insecurity.

Urban poverty and violence

The most popular theories explaining crime and violence place the blame not just on poverty, but also on the inequality experienced by poor people in the Global South, particularly in Latin America. According to this well-known hypothesis, Jonathan would become a delinquent and a killer because of his family's poverty, and as a reaction to the fact that he was living in destitution right beside a city full of wealth. But if those were the only two operative factors, why didn't Ederson become a criminal too?

The explanation of poverty and inequality as the causes of crime is rooted in a set of theories that originated in the Global North, which has social realities that are very different from those in Latin America. Applying those theories to this region's problems is an easy task, given the overwhelming evidence of poverty and inequality, and the weight of authority of the Northern academic and political tradition. For instance, we could explain Jonathan's criminal behaviour using the theories of functional "social disorganisation" (Shaw and McKay 1972; Finn-Aage and Huizinga 1990; Gottfredson and Hirschi 1990; Laub and Sampson 2003). We could also turn to Marxist theories of crime (Russell 2002; Sozzo 2008; Camacho and Guzmán 1990), since Jonathan's family could certainly be classed as dysfunctional and his feeling of exclusion from urban life and consumerism could well lead to a class struggle. But then how do we explain the hundreds of thousands of other Edersons, with the same family and social circumstances, who never become thieves or murderers?

The reality of Venezuelan society forces us to creatively rethink some of those standard theories. In the early 2000s, for instance—the decade in which the country was wealthiest, not most impoverished—Caracas was the capital city with the world's highest homicide rate (UNODC 2011). Furthermore, at this time the government had the nation's largest expenditure in social assistance. That period in Venezuela—when homicide rates tripled, and it became one of the five most violent countries in the world—was when official reports proclaimed it to be the least unequal country in Latin America (CEPAL 2004). Under those circumstances, how can we sustain theories affirming that poverty and inequality produce criminal violence?

The radical transformation of criminality in Venezuela, and the differences in the lives of Jonathan and Ederson, show us that we need to consider other factors. The working hypothesis of the research I present here focuses on the normative dimensions of a society. I feel that this is a highly relevant factor, and one to which the dominant theories on urban crime do not pay sufficient attention. It is the rules of the social contract, both formal and informal, which govern relationships and make life predictable. My thesis is that the social institution acts to control violence, and that the tragedy of urban exclusion is not based on the lack of material things. Rather, it is *normative* exclusion that leaves part of the population outside the rule of law, and fosters the rise of crime and violence.

The fragmented city

Venezuelan cities, like much of Latin America, developed with a different pattern than that of European and American cities. The standard theory of urbanisation is that the process of industrialisation brought with it the growth of cities: industrialisation preceded urbanisation. In Latin America, something very different occurred, there was a process of urbanisation without industrialisation. Not only did it not come first, but, in some cases, industrialisation never arrived at all (Quijano 1977).

The urbanisation of Latin America was the product of Spanish colonisation, which, as a tool of political domination, displaced or replaced pre-colonial urban centres. Some of those Aztec, Mayan, or Incan cities were very large, and were likely developed for commercial and ceremonial purposes. In other areas, such as Venezuela, only small villages existed. For more than four centuries, the colonial city of Latin America was built in the form of a chequerboard around a plaza, as established in the 1576 Ordinances of Felipe II of Spain. It grew in a slow and orderly fashion with new blocks added onto its fringes, where new inhabitants of the city lived.

In the twentieth century, the situation changed when a predominantly rural continent suddenly became urban. This process was marked by three major traits: speed, magnitude, and incapacity.

- Speed: The process of urbanisation was a very quick one. In 1950, only 43 per cent of the population of South America lived in cities; 50 years later, by the end of the century, this had nearly doubled, with 80 per cent of the population being urban.
- Magnitude: South America has a very large population and much of it moved into the cities at once. In 1950, there were 48 million urban dwellers; in 2000, there were 279 million. Those 230 million new inhabitants of the cities meant an almost 600 per cent population increase (CELADE 2004)—the equivalent of building, in just half a century, six times the total number of all of South America's cities.
- Incapacity: For cities accustomed to slow growth, it was very difficult to welcome so many new residents. This scant capacity for urban integration was evident in the overloaded systems for housing and also in the strains placed on urban infrastructure such as roads, water, and sewers, and on services such as hospitals and schools.

That inability to assimilate so much new population growth, due to its speed and magnitude, was what led to the illegal occupation of huge portions of marginal territory that was not suitable for urbanisation: the mountains and gullies where Jonathan and Ederson live. These informal new areas, created by the inhabitants themselves, were both integrated into and excluded from the formal city: they are an essential part of it, but lack both legality and services.

These areas, known variously as *favelas*, *barrios*, or *tugurios*, have a situation of material exclusion that has been widely studied in the region (Valladares 2005). They also, as I indicated earlier, are in a state of normative exclusion and this makes them areas not strictly governed by the rule of law. They are social spaces in which the formal law is rarely enforced. Due to the circumstances of this abandonment, these spaces are governed by an informal institutionalism that offers some advantages for those who live in them, but also a number of serious problems (Calderón 2005).

Social theories on crime in society

Among the social explanations for violence and criminality, there are two major schools of thought. One believes that crime arises from poverty and inequality, and the other that criminality is driven by normative and institutional deficiencies.

The poverty-based explanation says that individuals commit crimes in order to quickly obtain the things they lack in life; they feel justified in this because of the inequality they observe in society, where others have the things they lack (Kruijt 2008; Moser and Shrader 1998). According to this perspective, since the poor have no legal access to the things they need, whether vital or superfluous, they decide to snatch them illegally by force. The attractive thing about this theory is that it removes the justification of crime from the active individual and his environment, and turns instead to a collective explanation that aims more to understand criminals than to condemn them. Its origin is found in a 1939 book written by two German-American sociologists, George Rusche and Otto Kirchheimer, *Punishment and Social Structure* (1968). With all the prestige of the Frankfurt School to which they belonged (Wheatland 2009), they demonstrated their new hypothesis attributing the causes of criminality not to individuals but to an unjust social order.

The explanations of crime from poverty come in various forms. In some cases, it has been a micro-social analysis, such as ecological studies, in which poverty (expressed as low household income, substandard housing, or percentage of youth that do not attend school) is the cause of crime (Shaw, van Dijk, and Rhomberg 2003). Alternatively, the macro-social perspective argues that the conditions of poverty are themselves a type of violence, known as structural violence (Galtung and Hölvik 1971; Del Olmo 2000). Another widely accepted explanation is based on the theory of inequality or "relative deprivation". The idea, first formulated by Marx, is that a person might feel anger if a palace is built next to their little house. The difference between the two buildings makes the house look like a mere hut (Marx 1968). Many other studies have considered inequality as a cause of violence, including Blau and Blau (1982); Fajnzylber, Lederman, and Loayza (2002); and Buvinic, Morrison, and Shifter (2000), as well as publications by the World Bank (2011) and the World Health Organization (WHO 2000).

Some Latin American studies have sought an association between inequality and criminality (Cano and Santos 2001; Gawryszewski and Costa 2005; Bourguignon, Nuñez, and Sanchez 2003; Cramer 2003; Kruijt 2008; Moser and Shrader 1998). But they have found no convincing explanation.

A different perspective comes from studies that seek an explanation for violence in the interaction of individuals and the social norms that govern their coexistence. All societies have such standards and laws to regulate relationships, distribute duties, and establish which actions are acceptable and which are reprehensible. Society praises some behaviours and criminalises others with the result that the behaviour of most people is predictable (Guidice 2005). For simple societies, these mechanisms work well enough. But when urban society becomes more complex, they become even more crucial. Émile Durkheim, the founder of sociology, found that at times these normative provisions—the ones that set the guidelines for how individuals should act—are either not conveyed adequately, are not learned, or lose their impact. In such situations, the "criminal profession" arises (Durkheim 1978: 343). Criminal behaviour arises from shortcomings in society; it is learned in terms of relationships with other people and in the choices an individual makes between behaviour that accepts or breaks the rules (Sutherland 1955).

This perspective is revisited by Robert Merton, who interprets criminal behaviour as the result of the conflict that arises between an individual's desires and his limited means for achieving those goals (Merton 1965). Societies respond to those who break their rules; we might call this reciprocation "punishment" although Durkheim does not (Durkheim 1960). Punishment is the opposite of positive reciprocity in which kindness is met with kindness, and gifts with gifts (Mauss 1973). As a social norm, negative reciprocity translates into the willingness to inflict pain on a person in response to the pain that this person has previously inflicted on others. This process restores the universal value to the social norm that has been broken (Meares, Katyal, and Kahan 2004; Hart 2008).

This institutional perspective contends that the most important thing in society is the rules of the game since these allow individuals to control their behaviour, resolve conflicts without using force, and make life predictable. This normative dimension of the social contract is known as institutionality in sociology (Brinton and Nee 1998) and in economics (North, Wallis, and Weingast 2009), and has recently been adopted by criminology (Messner, Rosenfel, and Karstedt 2013). Institutions reduce the motivation of individuals to wander off the prescribed paths and commit crimes by applying formal and informal mechanisms of social control (La Free 1998). This might help us to explain the non-criminal behaviour of Ederson, even though his condition of poverty was similar to Jonathan's. In his case, perhaps the presence in the family of his father and the parental teaching of institutional norms, including the value of work, were what prevented his participation in crime.

Theories of crime: the institutional dimension

To understand the singularity of crime and violence in Venezuela and Latin America, I have identified eight important factors that serve as material and normative determinants either alone or in combination with one another (Briceño-León 2005, 2008). These factors are:

- changes in family structure
- the double exclusion of youth
- the secularisation of urban life
- unmet expectations
- urban fragmentation
- the culture of masculinity
- the drug market
- criminal impunity.

I explain each of these points in detail below.

Changes in family structure

In previous generations and in rural communities, families were extended ones, but now the urban family is nuclear. In addition, two-parent families are decreasing and single-parent families are increasing (Jelin 2000). With these changes, the capacity of the family as an institution to convey values to children, and impose rules on them, has diminished. Studies now show a reduction in the normative role of the father and an increase in the regulatory role of the mother (Hurtado 1998). While their parent(s) is (are) at work during the day, many children are left alone at home or in the care of other children (since there are now few grandmothers to help). As a result, socialisation mostly occurs in the street. Some teenagers from deprived areas do not go to school, either because there are no schools where they live or because their family does not send them. When they are able to attend, classes only last until noon, leaving young people unattended for the rest of the day.

The double exclusion of youth

In adolescence, young people in cities can choose between continuing their education or entering the work force. However, a sizeable percentage of youth leave school, but do not manage to enter the work force—which leaves them doubly excluded. This fact not only leaves them with no training and no income, it also segregates them from the regulated social world. Such excluded youth are vulnerable to the allure of criminal groups, which may provide them with both an income and a sense of belonging.

The secularisation of urban life

The loss of the power of religion to regulate social behaviours in daily life has left a gap, since secularisation and civil law have not adequately replaced religious control. These changes may well have modified people's relationship with the divine; they have certainly affected the impact of their religious beliefs as a mechanism of social control (Levine 2012). The commandments "Thou shall not steal" and "Thou shall not kill" have lost their force; yet, no effective substitute is available in either secular morals or in the criminal justice system. The known shortcomings of the latter, however, mean that the religious institution is maintained as a reference in terms of morals and punishment.

Unmet expectations

The process of urbanisation also brings with it a major transformation in the expectations of citizens. The opportunity for equalisation was one of the major purposes of urban development: to overcome the conformism of the rural population—their ingrained tendency to be resigned to the status quo, in both material and cultural life, and to lack any ambition or desire for personal or family improvement (Stavenhagen 1973). But the economy did not offer the chance of wealth to everyone. Market research today shows that both rich and poor youth in the city aspire to the same tokens of luxury consumption, such as name-brand clothing and cell phones—but they do not have equal funds to purchase them. This asymmetry often leads poor youth to obtain them in criminal ways. In the Global North, it may seem unlikely for young people to be willing to kill a person just to get some Levi's jeans, Nike sneakers, or the latest iPhone. But in Latin America, this is not surprising.

Urban fragmentation

The informality and illegality that mark the urban landscape of Latin America, and often the Global South in general, bring about two material conditions that encourage violence. One condition is demographic, the other is topographical: high population density and the irregular design and layout of these mountain or ravine areas, the result of adapting to the land in the absence of any planning (Bolívar 1995), combined with the shortage of roads to make access difficult for outsiders. Steps and streets are steep, narrow, and twisted, and the sprawling layout of the area is like a labyrinth. The police, in their regular patrol vehicles, can barely get into such an area without being ambushed by criminals, nor can they establish a permanent presence in these areas as that would require almost a military operation. This fact allows for easy control by gangs. The rule of law in such territories is precarious and they are largely lawless.

Urban fragmentation demonstrates exclusion not just in terms of the built environment, infrastructure, and services, but also security. People living in such areas also do not have security of calling on the police for protection; they can easily be victimised by criminals. They are excluded from the security that the state must provide to its citizens and also from the normative mechanisms of conflict resolution (Pedrazzini 2005). These mechanisms offer ways to resolve differences peacefully, and with some institutionality. For example, one man does not work and stays up late at night playing very loud music. His neighbour works in the early morning and wants to sleep at night. How can the state help citizens to resolve such a conflict? Or when two neighbours both claim that a property boundary belongs to them. How should this situation be handled peacefully? Absent formal conflict resolution mechanisms, one person must either submit or defend himself with violence, thereby generating more violence. Whatever their other faults, the gangs at least offer those mechanisms: they act as judges, deciding who is right and who is wrong (even in cases of domestic violence between couples). Absent any better alternative, the gangs assume the role of the state.

The culture of masculinity

Social norms in Latin America define a man as a person who must be bold and not avoid confrontation. One result of this is that of all the homicides that occur in the continent, in almost nine out of ten, both the victims and the killers are men. The origin of this violence appears to be less in the biology of sex, and more in the rules of society that define how males and females should behave (Zubillaga 2003; Pedrazzini and Sanchez 2001).

The drug market

In cities, the highly profitable market for drug manufacturing and distribution is very competitive and, despite its illegality, strictly regulated by the gangs that run it. The business is enforced either by threats of violence or its actual use. Fights over territory or murders over the collection of debts express the strict rules that govern this perverse institutionality.

Criminal impunity

The criminal justice system, which should be a means of containing violence, is barely able to catch more than a small percentage of those who commit crimes and only a negligible proportion of them are actually punished (Briceño-León 2012). This invulnerability to prosecution on the part of criminals exists because the justice system is so overwhelmed with such cases that it has no ability even to apprehend or try criminals, still less the prison capacity to lock them up. Overworked prosecutors deal with hundreds of new cases every week and they can only choose which few to take up. The majority are simply forgotten, meaning that the zone of impunity is ever-expanding. This situation means that law-enforcement authorities have lost all power in the cities of Latin America, and the gangs are well aware of it.

These eight factors help to explain the current state of institutionality in Latin America. They are present in all countries, but their magnitude and relevance varies from one society to another, which is why it is so important to study them in the field.

Methodological multiplicity

The study of institutionality and its impact on crime is a very complex matter. Some criminologists—such as Messner and Rosenfeld (2004)—consider it a difficult task, especially if only surveys are used. Indeed, qualitative studies are often too specific to be easily generalisable. To overcome those limitations, I developed an integrated model using both qualitative and quantitative methods to explore the diversity of institutionality (Briceño-León 2003). It used qualitative techniques at the beginning of the study (focus groups, interviews, and case studies) and this was followed by the quantitative technique of a random national population survey to evaluate the magnitude and significance of qualitative results.

For the qualitative part of this study, I used the case studies technique (Yin 1984), adapting the methodology in order to apply it to multiple cases. With the goal of obtaining greater diversity and reliability (Briceño-León 2016), I established seven case studies in four cities:

- Caracas, the nation's capital and the principal city for services, such as banking and commerce, and the seat of national government
- Guayana City, a port city in Bolívar state and also an industrial and mining town
- San Cristobal and San Antonio, both located on the border with Colombia and both specialising in livestock production and trade.

For the quantitative study, I used a population survey with a multi-stage randomised national sample. This allowed me to evaluate the results of the qualitative study.

Research results

The results of the study show the importance of the normative dimension in the context of security and inclusion in cities. This dimension has generally been overlooked in terms of providing evidence of poverty or physical exclusion, but it can be a very powerful tool for explaining increases in violence and the institutional responses to it. But with no institutionality to support social processes—to motivate people to behave well, convince them of the virtues of the norm, oversee its enforcement, and punish offenders—security policies will always have limited effectiveness. In the six sections below, I examine the research findings and how they may affect the design of sustainable policies related to citizen security.

The positive contribution of informal institutionality

"Informal" institutionality refers to common rules for coexistence that are unwritten and not sanctioned by any formal authority. This factor had an unexpected relevance in the results of my research. Its study was included in the theoretical design, but much less weight was originally allocated to it; this changed as we encountered the phenomenon increasingly during the research. Notably, this occurred in all the study zones: in poor city neighbourhoods, in the marginal areas, and even in the behaviour of the police.

As I indicated earlier, a community that sprang up from illegal occupation of land and self-built housing, with no construction permits or legal status, exists outside the rule of law. When residents launch housing rental or sales businesses in an informal marketplace, none of those transactions is technically legal; however, the citizens do not consider them exactly illegal. We could say that they fit into a dimension of "paralegality", as the rules are legitimised by the stakeholders themselves. Their strength lies in the fact that they have proven to be quite successful. A smoothly functioning system has been created that includes a rotating credit arrangement between neighbours and especially the "real estate" and house rental market. All these operate with strict, but not formal, rules. This informal institutionality allows some important levels of internal social cohesion and social functioning. The rules are different from the formal system, as they are based on trust and personal ties between the citizens involved, but they are nevertheless recognised as legitimate.

Certainly some authors have emphasised "institutional diversity" (Ostrom 2005), but the phenomenon of informal institutionality is something much more powerful. Other studies (Helmke and Levitsky 2006) show that it involves a large percentage of the population who live according to different rules from those that formally govern social life. This is an important distinction: informal institutionality is not a fringe part of society, but a component that contributes to society's proper functioning.

Informal institutionality can be perverse

However, there is also a "perverse" aspect to the regulatory framework offered by informal institutionality, since these are the kinds of rules that can replace the law. Informal institutionality does not cause violence if its establishment is the product of coexistence among citizens. But when this is not the case—when it is imposed from the outside by organised criminal groups—it takes on a different aspect, and becomes a source of fear and crime. In some marginal urban territories, the criminal gangs replace the state in three of its important functions: establishing regulations, collecting taxes, and imposing punishment. Under perverse institutionality, criminal gangs establish social rules as they like, at their whim. They charge "taxes" that simply extort money from people and businesses for the "protection" they offer—that is, usually to protect citizens from their own harassment. And they cruelly punish anybody who does not submit to their authority or obey their rules.

This situation is exactly what we encountered in the border areas where Venezuela meets Colombia and within the cities in the territories controlled by criminal groups. The criminal rules thus constitute an institutionality in themselves. Although perverse, these are still important to show the relevance of the normative dimension of social life; in order to do business, even criminals must establish and obey certain rules. Even perverse institutionality, when criminal gangs replace the state, can fulfil the same functions as the positive kind such as setting expectations (Luhmann 2005) and making people's behaviour predictable (North and Weingast 2000). The same perverse effect can be true of social capital with its virtues of trust and its networks of cooperation, when these are implemented by organised crime (Rubio 1999).

Response to violence: strengthening the rule of law

The individuals we spoke to in focus groups strongly supported the idea that the government must use the army to control criminals. Their attitude was "*plomo al hampa*"— "fight scum with bullets". But alongside their enthusiasm for a "kill the bandits" strategy, there was also vehement support for the ideas of "negotiating with gangs" and "creating peace zones". These would be territories handed over to the gangs by the government, where the police could not go and where the gangs would be officially in charge with a mandate to reduce violence. This was considered a "least harm" compromise to avert political scandal; the bandits could still engage in extortion and selling drugs on the condition that they reduced the homicide levels.

In the survey, people had very different responses to these two proposals. The majority (77 per cent) supported sending in the army and only 18 per cent agreed with the idea of negotiation. The other 5 per cent were undecided. They wanted severe and decisive action to combat crime, not talk. However, this popular demand for an iron fist against crime has the potential to lead to extrajudicial excesses by the police and the military that, paradoxically, could end up destroying institutionality rather than strengthening it (Cruz 2011). And, from a methodological point of view, it was interesting to compare the results of the qualitative and quantitative methods. The quantitative surveys showed there was little popular support for negotiation approaches that had a lot of support in the qualitative work.

The gender dimension in social control

Our study showed that the most efficient operators for institutionality were not men, police, or members of the criminal justice system, but women. In their roles as mothers, teachers, or nuns, women were able to create pacts, agreements, and initiatives to promote positive informal institutionality. The female figures acted as protectors of the people and regulators of violence. Mothers were able to scold gang members that no one else dared to confront, teachers denounced delinquents if they came to school with guns, and nuns held street processions of saints to reclaim the public space from drug dealers.

Despite the government's failure to protect the people and uphold the norms, the wage research team discovered that women have made it possible for "traditional" institutions of social control, such as family, school, and religion, to be revitalised. These institutions remained valid despite having lost much of the power they once had in rural society or in small urban nuclei. They have maintained some of their legitimacy and represent great potential for resistance to crime and insecurity. This reality challenges the theories of modernisation, which maintain that social control is now the responsibility of a civil, impersonal, and secular state.

Violence produces and increases inequality

Our research found a different dimension of the link between violence and inequality. The results showed that inequality did not produce criminal behaviour and it was not the cause of violence. However, the opposite relationship was true: crime and violence increased social inequality. This happens because victimisation is not evenly distributed throughout the city. The poor are more likely to be victims of crime than other socioeconomic groups and are also victims of more violent crime. This is the result of economic inequality in protection from crime. When the state fails in its duty of universal protection, citizens must protect themselves privately. Only the wealthiest people can afford to pay for private security, bodyguards, or armoured cars. The poor are more vulnerable because they cannot do this.

As well, there is inequality in the damage caused to the victims of crimes against property. Although the items stolen from the poor may be of lesser value than those of the rich, that lower value still represents a much higher percentage of the family assets than it does for high-income earners. The loss of the modest vehicle of the motorcycle taxi driver, for instance, whether due to robbery or because he had to sell it to pay the ransom in a kidnapping, represents a much greater economic burden to his family than the loss of a luxury car to a wealthy businessman.

There is even inequality in the impact of injuries and death. If a family member is wounded or injured in an assault, there is a large difference between rich and poor in the economic capacity to afford the medical treatment needed to heal that person, ensure their survival, or cope with their being unable to work, and, in the worst case, to deal with the consequences of their death. The poor have much less ability than the wealthy to remedy the damage caused by crime and violence. This further impoverishes the poor and causes greater inequality in society.

Crime undermines the social legitimacy of success

Finally, our research showed that crime sets a bad example for honest young people. Theft, kidnapping, and selling drugs provide criminals with the kinds of money that law-abiding people cannot hope to obtain legitimately through their education and hard work. The criminals are well aware of this, and look down on students and young workers. Their nickname for them is *chigüire*, the local term for a capybara, a South American rodent. On a weekend night, one low-level drug peddler said, “I earn double what one of those *chigüires* earns in a month.”

This means that the gap between youths' consumer expectations and their ability to satisfy them can only be bridged by criminal activity, which gives them access to large sums of money. As pointed out by Merton (1965), this reality devalues the accepted means of work, study, and saving as ways to achieve goals of social and financial success, and it reinforces the belief that only the prohibited means of crime can accomplish those goals. As Durkheim (1978) explained, these situations produce anomie: a breakdown of the social contract and the rules established by society.

Conclusion

The social sciences, and politics, have recently tended to view violence and insecurity in the light of theories marked by what Lahire (2016) has appropriately termed “the culture of the excuse”. Remember Jonathan and Ederson, who grew up in very similar environments: in poverty, in a country that boasted of general wealth and had generous social policies for the poor. According to these theories, Jonathan would bear no responsibility for his thefts and homicides; poverty, inequality, familial abandonment, exploitation, or capitalism (depending on preference of theory) would all be sufficient to excuse his behaviour. Such excuses disguise themselves as understanding in order to forgive criminals their transgressions and place the blame on others: divorced parents, an exploitative economic system, the larger social structure, etc.

However, the research on insecurity and violence in Venezuela, with its major investments in social programs and a political effort to reduce inequality, refutes these theories on a macro level. And the lives of hundreds of thousands of young people like Ederson—who study and work, hard and honestly, to achieve their aspirations (and who are occasionally victimised by people like Jonathan)—refute the theories on a micro level. There are no possible excuses for decisions made by individuals and for social policies that have negative consequences. These sociological and political theories were developed in the Global North, yet they are accepted without criticism in Latin America, continuing to affirm that insecurity has its origin in this kind of "violence of the rich" (Pinçon and Pinçon-Charlot 2013). But research in Latin America shows that violence is linked less to circumstances of poverty or misery, and more to social norms and managing expectations. It is significant that none of the people we interviewed rob or kill people to obtain basic necessities like food or shelter; they do it for luxury goods like fancy jeans, sneakers, or cell phones.

We must think of the difference between Jonathan and Ederson in terms of managing the legitimacy of the means and time required to achieve goals. The theories of rational behaviour affirm that some individuals choose the path of crime because they consider it an acceptable alternative, while to others crime is not acceptable (Wikström 2004). Hence Jonathan wants to achieve his goals of luxury consumption quickly, and he is not troubled by the fact that this can only be done by prohibited means. Ederson, on the other hand, does not accept the use of illegal means, his personal values and ethics forbid such a shortcut. His "institutionality", his sense of compliance with the law, and his preference for moral means to achieve his goals, all mean that deciding to become a thief or a murderer is not an option for him. Like many thousands of other law-abiding citizens, the vast majority in fact, Ederson is willing to make the effort of studying, working, and waiting until he can achieve his goals legally.

This mindset illustrates the social contract that makes it possible for society to work. Preventing or controlling crime cannot be done by the after-the-fact intervention of the police or criminal law. These institutions can play an important role in fulfilling the social contract and strengthening the norms by punishing offenders once a crime has been committed. But the framework of society relies on morals, values, standard rules of behaviour, and reliable mechanisms for conflict resolution. These mechanisms are intended to prevent people from behaving badly in the first place.

The theoretical difficulty is that the normative dimension has been understood exclusively from the perspective of law—that is, from formal institutionality (Robert 1988). This is not sufficient to maintain good order as the social contract and informal institutionality have a diversity of norms and agreements. They are both the shadow and the mirror image of the law: "shadow" because they maintain it as a reference and "mirror" because they tend to imitate it in an informal way.

Evolutionary psychology explains the predominance of young men as murderers and rapists in terms of biologically programmed youthful aggression. Young men are at their highest level of sexual desire and their violence constitutes a primitive expression of masculinity in terms of fighting to exercise reproductive domination (Collins 2008; Daly and Wilson 1988). So why can Ederson control his sexual and aggressive impulses, while Jonathan can't? Why did one choose a life of crime and the other not?

To control people's impulses, society educates; to dissuade people from a criminal life, society punishes. We can assume that for Ederson, as for thousands like him, his self-control of his impulses worked. He accepted the choice of prescribed means and he believed in the threat of punishment. None of these were the case for Jonathan or for the thousands like him in the city who kidnap, steal, assault, rob, rape, and kill.

When a society's moral, normative, and punitive mechanisms work properly (Luhmann 2005), it expectations can be established either in a formal or an informal way. Either way, people know how they must behave and what they can expect from others. Formal or informal institutionality makes society predictable (North, Wallis, and Weingast 2009), which reduces the potential for conflict and violence. This moral and normative dimension of informal institutionality allows formal institutionality and law to function. In the end, as maintained by Habermas (1996), what makes a society safe is not repression but the acceptance of a set of self-imposed norms that are valid for everyone. The same principle is true of Latin American cities: safety and security must be based on a renewal of the social contract. This contract includes everyone, not only in the material goodness of urban life, but also in the normative inclusion that allows the rights of citizens to be exercised.

References

Blau, Judith, and Peter Blau (1982). The cost of inequality: Metropolitan structure and violent crime. *American Sociological Review* 47(1): 114–129.

Bolívar, Teolinda (1995). Urbanizadores, contructores y ciudadanos [Urbanisers, builders and citizens]. *Revista mexicana de Sociología* [*Mexican Sociological Review*] 57(1): 71–87.

Bourguignon, François, Jairo Nuñez, and Fabio Sanchez (2003). A structural model of crime and inequality in Colombia. *Journal of the European Economic Asociation* 1(2–3): 440–449.

Briceño-León, Roberto (2016). La metodología de los múltiples estudios de caso [The methodology of multiple case studies]. In Roberto Briceño-León, *Ciudades de vida y muerte: La ciudad y el pacto social para la contención de la violencia* [*Cities of life and death: The city and the social pact for containing violence*] (113–124). Caracas: Editorial Alfa.

——— (2012). La impunidad como causa de la violencia homicida [Impunity as the cause of homicidal violence]. In Roberto Briceño-León, Olga Avila, and Olga Camardiel (Eds.), *Violencia e institucionalidad* [*Violence and institutionality*]. Caracas: Editorial Alfa.

——— (2008). *Sociología de la violencia en América Latina* [*Sociology of violence in Latin America*]. Quito: Facultad Latinoamericana de Ciencias Sociales (FLACSO) [Latin American Faculty for the Social Sciences].

——— (2005). Urban violence and public health in Latin America: A sociological explanatory model. *Cadernos de Saude Pública* [*Notes on Public Health*] 21(6): 1629–1664.

——— (2003). Quatro modelos de integracao de tecnicas qualitativas e quantitativas de investigacao nas ciencias sociales [Four models for integrating qualitative and quantitative techniques in social science research]. In Paulete Godenberg, Regina Marsiglia, and Mara Gomez (Eds.), *O classico e o novo: Tendencias, objetos e abordagens em ciencias sociais e saúde* [*The classic and the new: Trends, objects and approaches in social sciences and health*]. Rio de Janeiro: Editora Fiocruz.

Brinton, Mary, and Victor Nee (1998). *The new institutionalism in sociology*. Stanford: Stanford University Press.

Buvinic, Mayra, Andrew Morrison, and Michael Shifter (2000). *La violencia en América Latina y el Caribe: Un marco de referencia para la acción* [*Violence in Latin America and the Caribbean: A framework for action*]. Washington, DC: Inter-American Development Bank.

Calderón, Julio (2005). *La ciudad ilegal* [*The illegal city*]. Lima: National University of San Marcos.

Camacho, Alvaro, and Alvaro Guzmán (1990). Ciudad y violencia [Cities and violence]. *Revista Foro* [*Forum Review*] 12: 22–32.

Cano, Ignácio, and Nilton Santos (2001). *Violência letal, renda e desigualdad social no Brasil.* [*Lethal violence, income and social inequality in Brazil*]. Rio de Janeiro: 7 Letras.

CELADE: Centro Latinoamericano y Caribeño de Demografía, División de Población [Latin American and Caribbean Demographic Centre, Population Division] (2004). Transformaciones democráficas en América Latina y el Caribe y consecuencias para las políticas púlblicas [Democratic transformations in Latin America and the Caribbean, and their consequences for public policies]. *Panorama social de América Latina* [*Social panorama of Latin America*]. Santiago: CEPAL [Economic Commission for Latin America].

CEPAL: Comisión Económica para América Latina [Economic Commission for Latin America] (2004). *Panorama Social* [*Social Panorama*]. Santiago: Author.

Collins, Randall (2008). *Violence: A microsociological theory*. Princeton: Princeton University Press.

Cramer, Christopher (2003). Does inequality cause conflict? *Journal of International Development* 15: 397–412.

Cruz, José Miguel (2011). Criminal violence and democratization in Central America: The survival of the violent state. *Journal of Latin American Polities and Society* 53(4): 1–33.

Daly, Martin, and Margot Wilson (1988). *Homicide*. New York: Aldine de Gruyter.

Del Olmo, Rosa (2000). Ciudades duras y violencia urbana [Hard cities and urban violence]. *Nueva Sociedad* [*New Society*] 167: 74–86.

Durkheim, Émile (1978). *De la division du travail social* [*The division of social work*]. Paris: Presses Universitaires de France.

——— (1960). *Les reglés de la méthode sociologique* [*The rules of the sociological method*]. Paris: Presses Universitaires de France.

Fajnzylber, Pablo, Daniel Lederman, and Norman Loaysa (2002). Inequality and violent crime. *Journal of Law and Economics* 45(1): 1–40.

Finn-Aage, Esbensen, and David Huizinga (1990). Community structure and drug use from a social disorganization perspective. *Justice Quarterly* 7: 691–709.

Galtung, Johan, and Tord Hölvik (1971). Structural and direct violence: A note on operationalization. *Journal of Peace Research* 8(1): 73–76.

Gawryszewski, Vilma Pinheiro, and Luciana Scarlazzari Costa (2005). Homicídios e desigualdades sociais no município de Sao Paulo [Homicides and social inequalities in the municipality of Sao Paulo]. *Revista Saúde Pública* [*Public Health Review*] 39(2): 191–197.

Gottfredson, Michael, and Travis Hirschi (1990). *A general theory of crime*. Stanford: Stanford University Press.

Guidice, Michael (2005). Normativity and norm-subjects. *Australian Journal of Legal Philosophy* 30: 102–121.

Habermas, Jurgen (1996). *Between fact and norms: Contribution to a discourse theory of law and democracy*. Cambridge, MA: MIT Press.

Hart, Herbert Lionel Adolphus (2008). Prolegomenon to the principles of punishment. In Herbert Lionel Adolphus Hart, *Punishment and responsibility* (1–28). Oxford: Oxford University Press.

Helmke, Gretchen, and Steven Levitsky (2006). *Informal institutions and democracy: Lessons from Latin America*. Baltimore: Johns Hopkins University Press.

Hurtado, Samuel (1998). *Matrisocialidad: Exploración de la estructura psicodinámica básica de la familia venezolana* [*Matriciality: An exploration of the basic psychodynamic structure of the Venezuelan family*]. Caracas: Ediciones de la Bilbioteca Central de la Universidad Central de Venezuela [Library of the Central University of Venezuela].

Jelin, Elizabeth (2000). *Pan y afectos: La transformación de la familia* [*Bread and affects: The transformation of the family*]. Buenos Aires: Fonde de Cultura Económica [Economic Culture Foundation].

Kruijt, Dirk (2008). Violencia y pobreza en América Latina: Los actores armados [Violence and poverty in Latin America: The armed actors]. *Pensamiento Iberoamericano* [*Ibero-American Thinking*] 2: 55–70.

La Free, Gary (1998). *Losing legitimacy: Street crime and the decline of social institutions in America*. Boulder, CO: Westview.

Lahire, Bernard (2016). *Pour la sociologie: Et pour en finir avec une pretendue "culture de l'excuse"* [*Sociology: Ending the "culture of the excuse"*]. Paris: La Découverte.

Laub, John, and Robert Sampson (2003). *Shared beginnings, divergent lives: Delinquent boys to age 70*. Cambridge, MA: Harvard University Press.

Levine, Daniel (2012). *Politics, religion and society in Latin America*. Boulder, CO: Lynne Rienner Publishers.

Luhmann, Niklas (2005). *El derecho de la sociedad* [*The right of society*]. Barcelona: Herder.

Marx, Karl (1968). *Trabajo asalariado y capital* [*Wage labour and capital*]. Madrid: Aguilera.

Mauss, Marcel (1973). *Sociologie et anthropologie* [*Sociology and anthropology*]. Paris: Presses Universitaires de France.

Meares, Tracy, Neal Katyal, and Dan Kahan (2004). Updating the study of punishment. *Stanford Law Review* 56(5): 1171–1210.

Merton, Robert (1965). *Teoría y estructura social* [*Theory and social structure*]. Mexico City: Fondo de Cultura Económica [Economic Cultural Foundation].

Messner, Steven, and Richard Rosenfeld (2004). "Institutionalizing" criminological theory. In Joan McCord (Ed.), *Institutions and intentions in the study of crime: Beyond empiricism* (69–82). New Brunswick, NJ: Transaction Publishers.

Messner, Steven, Richard Rosenfeld, and Susanne Karstedt (2013). Social institutions and crime. In Francis Cullen and Pamela Wilcox (Eds.), *Criminological Theory* (405–423). Oxford: Oxford University Press.

Moser, Caroline, and Elizabeth Shrader (1998). *Crime, violence and urban poverty in Latin America: Towards an integrated framework of reference*. Washington, DC: World Bank.

North, Douglas, John Joseph Wallis, and Barry Weingast (2009). *Violence and social order: A conceptual framework for interpreting recorded human history*. Cambridge: Cambridge University Press.

North, Douglas, and Barry Weingast (2000). Introduction: Institutional analysis and economic history. *Journal of Economic History* 60(2): 414–417.

Ostrom, Elinor (2005). *Understanding institutional diversity*. Princeton: Princeton University Press.

Pedrazzini, Yves (2005). *La violence des villes* [*Violence in cities*]. Paris: Enjeux Planète.

Pedrazzini, Yves, and Magaly Sanchez (2001). *Malandros, bandas y niños de la calle: Cultura de urgencia en la metrópoli Latinoamericana* [*Crooks, gangs and children of the street: The culture of urgency in the Latin American metropolis*]. Caracas: Vadell Hermanos Editores.

Pinçon, Michel, and Monique Pinçon-Charlot (2013). *La violence des riches* [*The violence of the rich*]. Paris: La Découverte.

Quijano, Anibal (1977). *Dependencia, urbanización y cambio social en latinoamérica* [*Dependence, urbanisation and social change in Latin America*]. Lima: Mosca Azul.

Robert, Philippe (1988). Le crime entre déviances et normes [Crime between deviations and norms]. In Philippe Robert, *Normes et déviances* [*Norms and deviations*] (263–294). Neuchâtel: Les Éditions de la Baconnière.

Rubio, Mauricio (1999). *Crimen e impunidad: Precisiones sobre la violencia* [*Crime and impunity: Clarifying violence*]. Bogotá: TM Editores.

Rusche, George, and Otto Kirchheimer (1968). *Punishment and social structure*. New York: Russell & Russell.

Russell, Stuart (2002). The continuing relevance of Marxism to critical criminology. *Criminology* 11(2): 113–135.

Shaw, Clifford, and Henry McKay (1972). *Juvenile delinquency and urban areas*. Chicago: Chicago University Press.

Shaw, Mark, Jan van Dijk, and Wolfgang Rhomberg (2003). Determining trends in global crime and justice: An overview of results from the United Nations surveys of crime trends and operations of criminal justice systems. *Forum on Crime and Society* 3(1–2): 35–63.

Sozzo, Maximo (2008). *Inseguridad: Prevencion y policia* [*Insecurity: Prevention and policing*]. Quito: Facultad Latinoamericana de Ciencias Sociales (FLACSO) [Latin American Faculty for the Social Sciences].

Stavenhagen, Rodolfo (1973). *Siete tesis equivocadas sobre Ámerica Latina: Sociología y subdesarrollo* [*Seven misconceptions about Latin America: Sociology and underdevelopment*]. Mexico City: Nuestro Tiempo.

Sutherland, Edwin (1955). A theory of crime: Differential association. In Edwin Sutherland and Donald Cressey (Eds.), *Principles of criminology*. Chicago: J.B. Lippincott.

UNODC: United Nations Office on Drugs and Crime (2011). *Global study on homicide 2011*. Vienna: Author.

Valladares, Licia do Prado (2005). *A invenção da favela* [*The invention of the favela*]. Rio de Janeiro: FV Editora.

Wheatland, Thomas (2009). *The Frankfurt school in exile*. Minneapolis: University of Minnesota Press.

Wikström, Per-Olof (2004). Crime as alternative: Toward a cross-level situational action theory of crime causation. In Joan McCord (Ed.), *Institutions and intentions in the study of crime: Beyond empiricism* (1–38). New Brunswick, NJ: Transaction Publishers.

World Bank (2011). *World development report 2011: Conflict, security and development*. Washington, DC: Author.

WHO: World Health Organization (2002). *World report on violence and health*. Edited by Etienne G. Krug, Linda L. Dahlberg, James A. Mercy, Anthony B. Zwi, and Rafael Lozano. Geneva: Author.

Yin, Robert (1984). *Case study research: Design & methods*. London: SAGE Publications.

Zubillaga, Verónica (2003). *Entre hombres y culebras: Devenir un hommme et se faire respecter dans un barrio d'une ville latinoamericaine* [*Between men and serpents: Becoming a man and gaining respect in a Latin American barrio*]. Louvain-la-Neuve, Belgium: Université Catholique de Louvain.

Part IV

Interpersonal violence

9 Understanding Côte d'Ivoire's "Microbes"

The political economy of a youth gang

Francis Akindès

Introduction

With the development of criminology as a discipline, we have come to realise the extent to which crimes are a "social mirror" that reflects the health of a society (Kawachi et al. 1999). In this context, youth gangs are a universal phenomenon (Klein et al. 2006; O'Brien et al. 2013; Deuchar 2015; Hughes and Short 2015). Youth violence has even been identified as a global concern by the World Health Organization, in its *World Report on Violence and Health* (Krug et al. 2002) because of its impact on public health (Meddings et al. 2005). As a social phenomenon, youth violence is discussed in a large body of literature in the United States and Latin America, and to a lesser extent in Europe. However, it is rarely discussed in Africa, except in South Africa.

In this chapter, I discuss some of the results of the Safe and Inclusive Cities project that studied youth crime in Côte d'Ivoire.[1] Here, I focus specifically on Abidjan, the country's economic capital.[2] In 2010 and 2011, in the midst of the country's post-election crisis, a new form of criminality and criminal identity emerged: the *enfants-microbes*, or "germ children". These ultra-violent children and teenagers are criminals of a new breed. They are younger delinquents than their predecessors, and as a group they specialise in the violent group extortion of goods and money. Nobody seems to know quite how the name Microbe originated; it seems to have arisen spontaneously. But it's an accurate description: they act on society like germs in the human body, seriously harming the individuals they attack.

Who are these Microbes, and why have they appeared at this particular time? How do they differ from Abidjan's ordinary street children, called "*les enfants de la rue*"? What lessons can we draw from research in these risky fields (which is otherwise rarely conducted)? In the literature on gangs, there are four competing theories for the emergence of the phenomenon. These are:

- the criminal-sociology perspective (including social disorganisation), proposed by Thrasher (1927) and Shaw and McKay (1931)
- the ecological theory of crime, proposed by Sampson and Groves (1989) and Kawachi et al. (1999)

- the psycho-sociological perspective, proposed by Dupéré et al. (2007); Lacourse et al. (2006); Kakar (2005); Spergel (1995); Hill et al. (1999); and Dukes et al. (1997)
- most recently, the interactionist theories, proposed by Thornberry (1987); Hall, Thornberry, and Lizotte (2006); and Gatti et al. (2005).

In terms of these perspectives, how does my research on the Microbes in Côte d'Ivoire contribute to the general discussion on the gang phenomenon? This chapter will attempt to answer that question.

Background and context of the study

Criminal violence is nothing new in Ivorian cities, and has rarely attracted the attention of social scientists. The few recent studies of insecurity show a growth in criminal acts between 1970 and 1990, and in the last decade this activity has reemerged. This timing coincides with a period of economic recession in Côte d'Ivoire, characterised by a reduction in public spending and high unemployment (Duruflé 1988; Contamin and Fauré 1990; Diomandé 1997).

The turning point—from petty crime to organised crime—came in 1974, and this change raised some scientific interest in the topic of criminal violence (Touré and Kouamé 1994; Marie 1997). These studies on hardship in a city like Abidjan pointed out that "the last resort of the 'marginalised'," unable to adapt to the system, "was crime, which was said to threaten this city with an 'implosion-explosion'" (Touré and Kouamé 1994). From the 1980s onward, a combination of factors fuelled social frustrations: the economic crisis, increasing unemployment and employment instability, and the loss of social benefits (such as scholarships). Even the most educated youth were not immune, since they faced a greatly reduced possibility of socio-professional integration.

Among educated young people, particularly males, these frustrations gradually bred a culture of violent defiance of the social order. On university campuses, brutality increased: battles between political rivals were conducted with machetes, and students were killed. This criminal phenomenon drew the attention of researchers (such as Akindès 2000, 2009; Le Pape and Vidal 2002; Konaté 2003). Scholarly interest intensified with the sociopolitical crisis at the end of the 1990s and early 2000s (Banégas 2007; Bouquet 2005; Marshall-Fratani 2006; Strauss 2011; Bovcon 2009; Banégas 2010; Akindès amd Fofana 2011; McGovern 2011; Koné 2011, 2012). That turbulent time, which lasted more than 10 years, saw an escalation of politically motivated violence.[3] The political and military crisis that followed the 2010 elections also promoted the illegal proliferation and trafficking of firearms, which significantly contributed to the rise of urban crime.

But in terms of sociological research, interest in this criminalisation of the political sphere overshadowed lesser forms of crime. (Only the works of Eliane De Latour [1999, 2001] looked at the phenomenon of gangs in the ghettos.) As Ivorian society was transforming, so were the street gangs. The appearance of the Microbes was only one symptom of this evolution of criminality. Unlike the street children, the Microbes perpetrated new and more dangerous forms of robbery and physical assault. Armed with clubs, knives, and machetes, these children and teenagers terrorised city residents creating a kind of public hysteria.

While the northern Abidjan commune[4] of Abobo is the epicentre of Microbes activity, central Abidjan is also a hot spot. This phenomenon has spread to other cities in the various provinces, including Daloa and Gagnoa, although not to the same scale. The public panic caused by the Microbes is such that citizens have even turned to mob violence in addition to pressuring the government to deal with the gangs as part of its public security agenda. In May 2016, the police launched the highly publicised "Sparrowhawk" operation against the Microbes, with the goal of cleaning up the worst districts and rounding up young suspects.[5] But it has since become apparent that this action was merely for cosmetic purposes. It has not prevented the phenomenon from redeveloping and adjusting its operating modes to match police strategies.

A new form of criminality

The Safe and Inclusive Cities project in Côte d'Ivoire was initiated in 2013 with the objective of filling in the gaps in our research on the new faces of crime and better understanding the transformations of criminal violence. To this end, it identified the features, manifestations, and history of criminal violence by two factors: location and type. Widespread newspaper reporting over a three-year period identified many of the assaults as having been committed around hotbeds of crime such as bus terminals and transport hubs,[6] and the crimes attributed to the Microbes included not just robberies but also assaults and even murders. We sought to understand the relationship between these factors and the genesis of the Microbes—a category of "criminals" whose sociological characteristics are still poorly understood.

Methodological considerations: methods and data

Beyond being a research field that focuses on trying to better understand the individual and social reasons for these new forms of violence by children and adolescents, our work with the Microbes also yielded valuable methodological lessons.

Investigating the Microbes was viewed as troublesome

Engaging in a research program on the Microbes was perceived as politically incorrect by the government of Côte d'Ivoire, which was less than enthusiastic about the project, and our initial forays met with strong resistance. The social issue of the Microbes is one the authorities find troublesome, fearing that scientific interest in the phenomenon might establish it as a sort of indicator of the poor performance of their economic growth policies. For many public servants, especially the police, the Microbes deserve only to be "eradicated, not studied". In a 2013 interview, one senior police official said the kids should be "power-washed out" of the cities. This negative reaction to research on the Microbes is shared by the general public, who are terrified by these gangs. In 2016, to redefine the political stance on this issue, the Ministry of Justice rebranded the Microbes as "children in conflict with the law".

Transformation to a legitimate research subject

Despite several general publications on the matter (Agier 1997; Kovats-Bernat 2002; Wood 2006; Boumaza and Campana 2007), the methodological literature on how to address risky topics such as criminal gangs remains weak. Once we overcame the initial hurdles, our research—the first in-depth field study of the Microbes—took a qualitative approach, using semi-structured interviews. We engaged with a gang from the Clouetcha neighbourhood of Abobo, an area with a high concentration of poorly constructed housing and public spaces. It is home to many large households (an average of eight people) who live in small spaces, with an average of four people sleeping in each room. The heads of household are most often involved in precarious economic activity.

Our qualitative approach required some innovation, since we did not wish to compromise our research methodology or ethics. We identified five main challenges to the project, some related to collecting data and others to the safety of both subjects and researchers.

- Access: The Microbes know that the police are tracking them and distrust all strangers. This made it difficult to choose the best strategy for approaching them.
- Trust among family members: The immediate families of Microbes, who might otherwise be key informants, are reluctant to speak to researchers. They fear that their statements will be used against the gang members.
- Trust among associates: Other gang members tend to confuse research with police investigation. They are reluctant to answer questions about their involvement with the Microbes because they fear retaliation from their peers.
- Unsafe research environment: The lawless target population of this study poses serious risks to researchers, as do the study sites (such as smoking dens), which may be unsafe places. For this reason, it is important to mitigate these risks by establishing trust with the gang members, particularly about how our data will be used.

- Police territoriality: Some police officers see researchers as intruders, others as competition. Most are reluctant to share their information about the Microbes, which they view as "professional secrets". In their view, the gangs deserve a "zero-tolerance" approach. The police also have a hard time understanding why researchers treat these outlaws as legitimate subjects, whose statements have the same value as those of the police.

All five of these factors intersected to complicate our study and hinder our attempts at triangulating the data. Accordingly, our most essential task was building relationships of trust with the various actors—both gang members and police, with their competing priorities—allowing them a space in which to express themselves freely.

Building essential relationships of trust

How does one go about building trust? The methodology for research into such difficult topics requires the creation of "transferable relationships of trust". This means that subjects may be convinced to trust a researcher, based on a guarantee of trustworthiness offered by the person who introduces the researcher into the study environment—in other words, a de facto "sponsor". This person also acts as a mediator between the researcher and the study site, and its inhabitants.

For our study, this important process consisted of two phases. First, we identified an individual—the "introducer"—from within the Microbes' social circle, with whom they had an existing relationship of trust. Then we patiently worked to establish trust between that person and the researcher. We knew that the quality of the data we collected would depend on the quality of immersion into the research site, and that that immersion would depend on the quality of the trust the introducer transferred to the researcher. The chemistry of this two-way trust would not only make it possible for us to talk to the Microbes, but also to learn about their private lives through the stories they told us.

To accomplish this, we first shared our study objectives, protocols, and intended uses with our introducer. A vital component of this was our ethical commitment not to disclose the identities of the Microbes or of any of our informants. After two months of negotiations, this strategy was successful: the introducer understood and accepted the spirit of our research, and made it possible for us to contact the target population. We were finally able to speak with four small groups of people:

- 18 children—12 boys and 6 girls, all aged 10 to 12—who were Microbes
- 6 heads of families that included Microbes
- 10 victims and witnesses of violence committed by the Microbes
- 8 police and security services officers.

Our conversations with the Microbes took the form of semi-structured interviews asking about their life stories and personal family history. These focused on four points:

- the process of their involvement in a gang
- the factors that led them to become Microbes, and stay with them
- the initiation ritual they went through
- the respective roles of girls and boys within the gangs.

Following those four points, I present the results of our research in five parts. First, I focus on the gang's socialisation process. Second, I discuss how young people first get involved with the Microbes. Third, I analyse the importance of the socio-ecological factors in this new form of criminality. Fourth, the ritualised process of resocialisation in the gangs is presented. Fifth, I discuss gender relations within the gangs.

Results

From desocialisation to resocialisation in the gangs

The Microbes gangs are not an exclusively male territory: youth of both sexes, aged 10 to 20, are members. Most of the time, the gangs grow by recruiting new members, who tend to be at the younger end of the spectrum. This recruitment rejuvenates the criminal environment and ensures its continuation and renewal. As long as nothing cuts their criminal careers short, the more youthful members are able to stay in the gang longer and develop more refined skills. In effect, they serve an apprenticeship of violence.

Another characteristic of the Microbes is their specific modus operandi. They operate in groups of 4 to 20 individuals, sometimes more, but never on their own. They surprise, swarm, assault, and rob their victims, using weapons such as clubs, knives, and machetes. This form of crime is new in Côte d'Ivoire. Although there has been a long-standing issue of delinquency among the country's children and teenagers—especially Abidjan's regular street children—what sets the Microbes apart is their escalation of violence, and their unprecedented level of organisation.

While there is still no consensus among researchers defining what exactly constitutes a gang (Wood and Alleyne 2010; Deuchar 2015; Hughes and Short 2015), there is some basic agreement (Wood and Alleyne 2010; Papachristos and Zhao 2015) on their external features. These features, shared by the Microbes, are:

- engaging in criminal activity in public places
- perpetrating criminal acts in an organised group
- size of the group (at least three members per group)
- existence of codes of conduct within each group.

However, unlike youth gangs in the United States (Akiyama 2012) or Brazil, Microbes do not take the trouble to identify themselves with tattoos or symbols. This may be because the individual's identification with the gang is so strong: it represents a substitute family, one that reconfigures their personality and destiny. (From their stories, the Microbes certainly experience this sense of inclusion.) The literature on this point has extensively documented the process of belonging and identity (Watkins and Taylor 2016), which gives some meaning to members' lives. Their new identities are constructed around the control of violence. Unlike the Latin American countries, where a firearm in the hand is seen as a "symbol of power" (Stretesky and Pogrebin 2007), Ivorian gangs use the machete as a tool of self-expression. This helps these children and teenagers to reject the social invisibility forced on them by their low socioeconomic status. Indeed, this demographic is distinguished by signs of low status. They are likely to come from single-parent (most often female-headed) families, with low incomes or none at all; to be orphans; or to have left school very early, averaging only six years of education.[7]

This forced and early distancing from the norms of family and education are well-known indicators of desocialisation in the literature on street children in general, and gangs in particular (Bjerregaard and Lizotte 1995; Klein 1995; Vigil 1996; Stretesky and Pogrebin 2007). The life histories of most Microbes we spoke to reveal that they live in a breeding ground of social vulnerability, accustomed to breaking norms that are meant to be reinforced by institutions of socialisation: the family and the school. They view themselves as adrift from the society around them and refer to themselves as "vagabonds". In this milieu, the reference systems of their social adoptive family gradually develop and a new assumed identity emerges. This identity is socially co-constructed in the crucible of risk-taking. The community of practice is built on the collective planning of attacks, involving frequent gatherings at certain specific locations; the primary meeting places are the smoking dens where the children go to smoke marijuana or crack cocaine, or to take heroin, powdered cocaine, and other drugs. Their main affinity is to their clans, such as "Marley's Gang", "the Warriors", or "Boribana". The families of Microbes are organised by their neighbourhood or sub-territory, such as Clouetcha, Colombie, "Abobo derrière-rail", etc., and new recruits must give proof of their allegiance to the group.

The literature on gangs shows very clearly that cohesion is essential for their survival (Decker 1996; Hagedorn 1988; Suttles 1972; Klein 1971; Thrasher 1927). Groups are headed by a leader, and everyone feels responsible for the others. Despite the risks of belonging to a gang with such strict rules about security, if a member is disloyal, the others are required to kill him. As one male Microbe, aged 12, put it: "Often, often, we kill our fellow vagabonds. It hurts us. We weep for him. But tomorrow, we start again. And we talk about why and how we killed him."[8]

For the Microbes, internal cohesion means sharing information on potential threats, including police raids. This cohesion is facilitated by the fact that the criminal gangs have adopted a slang of their own, almost a private language, known as Nouchi, which only the initiated understand (De Latour 2001). Their social environment is one of semi-secrecy and hostility—not just against the authorities but also against rival clans, with whom they engage in turf wars on an almost daily basis: they need to defend and control their territory, the basis for their existence. They survive by resisting external pressures, especially attacks by the police.

Becoming a Microbe: Paths into the gangs

How do the Microbes recruit their members? Do children join because they are attracted to the possibilities for violence? And how did the crisis of 2010 fuel the emergence of this phenomenon? Thornberry et al. (1993) suggest three perspectives on the relationship between gangs and violence.

- The selection perspective: young people are already delinquents, with a taste for crime and violence before they self-select themselves to join a gang.
- The social facilitation perspective: for newcomers, the gang plays a normative role in socialising them in the values and social norms of gang life, which include crime and violence.
- The strengthening skills perspective: new gang members, who are not already delinquents, are recruited from among youths who have a predisposition to engage in crime and violence. Their brutality intensifies when they join the gang, since it provides them with a structure that encourages their criminality.

These three perspectives help us to analyse and better understand the Microbes' recruitment methods and their sociological configuration.

The first perspective, selection, helps to clarify the link between the violent conflicts of late 2010 to early 2011, and the appearance of the Microbes—who then increased in power over the next five years (and are, in fact, still increasing their power to disrupt society). That period created a window of opportunity for the Microbes to bloom. While the regular army opposed the rebel forces, the latter founded the Invisible Commandos militia group in Abobo. The children and teenagers of Abobo escaped being recruited as child soldiers, but they did carry bags and ammunition for the Commandos. This proximity taught the young people new skills: how to handle firearms and how to trivialise violence. During this lawless period of general disorder and fear in the adult world, these opportunistic youth found valuable economic opportunities. They took advantage of the chaos to extort goods that they lacked, such as food supplies, and they also stole consumer goods (laptops, cell phones, watches, jewellery, etc.) that they could quickly trade or sell. In fact, the goods most often extorted by gang members from their victims are almost always smart phones, which can be easily resold on the black market.

Many of the Microbes we interviewed were barely 10 years old in 2010; yet, during that period, many of them had used weapons such as clubs, knives, and machetes to assault and rob people. This violence was the distinguishing factor between the Microbes and the street children, whose activities were mostly confined to pickpocketing. The Microbes had only been petty delinquents themselves prior to serving the rebels; afterward they became the members and bosses of a new category of gang. Their criminal skills quickly helped some of them to prosper, and they became role models for others. Boosted by a group dynamic, this violence against others—and the escalation of transgression that distinguishes it from other forms of criminality—blew open the doors of what had previously been culturally and morally unacceptable among children and teenagers. As one male Microbe, aged 15, put it: "We even attack our mothers and grandmothers when we are roaming around looking for money. But we know that it's not good. ... But what are we going to do?"

Children tend to become Microbes via three routes:

- After gaining some experience with the Invisible Commandos. While the post-election conflict had an impact on the path of some children who became Microbes, only a few of them took this route to joining the gangs.
- Joining directly after leaving their families (usually unhappy ones from which the children felt compelled to run away), without any transition period in another group. In such cases, the Microbes directly resocialised these new recruits into the norms and values of the gangs, and taught them the skills they needed to commit crimes.
- After being recruited from among the *gnambros* at local informal transport (bus and taxi) hubs. The *gnambros* are young workers (mainly boys) who recruit clients for the bus and taxi drivers. Part of a sophisticated organisational structure, the *gnambros*' activity is coordinated by the *syndicalistes*, the senior managers of the organisations that run the transit hubs. Thes *gnambros* and *syndicalistes* organise themselves into rival clans that frequently clash with one another. This fighting experience, together with their talents for picking pockets and using bladed weapons, provide the *gnambros* with both social and violence capital that makes them attractive recruits for the Microbes. Most of the time, new recruits do not rise to be gang leaders, but the *gnambros* are often serious contenders for seniority and leadership within the clans.

Regardless of their route into the gang, all of the Microbes come from backgrounds marked by precariousness and vulnerability. They may have been the main providers for their families from an early age, their parents unable to meet their basic needs (perhaps because of sustained unemployment and economic hardships). Emotionally, their family situation may have become unbearable. Or they may have grown accustomed to taking care of themselves since childhood because they were orphans.

Whatever the cause, the children may feel strong resentment toward their degraded situations, unable to go to school and feeling fated to always live on the margins of society due to their lack of education. That resentment may fuel the feeling of being "justified" in preying on other members of society. Some comments made by several of the Microbes during interviews reflected these sentiments.

> "Nobody looks at us."
> "Nobody looks after us."
> "How are we going to eat if we don't do this?"
> "Being a Microbe, it's a job like any other."

Surviving as a child from Abobo means being able to use force and physical violence. This is necessary for personal protection, and also to "make oneself" in order to advance in the social hierarchy of the gang.

Another common reaction among male Microbes to the intolerable sensation of being socially marginalised, and suffering from "social invisibility" (Le Blanc 2009), is a deliberate decision to put their own lives at risk as a way of testing and demonstrating their masculinity. Suffering from several forms of inequality and exclusion, the Microbes try to resist by transgressing social values. They feel understandably bitter and disadvantaged when they compare themselves, for instance, to the privileged children from affluent Abidjan neighbourhoods such as Cocody, the most well-off of Abidjan's 10 boroughs and where most of the city's political elite lives. The Microbes we spoke to indicated their sense of the tremendous gap between the living conditions of children from Cocody, and their own: "They sleep at home, they have their parents, they go to school … they have everything. But us, the vagabonds, we have nothing … we have only *gbonhi* [group living]."

The Abobo Microbes define their own identity in opposition to the "normal" youngsters in other parts of Abidjan. They are characterised by the use of physical violence that they find necessary—both to protect themselves and to "make something of themselves". Perversely, the Microbes we spoke to feel a certain pride in their criminal accomplishments: "When we carry out our operations, this makes people see us a bit in Abobo; we're even in the newspaper. We—the children of the poor—people talk about us."

Another way for young Microbes to learn about new modes of criminality is by watching movies. Modern media know no borders, and, throughout Côte d'Ivoire, secret low-cost video clubs abound in unstable districts. All the children and adolescents we interviewed, male and female alike, had seen the 2002 film *City of God* made in a Rio de Janeiro *favela*.

Of all the modern mainstream films available, this must be the one that most closely reflects their own life experiences. One of the main characters in the film is Zé Pequeño (Little José), an ambitious child the same age as them, who grew up in harsh conditions of poverty and violence, and established himself as a drug dealer. In the imagination of the Microbes, Zé is their ideal role model: he acquires upward social mobility through transgression. Like the *gnambros*' bosses, the *syndicalistes*, this mobility represents social success. If social and military conflict and disorganisation led Abidjan society to trivialise violence, the socio-ecological environment depicted in *City of God*—and the norms and values the film defends—give the Microbes some powerful arguments for legitimising their own criminal practices.

The breeding ground of youth criminality

The phenomenon of the Microbes took shape in a specific socio-ecological environment. While the communities in the north of Abidjan, including Attécoubé, Adjamé, and Yopougon, are the most affected by the Microbes' activities, Abobo is still their main home. One of the most dynamic areas of Abidjan, its population increased rapidly from 638,237 residents in 1998 to 1,030,658 in 2014. Its annual growth rate was 3.2 per cent, with an average density of 17,000 residents per square kilometre, according to the 2014 General Census of Population and Housing (RGPH 2014). In other words, Abobo has all the characteristics of a neighbourhood where planning was quickly overtaken by demographic pressure. It developed by simply spreading out on its peripheries rather than as the result of a master plan. This promoted the sprawling development of unstructured housing in unplanned districts such as Abobo-Sagbé, Quartier Colombie, Abobo "derrière-rail", and Abobo-Clouetcha—this last being the true niche of the Microbes.

These slums, most often lacking proper roads and lighting, are usually made from scraps and salvaged material. The uncleared land around these "African favelas" is overgrown and harbours many smoking dens; the surrounding valleys serve as refuges for criminals. In these areas, a poor population that is economically weak and socially disadvantaged is concentrated. Heads of households, when they work at all, are active in the informal sector or work at low-paying jobs as chauffeurs, taxi drivers, construction workers, domestic servants, etc. Parents have generally lost control of their children, many of whom, as mentioned above, have become the main providers for their families. In short, everything about these districts favours the development and entrenchment of crime.

Throughout our interviews with the Microbes, the depressing quality of their family lives, and their own feelings of being neglected, were often mentioned. In their miserable situation, sample comments included: "Look where we live" and "Are we not Ivorians like the others?" Their wretched living conditions, and their lack of access to basic social services, make them feel like second-class citizens.

Two theories provide ways to understand the relationship between the Microbes' living conditions and the development of their violent activity. One is the study of the effects of the local environment on criminal behaviours (Copping and Campbell 2015); the other is the paradigm of human ecology developed by Robert Sampson (2012), which focuses on the "poverty traps" generated by "neighbourhood effects". In Abobo, these traps can be explained by the consequences of a downgraded environment on the psychology of its occupants, especially those children who became Microbes. Those poverty traps also play an important role in the children's social construction of their subjective reasons for violent acting-out, which they feel is justified by the need to "get out at any cost". As some of the Microbes told us in interviews, "Our life is like our death, we just have to die at the same time." This lends force to the general strain theory (Agnew 1992, 2001; Baron 2006), which attempts to link the onset of delinquency with the feeling of failure (strain). The burgeoning of Microbe gangs, and the escalation of transgression within them, can both be explained by this psychological disposition. The children perceive their living conditions as something to be rejected, and they consider resorting to violence as a triumph over failure and social degradation.

The moral economy of violence

As other studies in Latin and North America have shown, the decision to turn to criminal violence to make a living is essentially an economic one: people have no other options. The young criminals may feel that any increase in the overall economic prosperity of Côte d'Ivoire bypasses them. The current government's economic policy, dubbed "emerging in 2020" and promoted in the national and international media, promises a massive investment in new road infrastructures—not an aspect likely to have much discernible effect on the living conditions of the poor and dispossessed. When the Microbes talk about the issue, it is clear that they have some political awareness. They make comments like:

> "People talk about emergence in the country. But us, we don't see anything."
> "We can't eat tar [off the roads]."
> "People see us as not mattering."

Reading between the lines of such statements, we might view this as criticism of the national economic policy from the lowest rungs of society. The Microbes perceive their criminal activity as defiance against their own social marginality. One boy said in an interview: "Both my parents are old and sick; and me—a boy—I can't stay here looking at them, doing nothing. I'm going to fight." Another person pointed out: "The police kill us every day. But we are still here. We are numerous, we cannot disappear."

They also used an expression about mob justice inflicted on them by members of the general population when they are caught after one of their attacks: "People use Section 125 on us." In street language, this refers to buying 100 Francs worth of fuel and a 25 Franc box of matches and using them to set someone on fire. Section 125 was practised with impunity during the 1990s, and it gained momentum during the post-election crisis and civil war of 2010–2011: immolating one another became a method of settling scores between people of rival political factions. Today, this gruesome act is used against the Microbes, reflecting the popular vindictiveness against them whenever they are apprehended by incensed citizens. Confronted with such drastic responses, the Microbes in turn intensify their own violence. They often seem to feel a desire for revenge on the society that rejects them. One young male told us: "People say that the police just have to kill us ... if people kill us here, we too are merciless."

For virtually all of the Microbes we spoke with, resorting to violence is not a choice but a necessity. One asked: "If we don't do this, how are we going to [make a living]?" Most of the time, the spoils from their robberies are sold for cash. (Individual gang members keep their own takings; nothing is invested in the gang itself.) Those who have families use a portion of their ill-gotten gains to help and maintain them.

> "I give money to my parents, letting them believe that I won it in poker."
> "I take care of my mother and father, who are both sick, and I pay for my little brother's school."
> "I pay the rent whenever I stay with my aunt and mother, and I feed my family of eight."

The rest of their "earnings" is spent on consumer goods to boost their social prestige, to satisfy their need for self-assertion and their pursuit of social recognition. In this respect, the Microbes do not much differ much from the urban culture of consumption of other youth around the world. In Ivorian society, bluffing is an important aspect of the culture of appearance, which depends on the outward signs of success (Newell 2012). By the violence of their surprise attacks on richer citizens, the Microbes capture the resources that allow them to project a mimetic image of modernity and masculinity (Matlon 2011). Sasha Newell (2009a) has analysed the lavish spending of urban Ivorian youth, including the Microbes, on clothing—preferably made in the USA—on various accessories, and on luxury phones. They also demonstrate their conspicuous consumption in a bustling nightlife filled with sex, alcohol, and drugs, and even dance parties (where they perform *la simpa*, a dance from the 1960s still very popular with young Mande people).[9] The robbery, violence, fighting, and struggle of their daily lives are all designed to give the gang members the margin of extra cash to afford this power of action, this freedom, this ability to consume, that they dream of.

While the emergence of the Microbes illustrates the theories of social disorganisation and resilience to deprivation, we might also say that the political economy of their criminality involves three elements: the politics of survival, the politics of social recognition, and the politics of signs. The gangs transgress the social order to access goods, and having goods allows them to demonstrate their "affluence". In the Microbes' structuring of the world, this makes sense. Such ways of thinking, feeling, and acting can be viewed as local reactions to the inequalities of globalisation.

The socialisation rituals of criminals

The process of inducting new candidates into any criminal group often requires them to undergo an initiation ritual, to introduce them to the norms and values of the gang. For the Microbes, these rituals of affiliation play a significant role. Their process can be mapped out in three phases. In the first, young aspiring gang members start by "courting" friends who already belong to delinquent groups or networks: children who work at bus terminals, who hang around with other gang members, or former soldiers or rebels. Under their guidance, the youth show their willingness to smoke cigarettes and drink alcohol, which prepares them for using cocaine and heroin later. They also learn to take part in improvised or organised brawls, either between members of the group or with rival gang members.

In this first stage, there is an African particularity in the Microbes' practices: the association of narcotics with talismans. These are magical or religious objects that candidates can use as psychological crutches to help them to conquer fear; the novices believe that the talismans can even grant invincibility in risky situations. *Kanks*, in Nouchi, are special amulets with the "imaginary" ability to make those who wear them invulnerable against attack. Putting on such "protection" is known as "*se travailler*" (to get worked up) or "*se kanker*" (to wear a kank). The adolescent or child who is wearing an amulet (and under the influence of narcotics) feels ready to face the street, to take part in robberies, and to engage in assaults.

This belief in "gris-gris" charms and amulets is a common African tradition, based on the belief of the influence of the "forces of the invisible on behaviour" (Schatzberg 2000). In situations involving the economics of violence, it can be viewed as cultural risk management. Even before the Microbes adopted them, the widespread use of kanks to confer inviolability had already been noted in the colonial war of the Bani-Volta in 1915 (Royer 2003) and in many other armed conflicts in different parts of Africa. These include Sierra Leone and Liberia (Ellis 2000; Ferme 2001; Hoffman 2011), Zimbabwe (Lan 1985), and Casamance (Marut 2010). The psycho-sociological disposition to use such objects almost indicates a mindset of "mystical war" (Miran-Guyon 2015) in the combatants of the military-political conflict: its protagonists shared the same mental universe as the Microbes.

Once the novice has got used to being involved in the criminal environment, the second stage of initiation begins: actually committing a crime. Here it is worth noting that recently, since June 2015, the pattern of Microbes assaults has changed. Due to increased police crackdowns and patrols, robberies now take place more at night and less during the day. The usual thing now is for the gangs (at least 20 individuals) to target housing blocks, which are systematically robbed one after the other. Before the most frequently used weapons were knives, clubs, and machetes. Now the groups use pistols and Kalashnikov rifles. This transition to firearms has several meanings for the Microbes. For one thing, carrying them is a sign of "professional success" in performing their work. For another, the police crackdown has led the Microbes to change the way they operate, both offensively and defensively. When hold-ups or armed robberies are committed during the day, for example, the robbers may carry guns to threaten their victims while the "operation" is carried out.

The third stage of initiation takes place when the candidate succeeds in actually carrying out an armed robbery. This act marks his acceptance into the Microbes group with the potential for a future criminal career. But if he shows any sign of hesitation, fear of the unknown, or the consequences of risk-taking, then he fails the test and is disqualified from joining a band of "vagabonds". However, this happens rarely. Novices generally have such a strong desire to create a new life for themselves, and to pursue social recognition, that few give up on the initiation; they are nurtured by the thought of belonging to a new social family. They are willing to work hard to build trust between themselves and their new peers so they can be considered a member of the gang.

Gender relations within the gangs

The presence of girls in a masculine social space deserves some attention. As St. Cyr and Decker (2003) have pointed out, in the Microbes gangs of Abidjan, the girls have the same socio-demographic profile as the boys, virtually identical life stories, and the same social trajectories. They are introduced to the gangs by a member who tempts them with gifts, sexually abuses them, introduces them to narcotics, and keeps them in the group by feeding their addiction.

However, within the gangs, the roles of girls and boys are gendered. Beyond the sexual use made of girls by their sponsors, they also have some agency, serving in operations—either as a lure to target male victims, who are then assaulted and robbed by the group, or to incite brawls that the gang takes advantage of to commit their crimes. As the result of the sexual activity, some young girls have the gang members' babies. They are also often the cause of battles between Microbe gangs, as they leave one partner for another, often a more generous male from another group. The battles between Microbe gangs can be murderous, but they also serve to restructure the hierarchies in both the groups.

Conclusion

This study attempted to understand how the Microbes, the harbingers of a new form of urban criminality, appeared in the urban landscape of Côte d'Ivoire. We also looked at the various factors that contributed to their emergence. Overall, we learned five lessons from the study.

The first lesson has to do with methodology. Research on the topic of gangs—which is so difficult and dangerous that it is rare in Africa—requires stringent precautions to be carried out properly. We have codified our approach, including the strategy of transferable trust that facilitated our entry into the social circle of the gang and allowed us to gather the data reported in this study.

The second lesson involves theories of why children break away from their families, including the classical analysis of deviance and delinquency in at-risk populations with antisocial and criminal practices. The Microbes' deviance lends credence to theories of social and socio-ecological disorganisation that attempts to understand this burgeoning form of criminal violence. In their system of organised crime, the average age tends to be closer to 10 than 20. The fact that the criminal environment thrives on younger members poses a real problem for any future solutions.

The third lesson relates to the harmful and long-lasting effects of armed conflict on societies. Our study shows that the 2010–2011 post-election conflict encouraged the criminality of at-risk children in the marginal sections of society (even though they did not actually serve as child soldiers). Five years later, the Microbe gangs were prospering. Other factors that aided the growth of this phenomenon included the increasing poverty that resulted from the conflict, the socio-ecological effects on the disorganisation of the family circle, and the inversion of roles between parents and children, with children becoming the breadwinners, leading to a loss of parental control. The implication of these observations is that any political response to the challenge of dealing with youth gangs cannot focus merely on police activity alone. It calls for solutions that directly address the underlying parameters: poverty, uncontrolled and unplanned urbanisation, and a high density of poor populations in spaces that are insufficiently designed to cope with them.

The fourth lesson involves the aspect of magic and religion. The consumption of narcotics is universal in criminal environments, allowing gang members to dehumanise themselves and decrease their awareness of danger. But among the Microbes, drugs are less important than the assurance provided by their amulets, which they imagine grant them invincibility. This tendency is specific to Africa, rooted in a system of belief in supernatural forces.

The fifth lesson relates to the moral economy of crime among these children and teenagers. For the Microbes, criminality is partly a matter of sheer survival: they need to acquire, by any possible means, the necessities of life. Just as important for them, though, is the power to purchase signs for social recognition—the objects and activities that give them much-needed prestige within the reference systems of meanings and values in their urban society.

Finally, we learned that solving the problem of the Microbes is likely to be a difficult task. The increasingly young age of these criminals suggests that, with nothing to interrupt their social trajectory, they will have all the time they need to consolidate their violent skills. Faced with such a fast transformation of the criminal scene, police crackdowns cannot be the only solution. Combatting brutality with greater brutality is unlikely to work well. The ideal political response would incorporate more positive solutions, such as offering these wild children alternative education and training opportunities. This approach could resocialise them away from the street, the gangs, and their disadvantaged home environments, back into normal society, allowing them to reinvent and improve their lives. There must be action in two respects: territory, including infrastructure development and planning (roads, lighting, water, sanitation, etc.), and social initiatives to save these Microbe children from the need for criminal activity.

Notes

1 This contribution is a partial presentation of the results of my research into the phenomenon of violence in Côte d'Ivoire, which I have conducted since the 1990s. I thank the reviewers and my colleagues Walter Kra and Séverin Kouamé for their careful review of this chapter.
2 Abidjan is a megalopolis. Its population was estimated at 2,877,948 inhabitants in 1998; by 2014, it had increased to 4,395,243.
3 The crisis following the election of 2000 led to murderous clashes between government troops and the rebel forces that appeared in 2002. Sporadic conflicts afflicted half the country for over five years; recently a mass grave was discovered, containing 57 bodies from that time. And, in 2011, in the four-month turmoil after the 2010 election, the death toll was estimated at around 3000 people.
4 The city of Abidjan is divided into 10 communes, a municipal-level administrative unit.
5 In three months, more than 11,500 people were questioned, 250 of whom were brought to court. Hundreds of weapons were seized, including six firearms, Kalashnikovs, and automatic pistols. Some 166 "smoking dens" were closed, and 2.5 tons of cannabis confiscated (Cessou 2017).
6 Another part of the research program focuses specifically on the ethnography of violence in bus terminals and public transport hubs. See Kra (2016).
7 A report on the Ivorian educational system assesses the average school experience at 7.7 years in 2015, while in the same period it was 9.7 years in Africa as a whole, and 12 years in middle-income countries (World Bank Group 2017: 28).
8 To protect their privacy, we do not identify any of the individual interviewees that we quote in this chapter.
9 Money-dependent activities perceived by the Microbes as being extremely gratifying include buying drinks for their friends, accumulating and displaying empty beer cans as signs of wealth, and buying gifts for desirable girls and seducing them in short-stay "love hotels"—the type of small spaces that proliferate in low-income neighbourhoods for people wanting a brief private space for sexual activity.

References

Agier, Michel (1997). Ni trop près, ni trop loin: De l'implication ethnographique à l'engagement intellectuel [Neither too close nor too far: From ethnographic involvement to intellectual engagement]. *Gradhiva* 21: 69–76.

Agnew, Robert (2001). Building on the foundation of general strain theory specifying the types of strain most likely to lead to crime and delinquency. *Journal of Research in Crime and Delinquency* 38(4): 319–361.

——— (1992). Foundation for a general strain theory of crime and delinquency. *Criminology* 30(1): 47–87.

Akindès, Francis (2009). Côte d'Ivoire since 1993: The risky reinvention of a nation. In Abdul Raufu Mustapha and Lindsay Whitfield (Eds.), *Turning points in African democracy* (31–49). London: James Currey.

——— (2000). Inégalités sociales et régulation politique en Côte d'Ivoire: La paupérisation en Côte d'Ivoire est-elle réversible? [Social inequalities and political regulation in Côte d'Ivoire: Is impoverishment reversible?]. *Politique Africaine* [*African Politics*] 2(78): 126–141.

Akindès, Francis, and Moussa Fofana (2011). Jeunesse, idéologisation de la notion de patrie et dynamique conflictuelle en Côte d'Ivoire [Youth, homeland ideology, and conflict dynamics in Côte d'Ivoire]. In Francis Akindès (Ed.), *Côte d'Ivoire: La réinvention de soi dans la violence* [*Côte d'Ivoire: Self-reinvention in violence*] (213–250). Dakar: Council for the Development of Social Science Research in Africa (CODESRIA).

Akiyama, Cliff (2012). Understanding youth street gangs. *Journal of Emergency Nursing* 38(6): 568–570.

Banégas, Richard (2010). La politique du gbonhi: Mobilisations patriotiques, violences miliciennes et carrières militantes en Côte d'Ivoire [Gbonhi politics: Patriotic mobilisation, militia violence, and militant careers in Côte d'Ivoire]. *Genèse* 4(81): 25–44.

——— (2007). Côte d'Ivoire: Les jeunes "se lèvent en hommes": Anticolonialisme et ultranationalisme chez les jeunes patriotes d'Abidjan [Côte d'Ivoire boys becoming men: Anticolonialism and ultranationalism among the patriotic youth in Abidjan]. *Les Etudes du CERI* 137. http://spire.sciencespo.fr/hdl:/2441/dambferfb7dfprc9m2ki874b0/resources/etude137.pdf.

Baron, Stephen W. (2006). Street youth, strain theory, and crime. *Journal of Criminal Justice* 34(2): 209–223.

Bjerregaard, Beth, and Alan J. Lizotte (1995). Gun ownership and gang membership. *Journal of Criminal Law and Criminology* 86(1): 37–58.

Boumaza, Magali, and Aurélie Campana (2007). Enquêter en milieu "difficile" [Research in "difficult" environments]. *Revue Française de Science Politique* [*French Journal of Political Science*] 57(1): 5–25.

Bouquet, Christian (2005). *Géopolitique de la Côte d'Ivoire* [*Geopolitics of Côte d'Ivoire*]. Paris: Armand Colin.

Bovcon, Maja (2009). French repatriates from Côte d'Ivoire and the resilience of Françafrique. *Modern and Contemporary France* 17(3): 283–299.

Cessou, Sabine (2017). *Les "microbes" ivoiriens, séquelles de la crise* [*Ivorian "microbes": After-effects of the crisis*]. http://blog.mondediplo.net/2017-01-26-Les-microbes-ivoiriens-sequelles-de-la-crise.

Contamin, Bernard, and Yves-André Fauré (Eds.) (1990). *La bataille des entreprises publiques en Côte d'Ivoire: L'histoire d'un ajustement interne* [*The battle of public enterprises in Côte d'Ivoire: The history of an internal adjustment*]. Paris: Karthala.

Copping, Lee T., and Anne Campbell (2015). The environment and life history strategies: Neighbourhood and individual-level models. *Evolution and Human Behavior* 36(3): 182–190.

Decker, Scott H. (1996). Collective and normative features of gang violence. *Justice Quarterly* 13(2): 243–264.

De Latour, Éliane (1999). Les ghettomen: Les gangs de rue à Abidjan et à San Pédro [Ghetto men: Street gangs in Abidjan and San Pedro]. *Actes de la recherche en sciences sociales* [*Proceedings of Social Science Research*] 129(1): 68–83.

——— (2001). Du ghetto au voyage clandestin: La métaphore héroïque [Clandestine path from the ghetto: The heroic metaphor]. *Autrepart* [*Elsewhere*] 3(19): 155–176.

Deuchar, Ross (2015). Youth gangs. In James D. Wright (Ed.), *International Encyclopedia of the Social and Behavioral Sciences, Second Edition* (819–823). Oxford: Elsevier.

Diomandé, K. (1997). Finances publiques et poids des interventions de l'Etat dans l'économie ivoirienne [Public finances and state intervention in the Ivorian economy]. In Bernard Contamin and Harris Memel-Fotê (Eds.), *Le modèle ivoirien en questions: Crises, ajustements, recompositions* [*The Ivorian model in questions: Crises, adjustments, recompositions*] (109–122). Paris: Karthala.

Dukes, Richard L., Rubén O. Martinez, and Judith A. Stein (1997). Precursors and consequences of membership in youth gangs. *Youth and Society* 29(2): 139–165.

Dupéré, Véronique, Éric Lacourse, J. Douglas Willms, Frank Vitaro, and Richard E. Tremblay (2007). Affiliation to youth gang during adolescence: The interaction between childhood psychopathic tendencies and neighborhood disadvantage. *Journal of Abnormal Child Pathology* 35(6): 1035–1045.

Duruflé, Gilles (1988). *L'ajustement structurel en Afrique, Sénégal, Côte d'Ivoire* [*Structural adjustment in Africa, Senegal, Côte d'Ivoire*]. Paris: Karthala.

Ellis, Stephen (2000). Armes mystiques: Quelques éléments de réflexion à partir de la guerre du Libéria [Mystical weapons: Some thoughts from the Liberian War]. *Politique Africaine* [*African Politics*] 79: 66–82.

Ferme, Mariane C. (2001). La figure du chasseur et les chasseurs-miliciens dans le conflit sierra-léonais [Hunters and militias in the Sierra Leone conflict]. *Politique Africaine* [*African Politics*] 2(82): 119–132.

Gatti, Uberto, Richard E. Tremblay, Frank Vitaro, and Pierre McDuff (2005). Youth gangs, delinquency and drug use: A test of the selection, facilitation, and enhancement hypotheses. *Journal of Child Psychology and Psychiatry* 46(11): 1178–1190.

Hagedorn, John M. (1988). *People and folks: Gangs, crime, and underclass in Rust-Belt City*. Chicago: Lake View.

Hall, Gina Penly, Terence P. Thornberry, and Alan J. Lizotte (2006). The gang facilitation effect and neighbourhood risk: Do gangs have a stronger influence on delinquency in disadvantaged areas? In James F. Short and Lorine A. Hughes (Eds.), *Studying youth gangs* (47–61). Oxford: Altamira Press.

Hill, Karl G., James C. Howell, J. David Hawkins, and Sara R. Battin-Pearson (1999). Childhood risk factors for adolescent gang membership: Results from the

Seattle Social Development Project. *Journal of Research in Crime and Delinquency* 36(3): 300–322.

Hoffman, Danny (2011). *The war machines: Young men and violence in Sierra Leone and Liberia*. Durham: Duke University Press.

Hughes, Lorine A., and James F. Short (2015). Gangs, sociology of. In James D. Wright (Ed.), *International Encyclopedia of the Social and Behavioral Sciences*, Second Edition (592–597). Oxford: Elsevier.

Kakar, Suman (2005). Gang membership, delinquent friends and criminal family members: Determining the connections. *Journal of Gang Research* 13(1): 41–52.

Kawachi, Ichiro, Bruce P. Kennedy, and Ricard G. Wilkinson (1999). Crime: Social disorganization and deprivation. *Social Science and Medicine* 48(6): 719–731.

Klein, Malcolm W. (1995). *The American street gang*. New York: Oxford University Press.

——— (1971). *Street gangs and street workers*. Englewood Cliffs, NJ: Prentice Hall.

Klein, Malcolm W., Frank M. Weerman, and Terence P. Thornberry (2006). Street gang violence in Europe. *European Journal of Criminology* 3(4): 413–437.

Konaté, Yacouba (2003). Les enfants de la balle: De la Fesci aux mouvements de patriotes [The children of the ball: From the Fesci to the patriot movements]. *Politique Africaine* [*African Politics*] 89: 49–70.

Koné, Gnangadjomon (2012). The politics of counter-insurgency: How did the young patriots emerge in Côte d'Ivoire? In Yvan Guichaoua (Ed.), *Understanding collective political violence* (222–245). New York: Palgrave MacMillan.

——— (2011). Logiques sociales et politiques des pillages et barrages dans la crise post-électorale en Côte d'Ivoire. *Politique Africaine* [*African Politics*] 122: 145–160.

Kovats-Bernat, Christopher (2002). Negotiating dangerous fields: Pragmatic strategies for fieldwork amid violence and terror. *American Anthropologist* 104(1): 7.

Kra, Kouamé Walter (2016). Ethnography of crime in small-scale public transport hubs in Abidjan, *Les Cahiers du CELHTO* 2: 241.

Krug, Etienne G., Linda L. Dahlberg, James A. Mercy, Anthony B. Zwi, and Rafael Lozano (Eds.) (2002). *World report on violence and health*. Geneva: World Health Organization.

Lacourse, Eric, Daniel S. Nagin, Frank Vitaro, Sylvana Côté, Louise Arseneault, and Richard Ernest Tremblay (2006). Prediction of early-onset deviant peer group affiliation: A 12-year longitudinal study. *Archives of General Psychiatry* 63: 562–568.

Lan, David (1985). *Guns and rain: Guerrillas and spirit mediums in Zimbabwe*. London: James Currey and Berkeley: University of California Press.

Le Blanc, Guillaume (2009). *L'invisibilité sociale*. Paris: Presses Universitaire de France.

Le Pape, Marc, and Claudine Vidal (Eds.) (2002). *Côte d'Ivoire: L'année terrible 1999–2000* [Côte d'Ivoire: *The terrible year of 1999–2000*]. Paris: Karthala.

Marie, Alain (1997). L'insécurité urbaine [Urban insecurity]. In Georges Hérault and Pius Adesanmi (Eds.), *Youth, street culture and urban violence*. (413–417). Ibadan, Nigeria: French Institute for Research in Africa.

Marshall-Fratani, Ruth (2006). The war of "who is who": Autochthony, nationalism, and citizenship in the Ivorian crisis. *African Studies Review* 49(2): 9–44.

Marut, Jean-Claude (2010). *Le conflit de Casamance: Ce que disent les armes* [*The conflict in Casamance: What the weapons say*]. Paris: Karthala.

Matlon, Jordanna (2011). Il est garçon: Marginal Abidjanais masculinity and the politics of representation. *Poetics* 39(5): 380–406.

McGovern, Michael (2011). *Making War in Côte d'Ivoire*. Chicago: University of Chicago Press.

Meddings, David R., Lyndee M. Knox, Matilde Maddaleno, Alberto Concha-Eastman, and Joan Serra Hoffman (2005). World Health Organisation's TEACH-VIP: Contributing to capacity building for youth violence prevention. *American Journal of Preventive Medicine* 29(5): 259–265.

Miran-Guyon, Marie (2015). *Guerres mystiques en Côte d'Ivoire: Religion, patriotism, violence (2002–2013)* [*Mystic wars in Côte d'Ivoire: Religion, patriotism, violence*] (87–92). Paris: Karthala.

Newell, Sasha (2012). *The modernity bluff: Crime, consumption, and citizenship in Côte d'Ivoire*. Chicago: Chicago University Press.

——— (2009a). Godrap girls, draou boys, and the sexual economy of the bluff in Abidjan, Côte d'Ivoire. *Ethnos: Journal of Anthropology* 74(3): 379–402.

——— (2009b). Registering modernity, bluffing criminality: How Nouchi speech reinvented (and fractured) the nation. *Journal of Linguistic Anthropology* 19(2): 157–184.

O'Brien, Kate, Michael Daffern, Chi Meng Chu, and Stuart D.M. Thomas (2013). Youth gang affiliation, violence, and criminal activities: A review of motivational, risk, and protective factors. *Aggression and Violent Behavior* 18(4): 417–425.

Papachristos, Andrew V., and Sandy Y. Zhao (2015). Crime: Organized. In James D. Wright (Ed.), *International Encyclopedia of the Social and Behavioral Sciences*, Second Edition (170–175). Oxford: Elsevier.

RGPH: Recensement général de la population et de l'habitat [General Census of Population and Housing] (2014). *Résultats globaux*. Abidjan: Institut National de la Statistique [National Institute of Statistics]. Retrieved from www.ins.ci/n/resultats%20globaux.pdf.

Royer, Patrick (2003). La guerre coloniale du Bani-Volta, 1915–1916 (Burkina Faso, Mali) [The colonial war of Bani-Volta, 1915–1916 (Burkina Faso, Mali)]. *Autrepart* [*Elsewhere*] 2(26): 35–51.

Sampson, Robert J. (2012). *Great American City: Chicago and the enduring neighborhood effect*. Chicago: University of Chicago Press.

Sampson, Robert J., and W. Byron Groves (1989). Community structure and crime: Testing socio-organizational theory. *American Journal of Sociology* 94(4): 774–802.

Schatzberg, Michael G. (2000). La sorcellerie comme mode de causalité [Witchcraft as a mode of causality]. *Politique Africaine* [*African Politics*] 3(79): 33–47.

Shaw, Clifford R., and Henry D. McKay (1931) *Social factors in juvenile delinquency: Report on the causes of crime*, Volume 2. Washington, DC: National Commission on Law Observance and Enforcement.

Spergel, Irving A. (1995). *The youth gang problem*. New York: Oxford University Press.

St. Cyr, Jenna L., and Scott H. Decker (2003). Girls, guys, and gangs: Convergence or divergence in the gendered construction of gangs and groups. *Journal of Criminal Justice* 31(5): 423–433.

Strauss, Scott (2011). "It's sheer horror here": Patterns of violence during the first four months of the Côte d'Ivoire post-electoral crisis. *African Affairs* 110(440): 481–489.

Stretesky, Paul B., and Mark R. Pogrebin (2007). Gang-related gun violence: Socialization, identity, and self. *Journal of Contemporary Ethnography* 36(1): 85–114.

Suttles, Gerald D. (1972). *The social construction of communities*. Chicago: University of Chicago Press.

Thornberry, Terence P. (1987). Toward an interactional theory of delinquency. *Criminology* 25(4): 863–892.

Thornberry, Terence P., Marvin D. Krohn, Alan J. Lizotte, and Deborah Chard-Wierschem (1993). The role of juvenile gangs in facilitating delinquent behavior. *Journal of Research in Crime and Delinquency* 30(1): 55–87.

Thrasher, Frederic Milton (1927). *The gang: A study of 1,313 gangs in Chicago*. Chicago: University of Chicago Press.

Touré, Ismaila, and N'Guessan Kouamé (1994). La violence urbaine en Côte d'Ivoire [Urban violence in Côte d'Ivoire]. In Eghosa E. Osaghae, Ismaila Touré, N'Guessan Kouamé, Isaac Olawale Albert, and Jinmi Adisa (Eds.), *Urban violence in Africa: Pilot studies (South Africa, Côte d'Ivoire, Nigeria)* (59–108). Ibadan, Nigeria: French Institute for Research in Africa.

Vigil, James (1996). Street baptism: Chicago gang initiation. *Human Organization* 55(2): 149–153.

Watkins, Adam M., and Terrance J. Taylor (2016). The prevalence, predictors, and criminogenic effect of joining a gang among urban, suburban, and rural youth. *Journal of Criminal Justice* 47: 133–142.

Wood, Elisabeth Jean (2006). The ethical challenges of field research in conflict zones. *Qualitative Sociology* 29(3): 373–386.

Wood, Jane, and Emma Alleyne (2010). Street gang theory and research: Where are we now, and where do we go from here? *Aggression and Violent Behavior* 15(2): 100–111.

World Bank Group (2017). *Situation économique en Côte d'Ivoire, le défi des compétences: Pourquoi la Côte d'Ivoire doit réformer son système éducatif* [*The economic situation in Côte d'Ivoire: The challenge of skill in reforming the education system*]. Abidjan: World Bank Group.

10 Preventing violence in Cape Town

The public-health approach

Sam Lloyd and Richard Matzopoulos

Introduction

Worldwide, interpersonal violence is responsible for a wide array of detrimental effects on health and development. The places that bear the brunt of these violence-related harms, which include an estimated 1.6 million lives lost annually, are low- and middle-income countries (Krug et al. 2002). Among these, South Africa has particularly high levels of violence, with a 2009 homicide rate of 38.4 per 100,000 population—roughly six times the estimated 2010 global average of 5.91 per 100,000 population (IHME 2017; Matzopoulos et al. 2015). Within the country, there are wide disparities in rates of violence between regions, cities, and metropolitan areas.

The public-health approach to violence prevention identified a number of well-known risk factors and also several protective factors. These are best understood in terms of the socio-ecological model of human health and development. According to this conceptual model, individuals are embedded within interactive systems at multiple levels. The causes and consequences of interpersonal violence arise from the complex interplay of processes at four different levels: individual, microsystem, exosystem, and macrosystem (Ward et al. 2012). We describe each of these levels below.

At the individual level, known risk and protective factors (for becoming either a perpetrator or a victim of violence) include biological factors such as age and sex (Matzopoulos et al. 2010), mental illness or impairment (Corrigall and Matzopoulos 2012; Moffitt 1993; Raine 2002), and behavioural factors such as the use of alcohol or other drugs (King et al. 2004; Corrigall and Matzopoulos 2012).

The microsystem level relates to contexts such as family, school, and peer groups, where daily interactions occur, and that most shape an individual's behaviour (Ward et al. 2012). For example, family-related factors that can cause a child to later exhibit violent behaviour include low socioeconomic status, child abuse, and low family cohesion. Peer group-related factors include having violent friends (Butchart et al. 2004) and being involved in gang activities (Ward et al. 2012).

Next, the exosystem level comprises the contexts that shape the lives of families, such as neighbourhoods, extended families and social networks, socioeconomic factors, and the availability of legal and security services such as police protection. Factors at this level that negatively affect violence prevention include low levels of social cohesion, little social support, socioeconomic inequality at the neighbourhood level, and poor provision of services such as health, education, and social assistance (Matzopoulos et al. 2010; Ward et al. 2012). As well, some characteristics of the urban environment also shape the incidence and nature of violence; these include the design of urban space, and the physical and social infrastructure for providing services.

Finally, the macrosystem is composed of structural factors and processes such as sociocultural norms and ideologies, government policies, and wider socioeconomic influences (Ward et al. 2012). Contributory factors to violence at this level include gender and social norms that support violence (Krug et al. 2002), economic inequality (Wilkinson and Pickett 2010), the availability of firearms (Matzopoulos et al. 2010), and migration and urbanisation patterns (Burton et al. 2004; UNODC 2005). Figure 10.1 illustrates the four levels and their interaction with one another.

In recent years, with the goal of achieving sustained reductions in the incidence of violence, there has been a renewed focus on wider contextual factors (known as "upstream" factors, which act primarily at the exosystem and macrosystem levels) rather than on the more immediate "downstream" factors (CSDH 2008). However, while some types of interventions show great promise for achieving that goal, there is currently a dearth of evidence to support

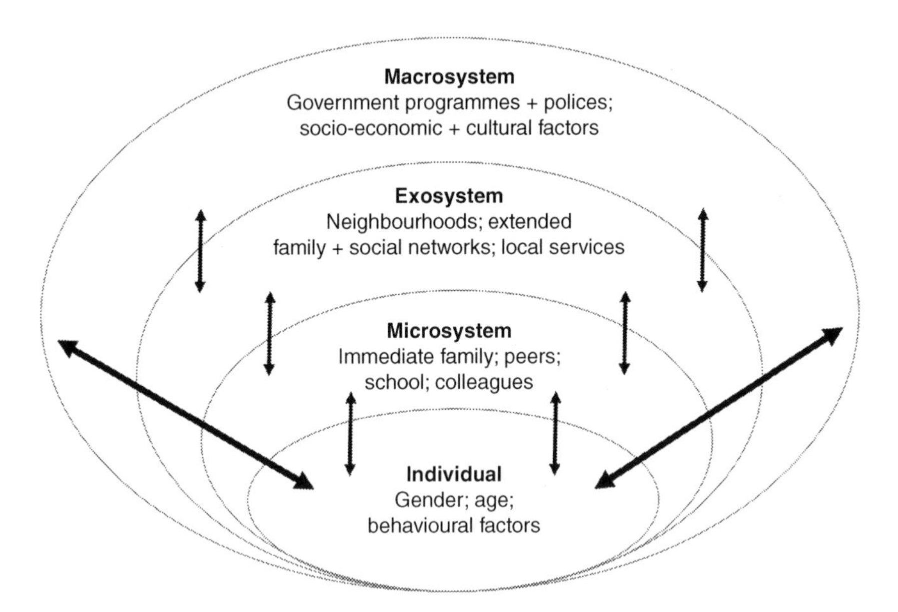

Figure 10.1 Ecological model for understanding and preventing violence
Source: Based on a diagram from Ward et al. (2012).

their use. The effectiveness of these interventions, which target the social determinants of violence at the structural level (such as unemployment, low education levels, low incomes, and the misuse of alcohol and other drugs), is difficult to quantify—mainly due to the difficulty of directly attributing to them any observed changes in violence rates. Stronger evidence is available for the effectiveness of interventions concentrated at the downstream level, which are more amenable to evaluation. The main reason for this is their more easily measurable targets, since these interventions have fewer interacting determinants of effectiveness to address. Consequently, despite its having less promise for large-scale changes in violence rates, the scientific literature is significantly biased towards downstream programming (Matzopoulos et al. 2010).

However, that limited evidence of effectiveness has not stopped urban upgrading in Cape Town from targeting multiple upstream factors. That strategy is included in two important initiatives: the new White Paper on Safety and Security (Civilian Secretariat for Police 2016), and the decade-old Violence Prevention through Urban Upgrading (VPUU) programme, established in 2006.

Conceptual framework: the public-health approach

In this chapter, our aim is to assess the feasibility of applying a public-health approach to the evaluation of such urban upgrading interventions in the context of Cape Town's township areas. Focusing particularly on the quality and suitability of the data available, we begin by describing the public-health approach, and how we used it in our research (which was ongoing at the time of writing). We also discuss the problems we encountered and how we adapted the approach in order to apply it successfully.

Evaluating upstream interventions

To evaluate interventions, the public-health approach is based largely on the quantitative paradigm (Williams et al. 2015) and focuses on how effective the intervention is at achieving its chosen outcomes. Research to determine *whether* an intervention did (or did not) work usually precedes the task of establishing *why*: the former would rely more heavily on quantitative approaches, the latter on qualitative.

The public-health approach comprises a well-established hierarchy of evidence (Rychetnik et al. 2002) with rigorous studies designed to approximate experimental conditions. Such studies randomly select and measure two groups to assess all factors that are relevant to the outcome. One group, the study group, receives the intervention; the other, the control group, does not. The study then follows the two groups over the same period of time. Any changes to the outcome are assumed to be attributable to the intervention, since that was the only difference between the groups. For this reason, randomised controlled trials (RCTs) are considered the "gold standard" of social science research.

The randomisation aspect—assigning individuals to either an intervention or a control group—is designed to create groups that are, on average, the same in terms of all factors other than exposure to the intervention. The goal of this is the lowest amount of bias in the results (Williams et al. 2015). However, conducting a RCT is not always feasible. In the real world, when action often arises naturally in response to local concerns, frequently an intervention has already been adopted when the study begins or an intervention group is selected in a non-randomised way. The public-health researcher must then consider alternative study designs. Among these, the *controlled before–after study* is considered the most robust.

This quasi-experimental type of study involves observing the outcome of interest, in our case the incidence of violence, both before and after the intervention. Since there is no formal ready-made control group, researchers create a sample of individuals, groups, or areas that did not receive the intervention. The first step in such research is obviously to decide which outcomes to use to measure violence prevention, and what indicators to use for the intervention. With these two components in place, a simple analysis tells researchers whether the intervention "worked". Using the VPUU initiative as an example, we could simply compare the changes in violence rates in areas exposed to the intervention with other areas (the "control" areas) that were not exposed.

But of course, research involving complex socio-ecological problems is rarely that simple. We must also understand the interrelationship of violence with a wide range of other factors, including the intervention. We need not only to measure its effect on the outcomes, we must also consider the effect of *intervening factors* that could affect the association. These numerous risk factors must also be controlled in the analysis, using statistical methods that allow us to isolate and measure the true effect. This is an extremely difficult task for interventions at the upstream level, because to definitively attribute any outcome to the intervention we would need to control for "the whole of society". This explains the relatively weak evidence for such holistic interventions, compared to the rather stronger evidence for more directed downstream interventions that are less affected by extraneous factors.

For example, if we observed that the high incidence of violence in a community was reduced over the same time period that a particular intervention was taking place, we might be tempted to attribute the reduction to the intervention. However, that might be a mistake. The intervention may, in fact, have simply *coincided* with some unrelated factor in the community: a vast increase in police presence perhaps or improved employment and recreational opportunities for young people. Those might be the true causes of the decrease; but since no one was looking at those factors, the intervention got the credit. The impact of an intervention in a community may also be greatly enhanced if it is implemented alongside other changes or initiatives, such as improved community cohesion. In other situations, it may work only for some groups (such as young people, or men), and not for others. Therefore it is important to identify concurrent interventions and measure the factors that we know are most likely to affect violence rates. That strategy allows us to rule out any alternative explanations for the associations we observe, and to better understand potential causal mechanisms.

Putting the public-health approach into practice

In order to control for the effect of intervening factors, we need to be able to identify and measure them. To do this, we develop indicators for each one, and they must meet three key requirements:

- validity: they must accurately measure whatever they are meant to measure
- reliability: they must measure consistently over time
- availability: the measurement data should be available for the entire period of the research.

A further challenge is examining the area-level effects on outcomes that are usually measured at the individual or household level. This is often the case with research on the effects of urban upgrading, since those effects occur differently in different spaces. For this reason, it is important that the basic geographic building blocks of the analysis be defined in terms of their *spatial resolution*—that is, the size of the area that will have the most meaning in terms of the research. The most commonly used area borders, for the sake of convenience, are usually official administrative boundaries. Nevertheless, the indicators chosen should be as fine-grained as possible so that they can be adapted for different levels of outcome (individual, group, or area). This allows researchers to explore the relationships between various factors, and the various ways an intervention might affect different segments of the population.

The theory may be relatively straightforward; but putting this approach into practice—actually collecting and incorporating all the various indicators—is where difficulties arise. This is why there is such a dearth of evidence for programmes that target multiple upstream risk factors.

Evaluating urban upgrading in Cape Town

In 2013, we began our research to evaluate urban upgrading programmes in three Cape Town communities: Khayelitsha, Gugulethu, and Nyanga. Our goal was to examine the VPUU in terms of its impact on community safety, using the public-health approach. In the following sections, we outline our strategies for putting this approach into practice, including the key challenges we faced and the ways we adapted the methodology to a real-world, low-income setting. Our initial outputs and early research findings provide an initial assessment of the relevance and feasibility of this approach.

The research context

Disparities in violence and crime levels are nowhere better exemplified than in Cape Town, South Africa's most violent city. The distribution of interpersonal violence there follows the geography of inequality, coinciding with differences in income and living standards: it is chiefly concentrated in the predominantly black and coloured townships.

Khayelitsha, Gugulethu, and Nyanga are three such communities. Originally designed as settlements for Cape Town's black workforce, under the government policy of apartheid, Nyanga was founded in 1948, neighbouring Gugulethu in 1958, and nearby Khayelitsha in 1983. The settlements are located between 15 and 30 kilometres from the centre of Cape Town, and are separated from it by several natural and man-made buffer zones. Since their inception, these areas have been underserved in terms of infrastructure, education, and other basic services. They have always been deprived areas and sites for political repression and violence—in stark comparison to the high standard of living and the relative security experienced elsewhere by the ruling white minority (Besteman 2008). While some efforts have been made, since the end of apartheid in 1994, to redress those historic inequalities, today all three of our study communities remain characterised by high levels of a range of well-established risk factors for violence. These include:

- abuse of alcohol and other substances (Peer et al. 2014)
- mental-health problems (Havenaar et al. 2008)
- family breakdown
- unemployment
- limited services and infrastructure
- unrestricted access to firearms
- negative gender roles that equate the use of violence with masculinity (Matzopoulos et al. 2010; Ward et al. 2012)
- inadequate policing (O'Regan and Pikoli 2014).

Another element in the communities is the recent proliferation of shack-dwellers in informal settlements, the result of high levels of inward migration. This new trend has only exacerbated the stress placed on local services. Taken together, all these factors have resulted in homicide rates that are double Cape Town's average and among the highest in the country. These three townships are almost a "perfect storm" of urban deprivation and violence. (For an illustration of what daily life can be like in such a community, see Nomfundo's story, below.)

Nomfundo's Story

Nomfundo, 35, has lived in Khayelitsha since 1996. She and her mother (who has since died) came to Cape Town more than 20 years ago, immediately after the country's first democratic elections in 1994. The two women were part of a massive internal migration to the cities by rural people, who previously under apartheid had been confined to impoverished *bantustans*—small settlements situated in remote and marginally agricultural lands. At that time, Khayelitsha was an informal community built in a wetland, some 30 kilometres from the city centre, and connected to it by a single railway line.

Nomfundo married in her late teens, and now lives with her husband, Mzolisi, and her three children—aged 16, 10, and 3—in a shack built out of scrap wood and bits of corrugated iron. Every winter, when the rains come, their home is flooded. Electricity is limited, and the family shares toilet facilities and a water pump with 30 other households.

She survives on a child care grant, plus her earnings from her part-time job as a domestic worker in the wealthy suburb of Constantia. To get there from Khayelitsha, Nomfundo must travel for an hour and a half every morning via train, minibus taxi, and by foot. In the evenings, on the return journey, she sometimes does not make it back to her settlement until after dark. Her route home takes her across an area of unlit wasteland notorious for muggings and sexual assaults, though so far she has been lucky.

Early in their marriage, her husband turned out to be a bad lot, with a taste for drinking and petty crime. When this escalated to armed robbery, he was caught and sentenced to serve time in Pollsmoor Prison. Recently released, he is unable to find work, so he has returned to his former lifestyle. Most nights he can be found in the local *shebeen*, spending his "earnings" on alcohol for himself and his friends. When he returns home drunk, he and Nomfundo frequently argue. Sometimes the argument escalates into a fight, and he beats her. Twice in the past year, Nomfundo has had to visit Khayelitsha hospital to have her injuries treated.

The intervention

Recognising the multi-faceted nature of violence in these areas, in 2013, the Western Cape provincial government launched its Integrated Provincial Violence Prevention Policy Framework. It adopted an intersectoral, whole-of-society approach that emphasised the importance of comprehensively targeting high-risk areas. Its aim was to move beyond mere law enforcement and use evidence-based interventions to address the wider social determinants of crime. These interventions included:

- infrastructural improvements
- the modification of public space
- the provision of after-school activities for children
- the development of life skills for youths
- long-term societal and structural interventions.

The long-term initiatives included interventions such as early childhood development programmes, economic development programmes, and measures to counter the social and cultural norms that support violence (Cassidy et al. 2015; Matzopoulos and Myers 2014).

In Cape Town, the city's flagship VPUU programme encapsulates the whole-of-society approach. Restructuring the urban environment is a key aspect, encompassing easier access to basic amenities and social services. Among its elements are the urban planning principles known as Crime Prevention through Environmental Design (CPTED). These focus on reducing the opportunities for individuals to commit crimes by a number of methods, including:

- promoting formal and informal surveillance
- constructing safe public spaces, infrastructure, and facilities, and engaging community ownership of these
- developing and strengthening physical barriers to crime
- enhancing area aesthetics to encourage feelings of safety and neighbourhood pride.

For example, one of the VPUU's key innovations is a series of "active boxes", small community buildings situated on major pedestrian routes in dangerous areas. These are used both as spaces of sanctuary for individuals who feel threatened or endangered, and for surveillance of the surrounding area and its activities by a caretaker and civic patrol groups. Other examples include the creation of well-lit pedestrian walkways between main activity centres, and the construction of "live-work units", mixed-use buildings with a business on the ground floor and a housing unit above. This combination enhances occupation of space throughout the day, and also has the desirable effect of increasing the number of "eyes on the street".

To facilitate civic engagement and community cohesion, these strategies are carried out in consultation and in partnership with the community affected: a cornerstone of the intervention is encouraging community members to volunteer. Other long-term social-development strategies try to:

- increase adult employment
- provide early childhood development programmes, with the goal of preventing young people from becoming involved in crime and violence

- support victims of crime
- construct new recreational and cultural facilities, such as a library and sports grounds (Cassidy et al. 2015).

Evaluating VPUU

The first step in our evaluation approach was to determine the basic geographic building blocks for the analysis. Urban upgrading is never applied quite equally all throughout a target community; certain areas always receive a greater share of the investment. The hypothesis is that the intervention will measurably affect the rate of violence at the neighbourhood level. In the Khayelitsha, Gugulethu, and Nyanga townships, we relied on community-defined areas that were small enough to detect the differential application of the intervention. Residents of the neighbourhoods participated in defining the boundaries, which differed slightly from the more commonly used political and jurisdictional borders (such as census zones). We felt that our boundaries would not suffer the limitations of the official kind: poor coherence and lack of recognition by the residents. Rather, they reflected the actual lived experience of each neighbourhood and had the added benefit of enhancing the homogeneity of area-level constructs of interest.

We also had to overcome the issue of incorporating data sources that did not follow our spatial framework. To this end, our geographic information systems (GIS) specialists devised innovative methods to allow us to aggregate our own primary data with higher-level data such as census enumeration areas, police precinct boundaries, and the like.

With this geographic framework in place, the next step was to select constructs and indicators to measure three vital elements:

- outcomes
- interventions
- intervening factors.

This was done in accordance with the key requirements indicated earlier: validity, reliability, and availability. To these was added the fourth factor of their *spatial resolution*. Those elements are each described in detail below.

Outcomes

A major problem with international research into violence prevention, particularly in developing countries, is the lack of data available on the actual incidence of violence. This is particularly true at the neighbourhood level, where systems for surveillance are usually lacking (Dahlberg and Butchart 2005). Studies must frequently rely on official data sources, which are generally of substandard quality, or on inferior proxies such as changes in local knowledge or attitudes (Dahlberg and Butchart 2005; Matzopoulos et al. 2010).

To select our outcome measures, we began by reviewing what was currently available from routine sources such as police crime statistics. These are a commonly used source of data on violence, but they are beset with problems. Most importantly, they represent only crimes reported to the police. This was an issue of particular salience in our study context, since the Khayelitsha Commission—established, coincidentally, at the same time as our research project, and tasked with investigating police inefficiency and the breakdown in police-community relations—found that only about 60 per cent of crimes were reported. In fact, this phenomenon is common in high-violence settings (Levitt 1998). As well, when these crime data are released in South Africa, they are aggregated to the police-precinct level, which makes specific neighbourhood-level effects difficult to ascertain. These two shortcomings meant that the data were not considered valid or reliable enough for our purposes, nor did they provide sufficient spatial resolution.

Another data source is the homicide statistics of the Forensic Pathology Service (FPS), which do meet the criteria of reliability and validity. However, the numbers involved are too small to be an accurate indicator of changes in violence at the neighbourhood level, and over such a relatively short time period. As well, given the fact that the subject is deceased, little contextual information is available. To address these shortcomings, we collected data from two original sources.

- Three surveys conducted between 2013 and 2015 that described the characteristics of more than 3500 Khayelitsha households, each of which was geocoded to a specific location in the study area.
- A series of biannual, cross-sectional studies of all trauma patients seen in the casualty departments of six health facilities located in Khayelitsha, Gugulethu, and Nyanga, over a one-week period. Data collected, through interviews, included the cause of injury (whether violence or a traffic accident) and, if the cause was violence, information about the perpetrator, whether either party had used alcohol or drugs, and the time and location of the injury.

These primary sources offer several advantages. They allowed us to collect data on a far wider range of violent outcomes than would otherwise be possible, painting a more detailed picture of our study context. This enhanced our understanding of potential differences in the effect of VPUU across different categories. They also enabled us to collect data on incidents not captured by official statistics—since, as indicated earlier, only 44 per cent of violent incidents involving strangers, and 49 per cent involving family members, were reported to the police. Similarly, only 48 per cent of reported incidents required a hospital visit (Cassidy et al. 2015)—hence the limitation of relying on hospital statistics alone.

A third advantage is that multiple forms of data allowed us to triangulate the results, thereby improving the validity of the estimates. Combined with other factors—the geocoding process in the community survey, the self-reporting of injury locations, and the more meaningful neighbourhood boundaries—we were able to analyse the effects of violence with a higher degree of accuracy than was previously possible. Overall, we believe that these benefits outweigh any potential inaccuracies in the self-reported data. The combination of all these activities enabled us to develop a solid set of outcome indicators for our study areas.

With regard to the nature of violence, the results of the cross-sectional studies of trauma patients offer a number of insights. The most common types of violent injury found, in descending order, were interpersonal violence, crime-related violence, and gang-related violence. Furthermore, as expected, violence differed in many important ways between men and women. The overwhelming majority of people presenting at health facilities with injuries were male, since men are most likely to suffer violence at the hands of other community members, who frequently use weapons such as knives. Women, in contrast, are most commonly injured by a spouse or partner—and the use of a weapon is less frequent (Mureithi et al. 2016). These results highlight the importance of disaggregating data by violence category, gender, and other factors.

In terms of our main research question, early findings indicate that the incidence of violence (along with other key outcomes, such as depression) is lower in areas that received the VPUU intervention than in those that did not. These findings offer hope that, at least to some degree, the intervention has been successful in achieving its goal.

However, a significant drawback of our sources is the fact that, in some areas, the intervention had already started by the time we commenced data collection. It is therefore not possible for us to determine whether the lower levels of violence in those areas reflect changes due to the intervention or simply pre-existing circumstances. To counter this, a key adaptation of our evaluation approach has been to use an additional source: robbery data, which dates back to 2002. This can be used as a proxy for violence and crime to determine whether there were any differences between the intervention and non-intervention areas in the preceding period. Should the temporality criteria be satisfied, we will use the robbery data to test for a *displacement effect* (or alternatively a *diffusion of benefits effect*). We will examine whether reductions in violence in the intervention areas have the negative result of a higher rate of violence in the surrounding areas or, conversely, whether they have the positive effect of a diffusion of benefits there.

Interventions

Although our early findings, as described above, indicated that violence levels are lower in intervention areas than in other locations, this analysis does not take into account the complexity of the VPUU programme or the differing degrees to which it has been implemented. The fact is that this programme of urban upgrading is not one single unit that can be clearly observed and measured, but rather a wide array of projects and activities of various sizes, functions, and scope. This means that we cannot simply treat all VPUU-affected areas as the same if we want to gain a true understanding of the intervention's impact.

To deal with this complexity, the first step in our measurement process was to determine the relative size of each individual component of the intervention at different points in time. This involved two elements:

- Scrutinising financial records to assess the level of financial investment in each component—on the assumption that the amount of money spent is directly correlated with the level of exposure.
- Calculating the level of each component's functionality (that is, the degree to which its capacity was exploited). We derived these qualitative data through discussions with VPUU staff based on criteria specific to the component.

With the relative *size* of each component of the intervention in place, the second step was to determine its relative *reach* or geographic footprint. Plotting each project on the map allowed us to determine its physical location, but this alone did not tell us the full story. To a greater or lesser extent, a project's influence always tends to extend beyond its physical boundaries. For example, the effect of the aforementioned "active boxes" on resident safety and violence reduction is relatively localised. In contrast, a library, which serves the wider community, may affect safety and violence levels both locally (by increased pedestrian traffic through its neighbourhood), and over a much wider geographical area. It accomplishes this through the educational and social benefits it provides to the community at large.

To establish the reach, or geographic footprint, of each project, we used a mixed-method approach. This included discussions with VPUU staff in charge of each project to determine its "catchment area" and using maps to analyse the relative positions of other projects with similar functions and transport links (such as roads and bus networks). We will combine the information derived from these different sources with the goal of developing accurate geographic footprints. This information on the size of each project's reach made it possible for us to quantify the *degree* of exposure to the intervention of each sub-area, a great improvement on the former simplified binary (intervention or no intervention) approach. By creating a more realistic picture of the intervention, this approach increases the validity of our results. It also allows for the possibility of further analyses based on different categories and combinations of projects. If combined, we hope the results of all these analyses might shed some light not only on the overall impact of the intervention, but also on how these effects occur.

Early results point to the benefits of this more refined approach. Our analyses, which defined sub-areas only in terms of whether or not they had ever been intervention sites, showed that the size of the intervention effect was significantly dampened. But when we scrutinised more closely, it became clear that some sub-areas had received the intervention only to a small degree, with limited functionality; therefore, we would not have expected it to have a significant effect. Yet when we removed these areas from the intervention group, the effect sizes were inflated. Both these situations indicate the importance of careful measurement and of correctly classifying the intervention and control areas. This also provides evidence for the idea that VPUU is effective when fully implemented, but that implementation is not always possible in all sites. There may be, for instance, certain factors that allow the VPUU to succeed in some communities, but not in others (where perhaps the intervention ended prematurely or never reached a reasonable level of functionality).

Finally, our approach highlights the importance of working with the implementers to evaluate complex interventions. Such partnerships offer researchers a wealth of data not otherwise available. It is also vital to incorporate both qualitative and quantitative methods as part of the measurement process.

Intervening factors

In an ideal research world, we would be able to develop indicators for every construct of interest; but in the real world, projects face considerable constraints of time and resources. The pragmatic requirement of time-relevant data with suitable spatial resolution, plus our discussions with key stakeholders and experts, led us to consider four thematic domains for our intervening factors:

- urban upgrading
- economic and human development
- alcohol
- safety and security.

We considered many other factors that might well have had an impact on violence, but we excluded them for various reasons. Either they were too difficult to measure reliably, or it would have taken us too long to see the results, such as changing cultural and gender norms, early child development programmes, and youth development initiatives. Having reduced the list to four factors, we describe each in detail below.

Urban upgrading

VPUU is only one of many governmental and non-governmental agencies that have the goal of improving the physical and social environment in Cape Town's low-income communities. Others work to deliver better housing, services, and infrastructural and social programmes. These efforts need to be measured concomitantly to isolate any additional effects of the VPUU. Unfortunately, we were unsuccessful in our attempts to acquire data on programme spending from those other agencies, which would have allowed us to disaggregate the temporal and spatial elements. So we reoriented our methodological approach to measure just the infrastructural aspects, using aerial photographs of the study area (including control communities), before and after the VPUU intervention. Going forward, this will allow us to identify changes in the urban environment over time.

Economic and human development

Not all individuals are equally likely to become either a perpetrator or a victim of violence: a range of biological, behavioural, socioeconomic, and cultural factors influence both possibilities. As indicated earlier, these risk and protective factors include age and gender. (A gendered approach was necessary for us, given that nearly all factors of interest are shaped to some degree by prevailing norms and power relations.) Also a factor is an individual's mental health, and their position in the community in terms of social cohesion and social capital. As well, poverty, low socioeconomic status (SES), and other deprivations negatively affect the incidence of violence (Matzopoulos et al. 2010). However, precisely measuring these constructs can be challenging. In South Africa, typical proxies for SES such as income and expenditure are considered to be of poor quality, since economic resources are usually shared within extended families and communities. As well, low SES often correlates poorly with formal education, given the historical under-resourcing of the education system for disenfranchised populations (Myer et al. 2004). In addition, economic and human deprivation affects SES characteristics at all levels: individuals, households, neighbourhoods, and communities.

For this domain, we developed multi-level indicators from a range of sources. These provided a finely detailed elucidation of poverty, and the different ways the socioeconomic landscape impacts on safety. They also allowed us to explore the relationships with other factors.

At the individual and household level, we used SES measures from community surveys, such as employment status, household economic contribution, and the education and assets of all household members. Other measures were self-reported social status, housing quality, and neighbourhood-level deprivation. To bolster measures of the last factor we used the South African Indices of Multiple Deprivation (constructed by the Centre for the Analysis of South African Social Policy). It measures deprivation across four domains at the individual level:

- income and material status (that is, having the basic necessities for an acceptable standard of living)
- employment status
- education status
- living environment (Noble et al. 2013).

As our understanding of the study environment evolved, informed by preliminary results, we were able to include a more nuanced measurement of mental health (and access to mental-health care). We also included additional measures of social capital and social cohesion to complement other projects within the Safe and Inclusive Cities programme.

Alcohol

Alcohol has long been known as a risk factor for interpersonal violence. This is true both for perpetrators—through heightened levels of disinhibition and aggression while intoxicated, particularly for men (Parry and Dewing 2006; Matzopoulos et al. 2010)—and for victims, due to the lowering of cognitive perception and motor coordination. This makes them more vulnerable to interpersonal and sexual violence (Matzopoulos et al. 2010; King et al. 2004). In some cases, individuals might be both victims and perpetrators. We heard many anecdotal reports of patrons leaving alcohol outlets being at increased risk of robbery or assault on their way home, and, once they arrived there, at increased risk of being perpetrators of domestic violence.

We developed alcohol-related indicators to measure its demand, supply, consumption and access, the harms associated with its use, and policy enforcement, including community members' perceptions of proposed policy initiatives. Most of the data were derived from our primary collection tools, in conjunction with a few secondary sources. Early results demonstrated the importance of these indicators. Alcohol was strongly implicated as a contributory factor to violence in the community survey; and, in health facilities, alcohol use was reported in over half of all violent injuries (Mureithi et al. 2016). We measured access to alcohol by including questions in the community survey, and we also mapped liquor outlets in a separate survey. It recorded characteristics such as capacity, operating hours, and type of outlet (onsite or off-site consumption, licensed or unlicensed). This information will provide the basis for an improved method of measuring access by incorporating a wider range of factors than existing methods.

Safety and security

The police and the courts are the standard tools employed by the state to control crime and violence. We aimed to develop indicators for relative security, whether provided by the police, private security firms, or community-based initiatives. Thanks to the Khayelitsha Commission mentioned earlier, we were able to access data on staff allocations for local police precincts (O'Regan and Pikoli 2014) and this, combined with salary data for the staffing complements, provided a relative measure of police presence. (We were unable to obtain more detailed information on resource allocation by any of the other agencies involved in security provision.)

A final note

Tables 10.1 to 10.5 attempt to illustrate the issues described in this chapter, and to summarise the indicators we used in our research so far (or will use going forward). The tables are arranged according to variable type: the first is *outcomes*, and this is followed by our four main *intervening factor* themes (as described earlier):

- urban upgrading
- economic and human development
- alcohol
- safety and security.

The information presented in separate columns for each indicator relates to:

- the construct: the type of outcome or intervening factor that needs to be measured
- the indicator(s) selected to measure the construct
- the data source for the indicator(s)
- the availability of data (what years and phases we could obtain)
- the measurement level for the indicator: area, household, individual, or a combination of these
- the spatial resolution, or geography, of the indicator—such as police precincts, or sub-areas of the VPUU programme
- the limitations of the indicator.

The range of indicators for which we collected data, the variety of sources we used, and the limitations they present all emphasise the complexity of the task of evaluating urban upgrading interventions and the difficulties inherent in the process.

Table 10.1 Outcomes

Construct	*Indicator*	*Source*	*Availability*	*Level*	*Geography*	*Limitations*
Violence and crime	Household experience of violence	Community household survey (CHS)	3 phases (2013–2015)	Household or area	Small areas delineated by VPUU	• Self-report
	Violent injuries	Cross-sectional studies of trauma patients	6 phases (every 6 months since 2013)	Area	VPUU	• Geocoded only to small areas
	Homicide	Forensic Pathology Service	July 2012	Area	Geocoded	• Access to data complicated; small caseloads
Mental health, including depression	Measurements of depression: Center for Epidemiological Studies Depression, 10-item scale	CHS	3 phases (2013–2015)	Household or area	VPUU	• Self-report
	Experience of mental-health problems, plus treatment	CHS	2 phases (2014–2015)	Household or area	VPUU	• Self-report

Source: Lloyd and Matzopoulos (2017).

Table 10.2 Urban upgrading

Construct	*Indicator*	*Source*	*Availability*	*Level*	*Geography*	*Limitations*
VPUU infrastructure development	Construction and maintenance expenditure; area of influence	Financial budgets, reports, VPUU staff	Since 2009	Area	VPUU	• Figures may not be completely accurate • Lack of security expenditure, as it mostly comes from City of Cape Town • Areas of influence still being developed
VPUU social crime prevention	Expenditure across intervention areas	Financial budgets, reports, VPUU staff	2014–2015	Area	VPUU	• Currently have for the last financial year only
Non-VPUU infrastructure development	Changes in urban land use	Survey of aerial photographs	2006–2012	Area	VPUU	• Only building locations; no indication of scale or cost of development

Source: Lloyd and Matzopoulos (2017).

Table 10.3 Economic and human development

Construct	*Indicator*	*Source*	*Availability*	*Level*	*Geography*	*Limitations*
Household economics	Household employment and economic contribution; plus dependency ratio	CHS	3 phases (2013–2015)	Household or area	VPUU	• Lack of income figures
	Perception of relative income	CHS	3 phases (2013–2015)	Household or area	VPUU	• Subjective self-report
Household wealth	Asset index	CHS	2 phases (2014–2015)	Household or area	VPUU	• Index not validated
Housing quality	Wall material, floor level, rain water, garden	CHS	3 phases (2013–2015)	Household or area	VPUU	• Variations in infra-structure and quality of dwelling not recorded
	Satisfaction with housing	CHS	3 phases (2013–2015)	Household or area	VPUU	• Subjective self-report
Education	Education level	CHS	3 phases (2013–2015)	Individual, house-hold or area	VPUU	• Self-report
Neighbourhood deprivation	South African Index of Multiple Deprivation (SAIMD)	South African Social Policy Research Institute (SASPRI)	2001, 2007 and 2011	Area	Data zones (agglomera-tion of census Enumeration Areas)	• At present only have data at the ward level • Same limitations as census data
	Poverty index	SASPRI	For 2011	Area		
	Perceptions of and satisfaction with neighbourhood (services, etc.)	CHS	3 phases (2013–2015)	Household or area	VPUU	• Self-report
	Formal-informal area	CHS	3 phases (2013–2015)	Area	VPUU	• Variations in infrastruc-ture and quality of set-tlement not recorded
Social capital (structural)	Group membership or community participation	CHS	3 phases (2013–2015)	Household or area	VPUU	• Self-report
Social capital (cognitive)	Perceptions of trust and social cohesion	CHS	1 phase (2015)	Household or area	VPUU	• Self-report
	Preference to continue living in area	CHS	3 phases (2013–2015)	Household or area	VPUU	• Self-report

Source: Lloyd and Matzopoulos (2017).

Table 10.4 Alcohol

Construct	*Indicator*	*Source*	*Availability*	*Level*	*Geography*	*Limitations*
Alcohol consumption	Young adult alcohol use	CHS	3 phases (2013–2015)	Individual or area	VPUU	• For young adults only
Alcohol abuse or dependency	Alcohol Use Disorders Identification Test (AUDIT)	CHS	3 phases (2013–2015)	Individual or area	VPUU	• For young adults only
Alcohol-related neighbourhood problems	Experience of alcohol-related problems	CHS	3 phases (2013–2015)	Individual or area	VPUU	• Self-report
Alcohol availability	Outlet data: number by type, capacity, hours of sale, location	Outlet mapping survey	Gugulethu and Nyanga (2013–2014) Khayelitsha (2015)	Area	VPUU	• Hours of sale not verified (self-report) • Only 2/3 of Khayelitsha surveyed in 2015 • Limited number of variables for Khayelitsha • 2014 data from Gugulethu and Nyanga of poor quality
	Distance to outlets, hours of nearest outlet	CHS	3 phases (2013–2015)	Household or area	VPUU	• Self-report
Alcohol and violence	Association of alcohol with experience of crime and violence	CHS	3 phases (2013–2015)	Household or area	VPUU	• Self-report
	Association of alcohol with trauma cases	Cross-sectional studies of trauma patients	6 phases (every 6 months since 2013)	Area	VPUU	• Geocoded to small areas
	Perceptions of alcohol as factor in violence	CHS	3 phases (2013–2015)	Household or area	VPUU	• Self-report
Alcohol policy perceptions	Perceptions of alcohol policy	CHS	3 phases (2013–2015)	Household or area	VPUU	• Self-report

Source: Lloyd and Matzopoulos (2017).

Table 10.5 Safety and security

Construct	*Indicator*	*Source*	*Availability*	*Level*	*Geography*	*Limitations*
Police presence	Police salary data	Khayelitsha Commission	2012–2013	Area	Police precinct	• Post-2013 data not currently available • Currently only have staff levels; need salary scales
Metro police and private security	Not available	Not available	Not available	Not available	Not available	• Currently unavailable
Enforcement of alcohol laws	Alcohol seizures	South African Police Service Provincial Liquor Control	For 2011	Area	Police precinct for all the Western Cape	• Limited detail on time, location, and type of alcohol (spirits or beer)
	Perceptions of alcohol policy enforcement	CHS	3 phases (2013–2015)	Household or area (aggregate)	VPUU	• Subjective

Source: Lloyd and Matzopoulos (2017).

Conclusion

The validity of our public-health approach may only be realised once information from all the data sources has been fully integrated. However, our preliminary findings certainly suggest that, with careful adaptation, the problems of complexity and limited data can be overcome when evaluating diverse area-level interventions. We focused our efforts on collecting complementary primary data and finding methods to integrate these with secondary sources. We also identified well-delineated outcome and intervention indicators for a range of intervening factors at multiple levels of the socio-ecological framework. The use of neighbourhood boundaries that are more meaningful to residents allowed us to collect accurate area-level outcome data and to construct more accurate aggregated neighbourhood-level variables. Adaptations to the data-collection instruments underline the importance of conducting repeat surveys and of allowing for flexibility in the data-collection process so that emerging knowledge can be built upon in an iterative way.

We are now able to test whether differences in violence between VPUU and non-VPUU areas do in fact correspond with the intervention itself or whether they instead correspond with other factors (such as differences in police practices or socioeconomic circumstances). If we do indeed find a strong association with the VPUU intervention, it will be important to explore temporality to strengthen or refute the argument for a causal association. Our acquisition of police robbery data, which we used as a proxy for community safety (or lack thereof), allowed us to establish whether any observed area-level differences pre-dated the VPUU intervention.

We believe that our Cape Town research illustrates the imperative need to strengthen the knowledge base for upstream approaches to urban violence initiatives of all types, especially given the impetus for these types of interventions in current South African policy and more generally in the Global South. Violence Prevention through Urban Upgrading is one of the more widely recognised initiatives in South Africa and, ideally, our research will indicate whether it is worthy of replication (in part or in whole) in other low- and middle-income country settings, both in South Africa and beyond.

References

Besteman, Catherine (2008). *Transforming Cape Town*. Berkeley: University of California Press.

Burton, Patrick, Anton Du Plessis, Ted Leggett, Antoinette Louw, Duxita Mistry, and Hennie Van Vuuren (2004). *National Victims of crime survey: South Africa 2003*. Pretoria: Institute of Security Studies.

Butchart, Alexander, Alison Phinney, Pietra Check, and Andrés Villaveces (2004). *Preventing violence: A guide to implementing the recommendations of the World Report on Violence*. Geneva: World Health Organization.

Cassidy, Tali, Sam Lloyd, Brett Bowman, Jonny Myers, Charles D.H. Parry, Prestige T. Makanga, and Richard Matzopoulos (2017). Alcohol, mental health and violence in Cape Town's poorest communities: Results of a community survey. Unpublished article submitted to *Journal of Interpersonal Violence*.

Cassidy, Tali, Melikaya Ntshingwa, Jakub Galuszka, and Richard Matzopoulos (2015). Evaluation of a Cape Town safety intervention as a model for good practice: A partnership between researchers, community, and implementing agency. *Stability: International Journal of Security and Development* 4(1): Article 27. doi: http://doi.org/10.5334/sta.fi.

Civilian Secretariat for Police (2016). *White paper on safety and security*. www.policesecretariat.gov.za/downloads/bills/2016_White_Paper_on_Policing.pdf.

Corrigall, Joanne, and Richard Matzopoulos (2012). Violence, alcohol misuse and mental health: Gaps in the health system's response. *South African Health Review 2012–2013:* 103–114.

CSDH: Commission on Social Determinants of Health (2008). *Closing the gap in a generation: Health equity through action on the social determinants of health*. Geneva: World Health Organization. http://apps.who.int/iris/bitstream/10665/43943/1/9789241563703_eng.pdf.

Dahlberg, Linda L., and Alexander Butchart (2005). State of the science: Violence prevention efforts in developing and developed countries. *Journal of Injury Control and Safety Promotion* 12(2): 93–104.

Havenaar, Juhan M., Mirjan I. Geerlings, Lauraine Vivian, Marh Collinson, and Brian Robertson (2008). Common mental health problems in historically disadvantaged urban and rural communities in South Africa: Prevalence and risk factors. *Social Psychiatry and Psychiatric Epidemiology* 43(3): 209–215. doi: http://doi.org/10.1007/s00127-007-0294-9.

IHME: Institute for Health Metrics and Evaluation (2017). *Global Health Data Exchange*. http://ghdx.healthdata.org/gbd-results-tool.

King, Gary, Alan J. Flisher, Farzad Noubary, Robert Reece, Adele Marais, and Carl Lombard (2004). Substance abuse and behavioral correlates of sexual assault among South African adolescents. *Child Abuse and Neglect* 28(6): 683–696. doi: http://doi.org/10.1016/j.chiabu.2003.12.003.

Krug, Etienne G., James A. Mercy, Linda L. Dahlberg, and Anthony B. Zwi, and Rafael Lozano (2002). *World report on violence and health*. Geneva: World Health Organization. doi: http://doi.org/10.1136/ip.9.1.93.

Levitt, Steven D. (1998). The relationship between crime reporting and police: Implications for the use of uniform crime reports. *Journal of Quantitative Criminology* 14(1): 61–81. doi: http://doi.org/10.1023/A:1023096425367.

Lloyd, Sam, and Richard Matzopoulos (2017). Urban upgrading for violence prevention in South Africa: Does it work? Research indicators. Unpublished.

Matzopoulos, Richard, Brett Bowman, Shanaaz Mathews, and Jonny Myers (2010). Applying upstream interventions for interpersonal violence prevention: An uphill struggle in low- to middle-income contexts. *Health Policy* 97(1): 62–70. doi: http://dx.doi.org/10.1016/j.healthpol.2010.03.003.

Matzopoulos, Richard, and Jonathan E. Myers (2014). The Western Cape government's new Integrated Provincial Violence Prevention Policy Framework: Successes and challenges. *Aggression and Violent Behavior* 19(6): 649–654. doi: http://dx.doi.org/10.1016/j.avb.2014.09.009.

Matzopoulos, Richard, Megan Prinsloo, Victoria Pillay-Van Wyk, Nomonde Gwebushe, Shanaaz Mathews, Lorna J. Martin, Ria Laubscher, Naeemah Abrahams, William Msemburi, Carl Lombard, and Debbie Bradshaw (2015). Injury-related mortality in South Africa: A retrospective descriptive study of post-mortem investigations. *Bull World Health Organ* 93(5): 303–313. doi: http://doi.org/10.2471/BLT.14.145771.

Moffitt, Terrie E. (1993). Adolescence-limited and life-course-persistent antisocial behavior: A developmental taxonomy. *Psychological Review* 100(4): 674–701. doi: http://doi.org/10.1037/0033-295X.100.4.674.

Mureithi, Leopold P., A. Africa, Muchiri Wandai, Nienke van Schaik, Tracey Naledi, Richard Matzopoulos, and René English (2016). *Injury morbidity surveillance in Nyanga and Khayelitsha, in the Western Cape*. Durban: Health Systems Trust.

Myer, Landon, Rodney I. Ehrlich, and Ezra S. Susser (2004). Social epidemiology in South Africa. *Epidemiologic Reviews* 26: 112–123. doi: http://doi.org/10.1093/epirev/mxh004.

Noble, Michael, Wanga Zembe, Gemma Wright, and David Avenell (2013). Multiple deprivation and income poverty at small-area level in South Africa in 2011. Cape Town: Southern African Social Policy Research Institute. http://saspri.org/wp-content/uploads/Docs/SAIMD_2011_ward_level_National_Report_for_Web.pdf.

O'Regan, Catherine, and Vusumzi Pikoli (2014). *Towards a safer Khayelitsha: Report of the Commission of Inquiry into Allegations of Police Inefficiency and a breakdown in relations between SAPS [South African Police Service] and the community of Khayelitsha*. Cape Town: Khayelitsha Commission. www.khayelitshacommission.org.za/images/towards_khaye_docs/Khayelitsha_Commission_Report_WEB_FULL_TEXT_C.pdf.

Parry, Charles D.H., and Sarah Dewing (2006). A public-health approach to addressing alcohol-related crime in South Africa. *African Journal of Drug and Alcohol Studies* 5(1): 41–56.

Peer, Nasheeta, Carl Lombard, Krisela Steyn, and Naomi Levitt (2014). Rising alcohol consumption and a high prevalence of problem drinking in black men and women in Cape Town: The CRIBSA [Cardiovascular Risk in Black South Africans] study. *Journal of Epidemiology and Community Health* 68(5): 446–452. doi: http://doi.org/10.1136/jech-2013–202985.

Raine, Adrian (2002). Biosocial studies of antisocial and violent behavior in children and adults: A review. *Journal of Abnormal Child Psychology* 30(4): 311–326.

Rychetnik, Lucie., Michael Frommer, Penelope Hawe, and Alan Shiell (2002). Criteria for evaluating evidence on public health interventions. *Journal of Epidemiology and Community Health* 56: 119–127. doi: http://doi.org/10.1136/jech.56.2.119.

UNODC: United Nations Office on Drugs and Crime (2005). *Why fighting crime can assist the development of Africa: Rule of law and the protection of the most vulnerable*. Vienna: Author.

Ward, Catherine L., Lillian Artz, Julie Berg, Floretta Boonzaier, Sarah Crawford-Browne, Andrew Dawes, Donald Foster, Richard Matzopoulos, Andrew Nicol, Jeremy Seekings, Arjan B. (Sebastian) van As, and Elrena Van der Spuy (2012). Violence, violence prevention, and safety: A research agenda for South Africa.

South African Medical Journal 102(4): 215–218. www.ncbi.nlm.nih.gov/pubmed/22464496.

Wilkinson, Richard G., and Kate Pickett (2010). *The spirit level: Why equality is better for everyone*. London: Penguin.

Williams, Damien J., Anna J. Gavine, Catherine L. Ward, and Peter D. Donnelly (2015). What is evidence in violence prevention? In Peter. D. Donnelly and Catherine L. Ward (Eds.), *Oxford Textbook of Violence Prevention: Epidemiology, Evidence, and Policy* (125–146). Oxford: Oxford University Press.

Conclusion

New perspectives on lasting solutions

John de Boer, Jennifer Erin Salahub, and Markus Gottsbacher

At the core of this book rests the ethos that lasting solutions to pressing problems such as urban violence and inequality are best developed locally. This is because issues of crime, violence, inequalities, and poverty are rarely resolved through technical means alone. As this book illustrates, these problems are often embedded in structural, legal, social, and political norms and practices that, in some cases, have been around for centuries. To change patterns and trajectories, a deep understanding of the local context and the factors that drive and influence human behaviour is required. People living and working in local contexts possess unparalleled insights into and understandings of these dynamics. Solutions need to be tailored to local realities and, moreover, have the capacity to influence the political economy that defines and perpetuates them across urban geographies and populations.

All of the cities researched in this book are facing a myriad of challenges. Each of them is growing at a breakneck pace. They face a combination of threats that include violence, crime, conflict, and climate change-induced hazards, as well as social and economic pressures. All of this is occurring within contexts of weak governance and a range of social, economic, and political inequalities, including gender inequality. Increasingly, these risks are converging and complicating the ability of local and national authorities to effect positive change for their urban residents.

As the world continues to urbanise with particular speed across Latin America, Asia, and Africa, cities will increasingly be on the frontline of challenges that have both local and global impact. Singular risks such as the unsustainable pace of unplanned urbanisation, climate change, or conflict cannot be seen or addressed in isolation. They cause a cascade of risks compounding the challenges for local and international actors. As such, it is not just these risks in isolation that worry urban planners and authorities most; rather, it is the convergence of these threats, which is becoming increasingly visible (de Boer and Patel 2016).

Research in this book has highlighted how rapid urbanisation and growing economic inequality are colliding to create pockets of chronic poverty and conflict. In many cases, this also leads to exploitation and displacement creating situations of acute crises layered over chronic crises. Given demographic trends, these tendencies are likely to continue, placing cities on the frontlines of a range of social, political, and humanitarian emergencies, ranging from flooding and famine exacerbated by climate change, to growing authoritarianism in countries that were well on the path to democracy, to migration fueled by war, fear, and hope for a better life (de Boer and Muggah 2016; Bosetti, Cooper, and de Boer 2016). Over the coming years, these trends will only increase, requiring local authorities—in collaboration with national and international counterparts—to radically change their practices (de Boer 2015).

Efforts are underway and much work is being done to help cities tackle some of the world's most pressing problems. In many cases, these efforts are being led by urban residents and city authorities who have established extensive networks for mutual learning and exchange. Networks such as the Global Alliance for Urban Crises, for example, bring together city authorities and civil society groups, as well as international actors and the UN, to try to harness the potential that cities and towns have to become more crisis-disaster proof. Other promising groups include the UN-Habitat-led Global Network on Safer Cities, the European and African Forums for Urban Safety, Mayors for Peace, Cities for Peace, the 100 Resilient Cities initiative, and the Municipal Alliance for Peace in the Middle East—all of which are serving as platforms to scale up solutions to tackle pressing problems.

Yet, despite these efforts, there remains a dearth of evidence on what works, and what does not, in tackling these pressing problems facing cities in the Global South. Importantly, perspectives and approaches from the Global South—from those best placed to provide context-specific insight and analysis—are noticeably absent from global debates. Existing models are more often than not based on theoretical frameworks and experiences from North America and Europe, which are implemented with varying degrees of success in the Global South. As a result, cities in the Global South are struggling to find answers to their pressing problems.

This brings us back to the core objective of this book: to enrich theoretical discussion and deliberation on how best to reduce urban violence and inequalities by investing in research from the ground up, based on local realities and local understandings. The chapters contained in this book reflect research undertaken in dozens of cities in Latin America, Sub-Saharan Africa, and South Asia. This research was led by experts who are embedded in these cities, have established networks based on trust, and are committed to a long-term process of problem solving and accompaniment in these cities.

The book touches on a number of themes that can be interpreted as important guideposts for practitioners and analysts seeking to better understand local dynamics on the ground. Part I tackles the complex gendered realities faced by women and men in cities ranging from Karachi to Maputo and Harare. The approaches and findings are as theoretically enriching as they are practical, allowing readers to understand the gendered complexities and violences that restrict women's full realisation of their rights, constraining them as they undertake everyday tasks. Anwar, Viqar, and Mustafa look beyond mainstream treatments of violence and examine the highly gendered realities that constrain mobility for girls and women in Karachi. They remind us how mobility in many urban centres is inherently gendered, particularly for working class women who rely on public transport to access the city and their livelihoods. For these women, exposure to sexual harassment, intimidation, and the threat of violence comes not at the hand of a knife or a gun from gang members, but from their daily exposure to harassment on buses and other modes of transport. These constraints on their mobility in public are mirrored by domestic, private constraints: fathers, husbands, brothers, and other relatives who police their movements, and prevent them from moving about the city because of fear for their safety as well as concerns about reputation and honour. This chapter, along with those by Mariano, Slegh, and Roque and Stewart, Katsande, Chisango, and Maseko, highlights the increasingly blurred lines between public and private spaces, particularly when it comes to gendered violences that target women.

These chapters are joined by Balsamanta and Reddy's work in providing rich description and detailed analysis of the extent to which structural, state, and physical interpersonal violence are normalised in two specific contexts. First, violence against women and girls, ranging from verbal abuse by male and female family members to structural violence and discrimination to shocking interpersonal violence in public and private. But the normalisation of violence also has a second, geographic dynamic to it, with communities living at the margins of the city and urban society—the slums, shantytowns, *favelas*, and other informal settlements that are growing globally and are home to most of the population growth in the Global South—suffering the most.

In their account of changing urban violence in post-conflict Maputo, Mariano, Slegh, and Roque remind us that changing gendered urban realities requires understanding not just the experiences of women, but also of men. Their research demonstrates how we need to go beyond fixed social roles assigned to men and women and seek to transform how they interact within the wider social context. Their chapter provokes a wide variety of innovations in how we could go about not just transforming gender dynamics but breaking multiple links in the chains that lead to and perpetuate multiple forms of violence and inequality in today's cities. Transforming gender roles and understanding how to push and pull young men along pathways of non-violence can have profound effects that ultimately prevent many of the challenges confronting cities. Doing so, however, requires dealing not only with the present but also with the past. This reality is clearly demonstrated by Stewart, Katsande, Chisango, and Maseko in their account of Harare, where the legal and historical legacies of a repressive colonial era live on and replicate existing forms of injustice and exploitation that have a disproportionate impact on women's lives.

The second part of the book picks up on this thread of analysis, but elevates it to discuss and dissect structural forms of state violence. Balsamanta and Reddy focus their analysis on state-inflicted violence on poor segments of the population in Delhi. Based on their survey of some 2,000 households, the chapter elucidates how vulnerabilities, and responses to them, shift and contest the state's apathy, hostility, arbitrariness, and inherent contradictions that further displace marginalised communities. Jayatilaka, Lakshman, and Lakshman take this analysis further by examining relocation and resettlement programmes in post-war Sri Lanka. Their conclusion points to clear differences in patterns of resilience between urban communities with a sense of mobility versus those who do not have the freedom to manoeuvre. These differences are visible in the social, economic, and psychological well-being of these communities, pointing to clearly different outcomes as a result of state resettlement policies.

Part III draws heavily from experiences in Latin America and, in so doing, challenges and suggests adaptations to dominant theories of violence and exclusion. Calderón Umaña examines the links that bind social exclusion and violence in cities in an inextricable knot. Illustrated through on the ground research on Central American gangs (*maras*), he demonstrates how the links between exclusion and violence constitute a vicious cycle with no easy way out. His research shows how social exclusion actually creates the conditions for violence while at the same time that violence reinforces and generates further obstacles for communities and individuals to overcome exclusion. As a result, residents are often cut off, materially and symbolically, from services and opportunities in the city, forcing them into enclaves over-burdened by ever increasing rates of violence and exclusion.

In their work, Arias and Tocornal Montt seek to understand the determinants of violent crime in highly disadvantaged neighbourhoods of Bogotá, Lima, and Santiago. Building on social disorganisation theory developed by Robert Sampson, the authors clearly articulate how the links between urban poverty, inequality, and violence vary across these three cities which have relatively similar levels of poverty. Their contribution helps elucidate the role that institutions and institutional capacity, especially of the state, play in either reducing or reinforcing violence through particular social and political practices, notably policing.

Their focus on institutions connects with Briceño-León's compelling study of cities and their institutions in Venezuela. The central question driving his analysis is: why do two young men, who grow up in the same conditions of urban poverty and exclusion, experience utterly different trajectories—one a life of crime and violence and the other of stability and safety? The factors that determine the difference, according to Briceño-León, are the set of self-imposed norms put forward by the informal institutions that govern everyday lives in these neighbourhoods. In the case of Venezuela, these informal institutions consist of family, schools, and faith-based groups and their importance is accentuated in contexts where the state has relieved or abrogated its social contract with urban residents. Important to the peace-building success of these institutions, notes Briceño-León, are women leaders, in their roles as mothers, teachers, nuns, and other community leaders.

Finally, the book assesses a fourth dimension of violence—namely the dynamics that shape interpersonal violence. With respect to the transformations taking place in criminal violence affecting Ivorian cities, Akindès analyses the emergence of youth gangs in Abidjan. His analysis reveals how the experiences and behaviours of these youth gangs are shaped and reinforced by the fact that the gangs have come to substitute for family in a context where war has ravaged society forcing youth to form "collectives of violence" for survival. Indeed, both boys and girls are drawn into gangs where, in addition to their specific gang roles—girls serve as lookouts and as lures for victims—they recreate nuclear family structures within the wider gang "community." Despite this sense of belonging, once enmeshed in these gangs, youth start to assume political identities that are shaped by their sense of marginalisation, invisibility, and demonisation. Labelled "Microbes", these youth are treated as ills of society, and the remedy proposed by authorities is eradication. Their awareness of this castigation ultimately reinforces a common identity within and among gangs where violence is used as a means for survival and resistance.

Finally, Lloyd and Matzopoulos conclude the volume by describing how South Africa's Violence Prevention through Urban Upgrading (VPUU) programme, which has been operating in Cape Town since 2007, is helping to transform communities through improvements to public infrastructure and community engagement aimed at reducing and preventing violence. Their work in the communities of Khayelitsha, Gugulethu, and Nyanga demonstrates how coordinated and thought-out programmes that combine urban upgrading with education, public health outreach, and clear indicators, can help promote social cohesion, improve livelihoods, and ultimately reduce violence. The pathways, however, are not always straightforward, and ultimately they are difficult to replicate in other localities.

In seeking to answer the question "*What happens when social theory—largely developed and tested in the Global North—meets the realities of life in violent parts of cities in the Global South?*" the answer is clear. Northern theories on their own are inadequate to explain and understand every day, structural, and sporadic forms of violence in the cities assessed. Local researchers, such as those featured in this study, are innovating and contributing to knowledge that can help tackle some of the most pressing challenges facing our world today. By including these voices and this literature in academic and policy discussions, experts and novices alike will be able to avoid adopting theoretical frameworks and approaches that are blind to the varied and contextual experiences (gendered, structural, and interpersonal) of urban violence as well as the related solutions.

In addition to the empirical value that the work embodied in this book demonstrates, the implications for those who fund research are also an important consideration. Research funders need to open up windows and opportunities that enable Southern knowledge to grow and flourish. In many ways, this could also contribute to what seems to be an emerging renaissance of comparative research in the field of urban studies. Global and local leaders and authorities are increasingly recognising that they cannot carbon copy policies or initiatives from other contexts. While lessons can be learned, in some cases deliberate divergence may be necessary.

As showcased in many of the chapters, cities in the Global South are often shaped by tension and friction between the state, communities, and citizens in urban contexts. As pressures driven by demographics, climate change, and resource constraints—as well as related opportunities—mount, these tensions will likely heighten, particularly when this change confronts often-rigid and gendered power structures. But instead of resisting or shying away from such tensions, researchers and policymakers should seek to identify and understand them in more depth. As this volume illustrates, it is essential that we map out the inter-linkages between social, political, and economic forms of inequality, exclusion, and violence if we are to resolve them. And perhaps this is the greatest contribution this volume makes: it recognises, names, and documents these tensions and frictions in cities around the world. What remains to be tackled is how to overcome these challenges and, in so doing, promote safer and more inclusive cities. This is the challenge we take up in this book's partner volume, *Reducing Urban Violence in the Global South: Towards Safe and Inclusive Cities*, also published by Routledge.

References

Bosetti, Louise, Hannah Cooper, and John de Boer (2016). Peacekeeping in cities: Is the UN prepared? UNU Centre for Policy Research. 12 April. https://cpr.unu.edu/peacekeeping-in-cities-is-the-un-prepared.html.

de Boer, John (2015). The sustanable development fight will be won or lost in our cities. World Economic Forum. 24 September. https://www.weforum.org/agenda/2015/09/the-fight-for-sustainable-development-will-be-won-or-lost-in-our-cities/.

de Boer, John, and Robert Muggah (2016). Are aid agencies ready to deal with war, terrorism, and crime in cities? Thomson Reuters Foundation News. 23 May. http://news.trust.org/item/20160523050942-7f0xo/?source=spotlight.

de Boer, John, and Ronak Patel (2016). Resilience in the future: 2025 and beyond. In *World Disasters Report 2016* (190–221). Geneva: International Federation of the Red Cross and Red Crescent Societies. http://www.ifrc.org/Global/Documents/Secretariat/201610/WDR%202016-FINAL_web.pdf.

Index

Note: Entries in **bold** refer to tables and entries in *italics* refer to figures.

Printed in the United States
By Bookmasters